REHEARSING
REVOLUTIONS

Studies in Theatre History and Culture

HEATHER S. NATHANS, SERIES EDITOR

REHEARSING REVOLUTIONS

The Labor Drama Experiment
and Radical Activism
in the Early Twentieth Century

≈ ≈ ≈ ≈ ≈

Mary McAvoy

University of Iowa Press
IOWA CITY

University of Iowa Press, Iowa City 52242
Copyright © 2019 by the University of Iowa Press
www.uipress.uiowa.edu
Printed in the United States of America

Text design by Judy Gilats

Printed on acid-free paper

Library of Congress Cataloging-in-Publication Data
Names: McAvoy, Mary, author.
Title: Rehearsing revolutions : the labor drama experiment and radical activism in the early twentieth century / Mary McAvoy.
Description: Iowa City : University of Iowa Press, [2019] | Series: Studies in theatre history and culture | Includes bibliographical references and index. |
Identifiers: LCCN 2018044536 (print) | LCCN 2019000789 (ebook) | ISBN 978-1-60938-642-9 (ebook) | ISBN 978-1-60938-641-2 (pbk. : alk. paper)
Subjects: LCSH: Workers' theater—United States—History—20th century. | Amateur theater—United States—History—20th century. | Experimental theater—United States—History—20th century. | College theater—United States—History—20th century. | Labor unions and education—United States—History—20th century. | Labor union members—Education—United States—History—20th century. | Labor unions and the arts—United States—History—20th century. | Socialism and theater—United States—History—20th century. | Political activists—Education—United States—History—20th century. | Radicalism—United States—History—20th century.
Classification: LCC PN3307.U6 (ebook) | LCC PN3307.U6 M35 2019 (print) | DDC 792.02/2209730904—dc23
LC record available at https://lccn.loc.gov/2018044536

TO WORKERS

CONTENTS

ACKNOWLEDGMENTS

I am grateful for the support I have received throughout the research and writing of this book. I would first like to thank the many archivists and staff members at the Kheel Center for Labor-Management Documentation and Archives at M. P. Catherwood Library (Cornell University), the Center for Urban and Labor Affairs at Walter Reuther Library (Wayne State University), the Smithsonian Center for Folklife and Cultural Heritage, the University of Arkansas Special Collections, the Tennessee Historical Society, the Rauner Special Collections Library (Dartmouth College), the Wisconsin Historical Society and Memorial Library (University of Wisconsin–Madison), the Oregon Historical Society, and the Highlander Research and Education Center. The project would not have been possible without these individuals' help and guidance.

Portions of Chapter 3 appeared previously in "The Variegated Shoots: Hazel MacKaye and the Advent of Pedagogical Drama at Brookwood Labor College, 1925–1926," *Youth Theatre Journal*, 29, no. 1 (2015): 45–61.

I would like to extend thanks to my mentor, friend, and colleague Dr. Manon van de Water for her early support of this project. I would also like to extend additional thanks to Dr. Adam Nelson, who introduced me to the histories of radical education and sparked my initial research on Hazel MacKaye's theatrical work at Brookwood Labor College.

This work has been presented to several professional organizations, including the American Society for Theatre Research, the Association for Theatre in Higher Education (particularly the American Theatre and Drama Society), the Mid-American Theatre Conference, and the American Alliance for Theatre and Education. Thank you to my colleagues for insightful comments, questions, and feedback through working groups and paper presentations.

Financial support from several institutions and organizations assisted with this study, including the Mellon-Wisconsin Summer Fellowship, the American Theatre and Drama Society's Graduate Student Award, the Helen Krich Chinoy Dissertation Research Fellowship from the American

Society for Theatre Research, the Vilas Travel Grant from the University of Wisconsin–Madison, the Winifred Ward Scholarship, and the Archie K. Davis fellowship from the North Caroliniana Society. My institution, Arizona State University, also provided time to support my work.

Thank you to the University of Iowa Press team, including my editors, Heather Nathans, Catherine Cocks, and Ranjit Arab. Thank you also to Meredith Stabel and Noreen O'Connor-Abel. Your feedback, questions, and investment in this project have sustained and improved my research and writing. Thank you also to the readers of my manuscript for challenging and supportive comments.

Last, I extend thanks to my colleagues, friends, and family who have inspired, challenged, and supported me through this process. A special thanks to Dr. Niccole Carner for her help and friendship. Finally, thank you to Dr. Kristin Hunt for her enduring commitment to and tolerance of my decade-long excursion into the world of workers, theatre artists, and radical education.

REHEARSING
REVOLUTIONS

CHAPTER 1

The Labor Drama Experiment

We make rich the world.
The Man and the Masses, in *Miners*, a play presented
at Brookwood Labor College, 1926

There is no labor audience for this theatre.
Louis Schaffer, editor of *Labor Stage*, Brookwood Workers' Theatre
Conference, 1936

On the weekend of February 19, 1926, Brookwood Labor College was
abuzz with activity. To celebrate a successful first year, this new residential
workers' education program invited more than thirty leaders from university programs and prominent labor organizations to its scenic campus in
Katonah, New York, for a workers' education conference. These leaders,
pioneers in a young and vibrant movement that set out to design education
opportunities specifically for workers, gathered to share ideas and report
on new initiatives sprouting up throughout the country. At the end of their
second day, the guests joined together in the student common room for one
of Brookwood's own experiments in workers' education, an original play
entitled *Miners* created by students in the labor drama program. Brookwooders had been rehearsing this new three-act piece for weeks, and this
evening's performance would be the premiere.

As guests settled into folding chairs in the common room, their attention turned toward a makeshift platform stage situated at one end of the
hall. Although the room was a tight fit for the more than twenty students,
teachers, and teachers' children who would perform that evening, student
efforts to transform the space were notable. Production teams sewed and
hung simple curtains, giving the illusion of a proscenium, and a few new
stage lights were mounted to illuminate the performers. The students also
conveniently installed the stage near a set of doors leading to the patio, and
in this makeshift backstage area, cast and crew rushed to set props, adjust

set pieces, and add final touches to their simple costumes. Once everyone settled, a student pulled back the curtain, revealing the silhouetted figures of men, women, and children against "a ruddy glow" from the new stage lights.[1] These "Masses," supported by a chorus of offstage performers, moaned and sighed, filling the space with sounds of strife. In the "shadowy foreground a single tall figure of a working man" appeared. "The Man" and the silhouetted Masses offered the following call-and-response chant to open the show:

> THE MAN: We will strike for the right to work!
> THE MASSES: We will strike for the right to work!
> THE MAN: We will die fighting for the right to live!
> THE MASSES: We will die fighting for the right to live!
> THE MAN: We want bread for our starved children!
> THE MASSES: We want bread for our starved children!
> THE MAN: We make rich the world!
> THE MASSES: We make rich the world.[2]

The play continued, chronicling the "heroism and suffering and grim humor" of West Virginia miners, a group that had traveled to campus in the previous fall semester to meet with Brookwood students.[3] The drama concluded with a rousing rendition of "La Marseillaise." Afterward, Brookwood president A. J. Muste, with a "catch in his throat," introduced student playwright Bonchi Friedman, a Russian immigrant and textile worker from New York City, and the rest of the amateur worker-student ensemble, presenting all members of the production team with flowers. With their production of *Miners*, the Brookwood Labor Players had indeed made rich the world that evening.

Overview

The theatrical enterprise at Brookwood was but one example of labor drama, the topic of this book. These pedagogical process-focused drama programs flourished in workers' education institutions in the United States during the interwar period (roughly 1920–40), influencing left-leaning socialist and communist theatre artists, shaping radical and experimental education initiatives, and diversifying amateur theatre movements. Through a series of case studies, I demonstrate how these programs evolved from experimental performance forms grounded in the legacies of progressivism and designed to teach and entertain a new class of union members and labor leaders in the 1920s to radically politicized projects that inspired overt, even militant, labor activism by the late 1930s. These programs showcase the rapidity with which art, activism, and education were transformed during the period between World War I and World War II, suggesting new lines of analysis about left-leaning theatre practices, radical education, and arts-based political activism before and after the New Deal. This study explicitly focuses on young adult workers and their instructors as they explored drama's usefulness as a method for imagining and enacting emancipatory alternatives to the oppressive status quo of U.S. industry during the interwar period. These labor-oriented pedagogical drama programs ("labor drama" for this book's purposes), which are distinct from but adjacent to the more well-known production-oriented workers' theatre movement, attempted to synthesize workers' education and theatrical arts and took many forms, ranging from informal drama courses to formal theatrical productions. This new perspective on drama's relationship to education in the United States is timely. Despite robust historical scholarship about theatre education programs for children both in formal learning environments like K-12 schools and in theatre for youth programs, drama-based education in the United States lacks the same rigorous contextualization within openly radical, political, and avant-garde efforts, particularly during the first half of the twentieth century. These pedagogically focused labor drama experiments also connect with the legacies of activist performance in unexpected places, including the civil rights movement, contemporary applied drama and theatre practices, and the histories of popular, political, folk, and mass cultural theatre forms.

I first situate the labor drama experiment within the equally experimental workers' education movement during the interwar period. U.S. workers' education, a vast early twentieth-century initiative rooted in European political education and U.S. progressive education movements of the same period, provided workers with opportunities to learn about the labor movement. It was most popular between 1920 and 1940, particularly after the stock market crash in 1929, and took on a variety of forms including night, weekend, evening, and residential programs, retreats, workshops, and institutes. At the phenomenon's zenith, hundreds of different workers' education programs appeared from coast to coast in practically all areas of industry. Thousands of workers participated. While this book primarily considers residential programs, as they housed some of the most robust and long-standing drama endeavors with the richest enduring archives, labor drama was widespread throughout workers' education institutions and attracted a diverse array of workers.

Although night and weekend programs were generally accessible to any worker who could afford the inexpensive tuition and secure transportation to the local labor temple or union hall, residential programs were more challenging to attend. Often, working-class young people (roughly ages eighteen to thirty), many with only an elementary education, departed their jobs in mills and factories and on farms for extended study of the labor movement. Most attended through union sponsorship or received substantial scholarships generated through donations to the schools. Upon arrival on labor college campuses, which were often located in geographically and/or culturally foreign regions, students committed themselves to a period of intensive study in the hopes of becoming leaders in local and national labor activism. By participating in these education programs, students engaged with new and often challenging academic subject matter including labor history, economics, English, public speaking, and labor problems. In many instances, the college's administration required additional courses including physical education, nutrition, and hygiene as part of experimental whole-learner educational ethos shaping these programs. Additionally, due to the egalitarian philosophies grounding many of the schools' missions, students were often expected to do manual labor, working the school farm or cooking meals for students and staff, in order to earn their keep and contribute to the spirit of community. In sum, labor college students were a dedicated group who endured great sacrifice in their pursuit of an education.

These labor college students simultaneously served as pedagogical guinea pigs for their instructors. Workers' education faculty, a pioneering group of mostly young adults who committed themselves to experimental, democratic, anti-authoritarian, and progressive pedagogies, set off on the labor college experiment with little in the way of a road map. They, perhaps even more than the students, found themselves in unfamiliar regions of the country, and they too had to earn their keep by working the school farm or cleaning the school grounds alongside students. They often worked without appropriate resources and with groups of students whose life experiences greatly differed from their own. Additionally, they rarely received a salary, working in exchange for room and board. These teachers were also in turn guinea pigs for these schools' administrations as much as the students were for teachers' pedagogical experiments. For its part, more often than not, school leadership regarded drama as a form of recreation and included it as an evening activity after the supposedly more academically rigorous classes ended for the day. In other instances, like the *Miners* production, schools used labor drama productions as publicity tools, presenting performances at fundraising events, union meetings, community meet-and-greets, and workers' conferences held on campus. Instructors initially hired to direct these publicity productions and evening theatricals drove efforts to evolve labor drama's role from extracurricular entertainment to crucial pedagogical pursuits, and they did so with fervor. In addition to directing and producing a great number of plays, labor drama instructors spent immense amounts of time theorizing drama as pedagogy, publishing essays about their ideas in school newspapers and labor publications, developing learning objectives, writing course plans, creating lessons, and promoting their larger programmatic goals with school administrators. Once these instructors established a purpose and flow for their programs, they advocated for increasingly visible and integral roles for labor drama on campus not only as recreation, but also as a specific and unique mode for learning.

In creating these new programs, students' and instructors' participation in these labor colleges exposed them to great danger due to the aura of mystery surrounding these schools, particularly as U.S. society increasingly conflated labor activism with controversial radical Left politics by the mid-1930s. The danger associated with representing the imaginary on stage has long troubled artists and thinkers, but the role of theatre as dangerous art was particularly important to these labor college institutions. Few of the people involved in these experiments had formal dramatic training, and many instructors were in the early phases of conceptualizing the form and function of their work. Accordingly, they were not sure what would come out of their experimentation, and worse, they often lacked a vocabulary to explain its political, ideological, or pedagogical function, particularly if the product was controversial. Furthermore, drama's role as the performance genre de rigueur of radical workers' movements in Russia and Germany at this time complicated these concerns, resulting in constant worry over the potentially propagandistic nature of labor drama productions. However, school leadership often sought out drama to show the *lack* of radicalism at each of the colleges, especially when rumors brewed about the school's political leanings. Drama's public role on campus challenged many instructors to balance their programs' missions within larger plans for advocacy and activism. Occasionally, tensions arose between dramatics instructors and leadership. One instructor, Hazel MacKaye, was probably excused from her position for not being mindful of her responsibility to present a positive, polished face of the school with her productions. Other teachers and students were subject to criminal investigations or were expelled by labor organizations that once supported them, and still others fled the country under the threat of blacklisting.

Even though few productions produced substantial controversy, most labor drama teachers and students faced persistent crises endemic to these experimental institutions. At any given moment, a school might face threats of closure due to political controversy, acute financial strain, leadership change, or lack of students. Thus, instructor turnover was high. Once a program gathered steam, instructors often left, with new instructors taking the reins. These conditions resulted in perpetual debates among instructors, students, and leadership about appropriateness of material, the value of process over product, the role of drama as an academic course versus a recreational club, the manner by which students should study labor drama, and the program's ultimate goals. As such, these programs were wholly experimental, with teachers and students testing methods and ideas for teaching about drama, for making performance, and for generating dramatic material. As with many experiments, some were successful, and many were not. As expected, the enduring plays from these labor drama experiments are often simplistic and heavily influenced by popular culture. Labor drama programs also clearly tailored their plays to their immediate communities and, often, the enduring playtexts lack relevance for wider readership. These realities further threatened archives that are sadly incomplete. Labor drama was rarely publicized beyond school campuses; infrequently reviewed, particularly by someone other than a new labor journalism student; even more infrequently photographed; and occasionally, entirely improvised or written and rehearsed but never performed. In addition to simply having neither time nor resources to document goings-on, many of these schools had their records destroyed by adversarial government officials, particularly in the South, in an attempt to quite literally erase them from memory. While I have worked to reconstruct these labor drama courses and productions in each chapter, I also acknowledge that the archive leaves substantial gaps. Although extant labor drama archives reveal formidable challenges to the form, they also highlight the power of resiliency in forging new paths for art and education in the United States. As these teachers and students engaged in risky experimentation, they created an opportunity for messy, creative, and path-breaking work not only for pedagogical dramatics, but also more broadly for both activist-oriented arts and adult education. Through a series of case studies, I trace the labor drama's evolution at several institutions throughout the United States, including:

- ► Portland Labor College (Portland, Oregon), 1922–26;
- ► Brookwood Labor College (Katonah, New York), 1921–37;
- ► Southern Summer School for Women Workers in Industry (western North Carolina), 1927–37;
- ► Highlander Folk School (Monteagle, Tennessee), 1932–present; and
- ► Commonwealth College (Mena, Arkansas), 1923–40.

I selected these institutions due to their diverse student populations, foundational philosophies, geographies, and program designs. These schools also have rich and underexamined archival records that I integrate into each chapter.

While these programs diverged in regard to method and philosophy, several meaningful commonalities help define the labor drama programs that all employed as both pedagogical and artistic pursuits. First, each of these schools focused on drama as a method to teach about labor activism. No institution introduced labor drama solely as recreation or entertainment; labor drama's potential pedagogical benefit was key to its inclusion in curriculum even if it appeared as an end-of-day recreational offering. Given this focus on recreation and education, none of these programs aspired to train workers for virtuosity on the stage or in advanced stage-craft techniques. Instead they aimed to present students with opportunities to experience creation of performance with a clear pedagogical connection to exploring the labor movement. Finally, all of these programs included process-based experiential learning opportunities for students that involved discussion and reflection. Even formal productions involved ancillary processes whereby worker/students incorporated their real-life experiences into classes and productions through playwriting, talkbacks, reviews, and other forms of performance reflection. Given these programs' diversity, the term "labor drama" was inconsistently adopted, a testament to this performance phenomenon's experimental and emergent nature. Instead, specific terminology varied by institutions, drama groups, instructors, and the time period in which they worked. Sometimes instructors or schools used terms like "workers' theatre" and "labor dramatics" synonymously. In other instances, distinctions between the terms appear, particularly in regard to theatre as a product and drama as a process. Some groups had only a vague idea how they were using the term since they were in the process of defining a program through a series of performance experiments. Struggles to define this interdisciplinary performance genre were endemic to the larger focus on experimentation in these programs.

In regard to differences, some of these programs, like those created at Portland Labor College (Chapter 2) and Brookwood Labor College (Chapter 3), focused on production and generated touring plays based on extant dramatic works that may or may not have had explicit labor themes. Other programs, like those at North Carolina's Southern Summer School for Women Workers in Industry (Chapter 4), Tennessee's Highlander Folk School (Chapter 5), and Arkansas's Commonwealth College (Chapter 6), were more pedagogically focused, generating original plays in class and performing largely for school and local communities, if at all. In each chapter, I analyze the ways in which specific instructors and institutions generated their approaches, how they created their pedagogical objectives for the programs, and how they evaluated their work in an effort to clarify their specific definition of labor drama. With these ideas framing my analysis, in each chapter I weave together the influences of theatre, education, and labor activism while also contextualizing how labor drama evolved in response to political developments and the ancillary workers' theatre movement.

A Theatre with No Audience:
Contextualizing the Labor Drama Zeitgeist

Despite innumerable factors that directly shaped the practical and theoretical approaches of these programs, the interwar period's domestic and geopolitical turmoil exerted profound pressure on labor drama. Between 1919 and 1941, these small experimental initiatives, along with the rest of the United States, navigated the end of World War I, the Roaring Twenties, the rise and spread of communism, the Great Depression, the relief programs of the Federal Emergency Relief Act and the Works Progress Administration, the rise of fascism, and the advent of World War II. This global unrest challenged even the most well managed national-level labor organizations, including the American Federation of Labor (AFL) and Congress of Industrial Organizations (CIO). Expectedly, small experimental workers' education institutions housing labor drama programs likewise struggled to navigate these larger developments.

To contextualize the artistic, cultural, and political milieu in which the labor drama movement developed, I return again to Brookwood Labor College almost ten years after the premiere of *Miners*. Once again, Brookwood hosted a conference, but this time, they welcomed a veritable who's who of labor drama and workers' theatre leaders. By this point, the workers' theatre movement and labor drama programs were beginning to work more collaboratively, and early efforts were in play to establish labor drama programs as training grounds for workers' theatre artists to prepare them for producing professional theatrical works specifically for labor audiences.[4] The conference, a standing event in its fourth year, had previously provided artists and organizations opportunities to share ideas, reflect on the field, and plan for the future during the early 1930s. Generally, these events were energizing and inspiring affairs. However, in 1936, a fog of uncertainty lingered over the proceedings. This sense of unease manifested itself in the conference minutes, a laundry list of frustrations. In this conversation, Labor Stage manager Louis Schaffer provocatively insisted, "There is no labor audience for this theatre."[5] Schaffer's assertion captured a moment of crisis for the workers' theatre movement and more broadly for the labor movement toward the end of the 1930s. As New Deal policies, an improving economy, and geopolitical unrest coalesced in the run-up to

World War II, a recently invigorated labor movement once again found itself on unsteady ground, destabilizing the workers' theatre movement and labor drama programs with it. In an attempt to make sense of these concerns, Schaffer called out artists, accusing them of nostalgia for time gone by: "Intellectuals know of the progressive labor movement of twenty-five years ago, an immigrant labor group desiring culture, imbued with revolutionary spirit."[6] Similarly, the International Ladies' Garment Workers' Union's Fannia Cohn, who had been recently stripped of her executive secretary title in the union's fraught reorganization, criticized artists' lack of understanding regarding actual workers and recommended they "get closer to the labor movement to get the story."[7] The Rebel Arts Group's Samuel Friedman blamed the left's reliance on Soviet Russia's propagandistic theatrical forms and the influence of Popular Front ideologies: "Out of agit-prop theatre developed the workers' theatre and then the united front. There the vigorous thrust necessary to a workers' theatre was lost in an effort to gain a broader base. This was a vital loss."[8] *New Theatre* magazine's editor Herbert Kline criticized the material, stating, "The big problem is plays. The audiences don't want bad plays. Only good plays will form a theatre habit." Artist Margaret Larkin castigated the movement's failures in organizational management while others targeted the group's New York City bias, suggesting that artists failed to find resonant stories of U.S. workers outside cosmopolitan industrial centers. The rising popularity of movies, worsening working conditions for labor drama troupes as compared with professional theatre companies, increasing costs for theatre tickets, the overly intellectual bent of plays, and even the inability of labor organizations to pay playwrights for their scripts received mention in the discussion as well. Playwright Albert Maltz summed up the state of affairs regarding both workers' theatre and labor drama in sobering terms: "There is too much pessimism."[9] Something was indeed amiss.

The manifest sense of unease at the 1936 Workers' Theatre Conference might initially seem misplaced in light of several meaningful and potentially positive developments for workers' theatre in the mid-1930s. First, the Group Theatre's productions of *Waiting for Lefty* at the Civic Repertory and Longacre Theatres in the first half of 1935 had been undeniable successes. The League of Workers' Theatres, which had formed in late 1931, also grew its membership across the nation by 1935. Even more exciting were recent legislative developments. The 1934 election ushered in a supermajority for Democrats in the Senate and a significant gain of seats in the House. These victories marked the first time an incumbent president's party gained ground in a midterm election since 1866, and many read these results as a loud and positive referendum on President Franklin Delano Roosevelt's unprecedentedly left-leaning New Deal agenda. Soon after, Congress passed the Wagner Act, establishing the National Labor Relations Board (NLRB). Even more important, the legislature passed the Emergency Relief Appropriations Act, which ushered in the Works Progress Administration and a $27 million investment into Federal One, an umbrella project supported federally funded arts and culture programs including the Federal Theatre Project. The tide was rapidly turning toward the leftist agenda and, for the first time in the United States, arts and culture were central to these large-scale government initiatives.

Despite these positive developments, labor drama leaders were correct to view the rapidly evolving political and artistic landscape with some concern. Arts-based activism, along with the entire leftist political movement in the United States, changed dramatically in response to World War II and the Cold War. First, the rise of the new entertainment modes of film, radio, and later television rapidly destabilized theatre's prominence in society. The NLRB exacerbated these concerns for workers' theatres by galvanizing labor organizing in the film and radio industries, especially on the West Coast. These developments focused attention away from theatre centers like New York City and, more troublingly, away from theatre in general.

Additionally, New Deal successes opened space for pushing the limits of leftist ideology in politics and culture, and the results produced a particularly salient example of turmoil brought on by the social, economic, and political phenomenon of rising expectations. A well-established concept in economics and social science discourse, this phenomenon suggests that economic growth and change, along with political accomplishments, lead constituencies who benefit from these developments to accelerate their expectations, outpacing the sustainable rate of change that has led to the initial cultural, political, or economic improvement.[10] In keeping with this principle, the communist-affiliated Popular Front, a coalition of the left's more radical elements—including the young CIO; the Wobblies; the antifascists; and (significantly for labor drama) communist-aligned intellectuals, artists, and activists—tested the limits of leftist possibilities in the United States. The Communist Party of the United States of America's larger goals of uniting workers to form a new labor-focused political party that might challenge the anti-labor policies in Democratic southern states is one example of these rising expectations. Now understood as aligned with the Communist Party in the USSR and glowing red with Marxist-Leninist influence despite the reality being much more nuanced, the Popular Front movement not only splintered FDR's Democratic Party–led alliance, but also collapsed labor activism into a broader platform that included battling racial and religious injustices outside the Northeast.[11] For labor-oriented theatre, the affiliation of U.S. activist art with the Popular Front shifted activist rhetoric from around the labor movement to broader notions including reawakened and reimagined progressivism, collectivism, and general understandings of newness regarding political thought, likely a reflection of "New Deal" rhetoric in political goings-on during the 1930s. This Popular Front influence is most evident in the name shift from the League of Workers' Theatres to the New Theatre League and the related name change of their most popular publication from *Workers Theatre* magazine to *New Theatre* in 1935, as the organization moved away from exclusively focusing on labor activism. Furthermore, the much-lauded Federal Theatre Project (FTP) further impacted workers' theatre by diverting resources and recruiting artists to work on the FTP's socially minded but not explicitly labor-oriented productions. Several FTP productions would face scrutiny for their inclusion of socialist and communist overtones, most notably illustrated by the outrage over the 1937 children's production of *Revolt of the Beavers*.[12]

If the Federal Theatre Project's subsequent decline by 1939, the renaming of *New Theatre* magazine to *New Theatre and Film* in 1937, and the shuttering of theatre companies like the Theatre Union in 1937 and the Group Theatre in 1940 are taken as clues, the 1936 workers' theatre conference now reads as a bellwether of impending strife. Even Brookwood, the conference host site and bastion of the experimental workers' education movement, would close in a state of political and financial turmoil by the end of 1936. Likewise, the short-lived pedagogical drama experiments in workers' colleges would soon retreat into relative obscurity, a fate sealed by World War II, the second Red Scare, the Dies commission and House

Un-American Activities Committee, and, finally, the advent of the Cold War in the late 1940s.[13] This 1936 Workers' Theatre Conference, with nervous labor drama artists gathered at one of the most prominent workers' education outposts as both faced imminent decline, captures the tumult defining experiments in labor, education, performance, and radicalism in the United States during the interwar period. These four threads of influence shape and define the labor drama experiments discussed in this study and thus require additional attention in order to properly contextualize the challenges labor drama faced.

Labor

The rapid evolution, diversification, and contraction of the U.S. labor movement between 1920 and 1940 profoundly influenced labor drama. These shifts begin with the formation of the American Federation of Labor (AFL) in 1886. Although revolts against poor working conditions, joblessness, and poor pay feature heavily in narratives of the early United States, by the mid-1880s these protests grew more organized and more militant, especially among industrial unionists affiliated with the Knights of Labor, founded in 1869, and other radical left labor organizations. This turn toward militancy culminated in the 1886 Haymarket Square Riot, during which a bomb killed seven police officers and several civilians, leading to the conviction and public hanging of four men despite a lack of evidence linking them to the crime. In a reactionary response, moderate labor activists distanced themselves from perceived labor radicals and coalesced around the AFL. Samuel Gompers, who was president of the organization from 1886 until his death in 1924, established the federation as the U.S. home for trade and business unionism. As a result of these deradicalizing efforts, the AFL became one of the largest and most influential U.S. labor federations in regard to labor as a whole and to the workers' education phenomenon. The organization's agenda primarily focused on rights in the workplace, including working conditions, pay, and safety. Leadership stridently avoided any and all affiliation with the more radical aims of worker's movements, including tepid alliances with social unionists and an outright rejection of industrial unionization. The AFL was steadfastly conservative, careful in choosing its agenda, and committed to maintaining its legitimacy and longevity by avoiding scrutiny and critique. The AFL's controversy-averse influence on labor drama programs is a constant refrain in subsequent chapters.

Despite the AFL's ubiquity in workers' education and, by proxy, labor drama, it was not the only major contributor in debates about how the labor movement would best serve their workers and maintain a relevant and respected position in the U.S. capitalist economy. As the industrial age churned forward during the late nineteenth and early twentieth centuries, the labor movement expanded and diversified. Part of this evolution included newly incorporated workers such as unskilled laborers, women, immigrants, workers of color, and southern agricultural workers who founded new organizations with different philosophical foundations and practical agendas. Organizations interested in communism, socialism, neo-socialism, new unionism, and other -isms rose to prominence in the first decades of the twentieth century, and many of these new labor groups maintained tense relationships with the AFL. Among the most notable was the Industrial Workers of the World (IWW), which set out industrial and social unionization agendas, allied itself with several of the U.S. socialist parties, and was widely regarded by opponents—including the AFL—as a radical force. The IWW organized hundreds of strikes, some of them massive, including the Bread and Roses strike in 1912 and the Paterson Silk strike in 1913. By the mid-1910s, the IWW's agenda was so influential on the labor movement that a reactionary crackdown began, now known as the first Red Scare.[14] The turmoil brought on by the Great War only exacerbated concerns about the IWW's radical reaches, particularly as the chasm widened between the AFL, which supported the war, and further left groups, which opposed it, over United States involvement in World War I.

By World War I's conclusion, the labor movement was in dire straits. First, the Palmer raids in 1919 and 1920 decimated the U.S. radical left as government officials and law enforcement rounded up, imprisoned, and deported IWW members, anarchists, and other perceived radicals, details of which are discussed in the next chapter. The economy factored in as well. After a series of postwar recessions that galvanized labor activism in the early 1920s, the Roaring Twenties' widespread prosperity put many disgruntled laborers happily back to work with better wages and working conditions—no thanks to their unions. Simultaneously, pro-business

alliances, aided by sympathetic Harding, Coolidge, and Hoover administrations, waged an aggressive campaign conflating labor activism with
un-Americanness. As a result of these developments, union membership
rapidly declined, labor leadership was gutted and demoralized, and the U.S.
peacetime economy had little use for the once-powerful labor movement.
In the midst of this downturn, a group of visionary politicians, thinkers,
teachers, and artists with sympathies toward radical labor activism forged
plans for new workers' education initiatives in hopes of reinvigorating the
movement. Labor drama emerged from these efforts. However, given the
labor movement's sudden seeming irrelevance to workers' lives in the early
1920s, not to mention geopolitical turmoil left behind in the Great War's
aftermath and the active destruction of radical left groups by the government, these new programs faced uphill battles.

And then came the crash. From 1929 to roughly 1933, the Great Depression eclipsed practically all other social issues. By late 1932, the same year
Franklin Delano Roosevelt successfully campaigned for president on a platform promising "a new deal for the American people," the U.S. economy
reached its nadir.[15] Roughly a quarter of U.S. workers were unemployed,
and the country's gross domestic product was down by almost 50 percent
from a high in 1929. The nation's banks failed, and increasing numbers of
people were homeless and living in large Hooverville camps with little relief
in sight. In regard to the labor movement, as companies laid off workers, cut
wages and benefits, and undid many of labor's advances gained during the
prior thirty years, the need for a stronger labor movement grew increasingly
salient. Without protections from organized labor, workers were subject to
the whims of corporations as both navigated economic free fall. In response,
newly elected President Roosevelt moved swiftly to reshape corporate
influence and protect workers, collaborating with a politically aligned Congress to pass numerous pieces of legislation designed to stave off economic
decline and bolster government support for labor organizations in the first
half of 1933. As part of the president's "first hundred days" agenda, Congress
swiftly passed the Emergency Banking Act, the Securities Act, the Agricultural Adjustments Act, and, most important for the labor movement, the
National Industrial Recovery Act (NIRA). NIRA protected collective bargaining rights; established standards for pay, work hours, and basic working conditions; and authorized the creation of the National Labor Board

(precursor to the National Labor Relations Board). The labor movement was suddenly and surprisingly relevant once again.

Despite these developments, the labor movement struggled to find its footing. In addition to the lingering effects of the Great Depression and none-too-distant memory of the early 1920s government crackdown on radical labor activists, the movement's sudden prominence both troubled pro-business contingencies and challenged the otherwise decimated labor leadership. These growing pains, which included shifting views about how new union organizations might best serve their members, also shaped the labor drama experiment for good and for ill. Much of the debate centered on the union's role within workers' lives, particularly in response to international workers' movements. Determining where the union's influence started and stopped was a source of continuous debate among unions, labor federations, and political groups in the United States. The 1935 founding of the Congress of Industrial Organizations (CIO) helps illustrate these negotiations and how they evolved during the interwar period.

The CIO formed as an alternative for members interested in a more wide-reaching approach to labor advocacy. A small but significant faction of the AFL believed labor organizations had a responsibility to industrial unionization efforts that would help organize the masses of unskilled U.S. workers. Still others thought the AFL should involve itself in social justice causes germane to workers' lives, including women's suffrage and rights of workers of color to sit at the bargaining table. Still other members felt the AFL had a responsibility to workers' cultural lives and should support programs in labor arts, entertainment, and recreation in addition to securing better working conditions. Members advocating both industrial unionization and engagement in workers' political, social, and cultural life, otherwise known as a social unionization agenda, incited a rift within the organization. This dissenting faction founded the CIO as an alternative labor federation within the AFL.[16] However, with the IWW's history not far from memory, AFL leadership viewed the CIO's formation as a threat. They responded to this perceived danger by booting all unions affiliated with the CIO in 1935.[17]

By virtue of their interest in workers' education, labor colleges aligned themselves with social unionization ideology, closer to the CIO and IWW than the AFL. Conservative labor leaders conflated an interest in social unionization with radical left politics and believed that any association with radicals exposed the labor movement to scrutiny. These concerns were not unfounded. U.S. workers' education drew inspiration from Great Britain's controversial Plebs' League and labor college programs, the Russian Prolet-kult movement, and the influence of figures like Walter Vrooman regarding the importance of educating the worker both in and beyond the issues of the workplace. None of these influences was politically neutral. Unsurprisingly, teaching multiple variations of Marxist theory, along with an array of labor-oriented curricula, brought many schools under fire. Presumptions regarding these schools' interests in exploring all facets of the labor movement led to opposition from more mainstream organizations like the AFL, as well as from religious institutions, political groups, law enforcement, and the communities surrounding these schools. For example, in 1928, the AFL's new president, William Green, denounced Brookwood, subject of Chapter 2, as "communistic, atheistic and anti-A. F. of L.," and demanded that affiliated labor organizations sever all ties with the institution.[18] Similarly, both Highlander Folk School (Chapter 5) and Commonwealth College (Chapter 6) were subject to formal FBI investigations in the mid-1930s after reports appeared suggesting that the schools harbored and trained communists. Even Bryn Mawr College (Chapter 3) terminated its Summer School for Women Workers in 1938 after seventeen incident-free years when program leaders were falsely accused of supporting a strike and generating scandal for the alumnae and administration. The ever-present danger of radicalism in these programs was a constant source of strain.

Radicalism and Progressivism

Given these threats and accusations, a working definition of radicalism is critical for understanding the unique pedagogical approaches and political underpinnings of each institution. I borrow from Egon Bittner's seminal work, "Radicalism and the Organization of Radical Movements," and define the term as a "sociological and psychological" phenomenon that relies on both thought and action that "differ from the normal, ordinary, traditionally sanctioned world-view prevalent in any society" and that are "not a difference of degree but a juxtaposition of opposites."[19] In effect, radicalism is not simply a straying to the left or right on the path of culturally sanctioned belief, but, instead, an entire rejection of the path and every-thing it might represent. Furthermore, this understanding of radicalism requires the mind and the body to act in tandem; radical thought must become radical action to qualify as radicalism. In effect, the act of being radical requires that agents not only articulate juxtapositions in thinking about perceived dominant codes and ideas, but also embody those rejec-tions or inversions as part of a performance of radical values and ideolo-gies. This slippery definition is further complicated by the concept's ten-dency to rapidly change. Radical spaces mutate as participants negotiate their position relative to and often against both dominant codes and others in the movement. In effect, radicalism resists codification due to the variety of perspectives of the participants drawn to radical movements who desire to reject the mainstream. Thus, radicalism is the enactment of opposition-alism. Often in the context of labor drama, this oppositionalism took the form of revolutionary rhetoric and calls to upend dominant cultural and political structures and institutions.

Given this definition, even though their more conservative critics would disagree, many workers and artists considered in this study were *not* rad-ical. While many of these artists and teachers supported communist or socialist political philosophies—both of which were often conflated with radicalism in the United States during the first half of the twentieth cen-tury—they do not qualify as radicals because they most often hoped to fuse together their ideas with capitalism in order to evolve U.S. cultural and economic institutions into a more equitable playing field for all. They rarely aimed to topple societally sanctioned political, economic, artistic, or education systems, and, instead, set out to work from within extant polit-ical systems. Despite their tangential affiliations with actual radical move-ments during this period, each institution examined in this book negotiated accusations of radicalism. Even more, each group navigated differences between political radicalism, artistic radicalism, and educational radical-ism as they developed their work. For example, a group might express undeniably radical ideas about politics, but choose a very rigidly conform-ist style of artistic production to explore these ideas through performance. For instance, Brookwood dramatics instructor Hazel MacKaye, the subject of Chapter 3 and a suffragist, probably considered herself quite radical in the late 1910s while advocating for women's voting rights. However, as I will demonstrate, the suffragists' radicalism quickly morphed into a legitimate and socially sanctioned form of activism, leaving behind MacKaye as an old-school relic less than a decade after she led the vanguard of political performance. Some groups, like the women workers of the Southern Summer School (Chapter 4), vehemently rejected ideas that they harbored any radicals or supported radical thought. They launched aggressive publicity campaigns, going so far as to include a statement on all published literature indicating programs were "non-sectarian, non-political experiments in Workers' education sponsored by an independent committee" to reinforce their political neutrality and rejection of radical groups.[20] In contrast, a few of these subjects of study, like Commonwealth College's president Lucien Koch, *were* radical; they believed in overturning the current state of affairs and generating a new world order aligned with radical communism. However, Commonwealth performances were not particularly radical in their aesthetic orientation, choosing oft-critiqued variety forms including minstrelsy and Toby shows to engage rural southern workers.

Although accusations of radicalism ripple through each chapter, it is also important to acknowledge the influence of the complex and historically situated philosophy of progressivism in these programs. Progressivism, a multifaceted series of efforts that responded to rapid industrialization in the United States during the late 1800s, directly shaped labor drama.[21] The historical Progressive Era, demarcated by the Gilded Age's conclusion and the advent of the Roaring Twenties, ushered in a new focus on social uplift and government involvement in protecting the common good. The Progressive Era also contributes to twentieth- and twenty-first-century understandings of progressivism as a broad political strategy. Between the late 1800s and early 1900s, progressivism evolved and expanded, providing the philosophical foundation for Theodore Roosevelt's short-lived Progressive Party and shaping the platforms of William Howard Taft and Woodrow Wilson. Some of the many Progressive Era reforms included an increased focus on scientific inquiry and a rejection of social Darwinism, the growth of conservation efforts, women's suffrage, the formation of settlement houses, temperance and Prohibition, and the passage of antitrust and child labor laws. Even though many of these efforts were laudable as steps toward a more just society, the Progressive Era was also an undeniably racist period, with reform efforts reinforcing white supremacy thanks in large part to the rise of a new middle-class white elite, the influence of eugenics as a last gasp of pseudo-scientific racism, and a largely unchecked commitment to imperialism.[22] While many of the workers' education institutions discussed in this book were not radical, they most certainly navigated the Progressive Era's lingering influence. Through these struggles, many of these labor drama programs reveal profound challenges inherent in making the seeds of good ideas less tainted by white supremacism, particularly after the New Deal. Given their aims to reshape society, many of these institutions were easy targets for political and organizational backlash. Therefore, I examine how the influences of radicalism and progressivism, broadly construed through political, artistic, and educational thought, manifested throughout each program.

Education

The influence of progressive education philosophies on labor drama provides one particularly salient example of progressivism's evolution during the interwar period. Though many labor education initiatives in the early 1920s drew inspiration from pedagogical experiments based on the social unionism rhetoric from Europe, discussed in greater detail in Chapter 2, by the mid-1930s labor groups sponsored education programs as part of a larger interest in rehabilitating the legitimacy of the workers' movement as part of the progressive education movement. Progressive education theories and pedagogy developed alongside workers' education programs in this period. This work took many forms, with John Dewey anchoring the U.S. school of thought, particularly in the Northeast. Dewey, like other progressive education proponents, looked to new educational paradigms outside formal schooling, from scouting to workers' education, as laboratories for testing out new pedagogical theories and practices. Dewey's ideas about individuality, pragmatism, art, and experiential learning are most relevant for this particular discussion of progressive education and its connection to labor drama in workers' colleges. As one of the preeminent U.S. philosophers writing in the late nineteenth century and first half of the twentieth century, Dewey promoted ideas about progressive education that transformed and continue to exert influence on the ways in which U.S. teachers and students operate, especially in arts education fields. However, even when taken independently of other contemporaneous progressive education theorists, Deweyan progressivism was a complex and expansive theoretical project that evolved as rapidly as other facets of society during the interwar period. In the broadest strokes, Deweyan progressivism is defined by its focus on pragmatism and the idea of positively moving forward as a society. Both of these ideas require educational institutions to function as crucibles and as active agencies in negotiating the meaning of democracy and societal progress. In addition, Dewey's focus on pragmatism positions educational spaces as sites for working out the contours of societal progress through actual problems of the day. Thus, Dewey crafted his philosophical writings in response to contemporary social issues, including the labor movement.

In addition, Dewey's ideas about the act of *doing* in the processes of both education and art-making were equally important to labor drama's founding philosophies. Dewey believed that learning relied upon specific life relevancy, an act of doing or practicing doing. These principles extended to aesthetic experiences as well, whereby learners practiced skills and developed knowledge in understanding, appreciating, and making art, a term Dewey deliberately left open for interpretation. These experiences would support learners as they cultivated understandings of life's aesthetic dimensions both in and beyond school. Dewey's synthesis of aesthetic education and experiential learning appear in his seminal work *Art as Experience* (1934). In the book he critiques the tendency to "set Art upon a remote pedestal":

> In order to *understand* the esthetic in its ultimate and approved forms, one must begin with it in the raw; in the events and scenes that hold the attentive eye and ear of man, arousing his interest and affording him enjoyment as he looks and listens: the sights that hold the crowd. . . . The sources of art in human experience will be learned by him who sees how the tense grace of the ball-player infects the onlooking crowd; who notes the delight of the housewife in tending her plants.[23]

Dewey believed that an authentic experience with art rested with an individual's personal connection to the aesthetic dimension of everyday life, from cultivating houseplants to the aesthetic virtuosity of athletic performance. These ideas about the aesthetics of life provided the foundation for art and creativity, particularly drama, as a modality for learning in many labor drama classrooms. Dewey's suggestion that all learners might access an aesthetic dimension of life through experiential education echoes through each labor drama experiment discussed in this study.

Dewey was front and center for many developments in New York labor activism given his professorship at Columbia University, his membership and participation in the American Federation of Teachers, and his work as vice president of the Teachers' Union of New York. Between 1920 and 1940, Dewey developed many of his most influential writings via work with educators in the labor movement.[24] By the labor leaders' logic, if workers understood economic disparity in both practical and academic terms, they would rally around the core issues of the labor movement, calming some of the organizational tumult as the labor movement quickly gained power during the early years of FDR's administration. In particular, Dewey maintained a strong relationship with Brookwood, offering guest lectures on campus on several occasions in the late 1920s. In addition to his relationship with Brookwood, he published numerous essays in a variety of labor press publications, consulted with Highlander faculty, and worked with pro-labor organizations like the League for Independent Political Action, a political organization that hoped to unify socialists and progressives into a new political party in the late 1920s. The AFL even endorsed Dewey as a leading voice in educational theory before later admonishing him in the Brookwood/AFL split in 1928.[25] In response, Dewey directly addressed attacks on labor education in a 1929 article: "It is a part of the policy to eliminate from the labor movement the schools and influences that endeavor to develop independent leaders of organized labor who are interested in a less passive and more social policy than that now carried on by the American Federation of Labor."[26] Dewey was deeply invested in not only the pedagogical function of labor education, but also the political challenges faced by experimental left-leaning learning initiatives in this period of cultural upheaval. His ideas about how education might immediately and practically change the world formed a philosophical core for most programs discussed within these chapters.

Several other key concepts from Deweyan progressivism likewise influenced the schools' approaches to teaching workers through drama. The idea that schools were communities instead of simply sites for knowledge acquisition was a central value in many programs. For example,

Commonwealth Labor College, the subject of Chapter 6, supported a working farm where teachers and students worked alongside one another in the fields to help fund their education. Commonwealth's educational community demonstrates progressive educators' pioneering use of experiential learning practices, curricular development focused on students' needs and desires, and reconceptualization of the school's social dimension as a site where learners could acquire knowledge about being a citizen in the larger society by living together as citizens in an educational context. Furthermore, this focus on community-centered learning exemplifies progressive beliefs about schools as sites for social reform. Accordingly, the workers' programs studied here focused on how their educational programs would inspire worker-students not only to learn about the labor movement, but also to prepare for a role in labor activism. Deweyan progressivism was both an undeniably important component of these schools' missions and another form of experimentation within these institutions.

Performance

Drama's popularity during the interwar period undoubtedly inspired its inclusion in labor college curricula. During the early twentieth century, theatre approached its apex as a cultural form. In the early days of radio and film, theatre provided the most accessible and common avenues for entertaining the growing middle-class masses. As theatre historian Thomas Postlewait writes about the period, "American entertainment became one of the largest industries in the country, encompassing not only dramatic performances and musical theatre (from revues to opera) but also minstrelsy, vaudeville, amusement arcades and parks, circuses, and the new media of film and radio."[27] These developments in theatrical popular culture advanced alongside a more widespread visual culture. The interwar period was a period of spectacle, pictures, glossy magazines, elaborate stage technology, and celebrities. In many ways, the popular entertainment of the 1920s and 1930s might be thought of as akin to cotton candy: light, fluffy, saccharine, easy to digest, and usually featuring many lovely colors. This trend was a natural adaptation for audiences, a group fatigued by economic woes, wars, international instability, and growing pains associated with making a go of society as a rapidly changing nation.

As theatre diversified and workers acquired leisure time, interest in amateur dramatics similarly increased. Audiences were not only attending performances in unprecedented numbers, but also creating theatre in their newfound free time. Throughout the twentieth century, recreational performances, from plays to skits to vaudeville and variety shows, served as important pastimes in churches, cultural centers, schools, immigrant community groups, Little Theatres, and community drama groups. As amateur and folk theatre programs flourished, formal theatre and performance likewise responded to the desires of larger groups of audience members. These developments helped bring aesthetic values to ordinary people, directly shaping mass and popular cultures.

This shift toward theatre for the masses, however, was not without concerns. For example, hierarchies shaping elite, popular, and mass artforms grew increasingly salient in formal theatre. These tensions present themselves as a challenge time and time again in labor colleges. In contrast to the expanding popular and mass cultures, most pioneering labor drama instructors were not interested in cotton candy art. As intellectuals-cum-instructors took up teaching labor drama, they introduced plays they found thoughtful and stimulating, most often from European political theatre movements. The influence of German theatre artists like Erwin Piscator and Bertolt Brecht, as well as the Russian proletkultists Sergei Eisenstein, Vsevolod Meyerhold, and others, presented challenges to the U.S. theatre artists interested in workers' theatre. As Herbert Kline, editor of *New Theatre* magazine from 1934 to 1937, noted in a 1934 article, "The difficulty in writing a revolutionary play that encompasses not only the lives of individuals, but also the manifold ramifications and interlacings of class relationships and conflicts," is "great."[28] Kline's statement exemplifies anxieties and ambivalence experienced by many artists interested in U.S. political theatre due in part to the imperfect transfer of techniques and forms from countries like Russia and Germany to the U.S. capitalist landscape. Many labor drama instructors hoped to adopt theatrical techniques from these artists in order to think deeply about complex labor issues, and they wanted theatrical works that were gritty, honest, and truthful. In contrast, students were much more likely to view dramatics as pure recreation and could not yet fully engage with the more challenging concepts presented in their courses, let alone interpret those ideas through drama. These tensions resulted in important negotiations among students, instructors, school leadership, and the greater school community about what aesthetic values to uphold in their institution's particular brand of dramatics. Interestingly, in most cases, instructors yielded to their students' interests, and many of the enduring plays from these programs are odd political-variety-show-musical-melodrama hybrids that more often reflect the influences of popular culture than the larger workers' theatre movement, let alone avant-garde and political theatres. These interesting but somewhat peculiar works provided challenges for many instructors; by capitulating to their students' interests, they crafted, in their view, theatre of questionable quality despite its relevance to those who created it. The challenges of navigating labor education themes, theatrical trends of the day, and the ideological and political values of the institution in regard to performance pedagogy and theatrical production are constant refrains in each of these case studies.

Weaving Together the Threads: The Labor Drama Experiment

As an experiment attempting to help workers make sense of larger political, cultural, and social issues through theatre-as-pedagogy, labor drama changed rapidly between the late 1910s and the early 1940s. Accordingly, this study reconstructs histories of labor college dramatics by acknowledging and including popular culture, politics, labor agendas, and educational innovation in tandem with the historical record and contemporaneous artistic and political avant-gardes surrounding these programs. In Chapter 2, I describe some of the first documented courses in labor drama as part of Portland Labor College's experiments in workers' education. I focus on dramatics instructor Doris Smith and her leadership of the Labor College Players. Smith, an actress who worked in Chicago and in New York's Little Theatre scene, began her experiment in labor drama with little in the way of a roadmap. Smith took inspiration from pageants and the complex progressive politics in early 1920s Portland, Oregon, utilizing her classes as laboratories for transforming Portland's Labor Temple into the United States' first and, at the time, only workers' theatre. This study of Smith frames the subsequent chapter about Hazel MacKaye, a former radical suffragist who pioneered activist pageantry and taught dramatics at Brookwood Labor College between 1925 and 1926. MacKaye, daughter of prominent actor, director, manager, and inventor of stage technologies Steele MacKaye, shaped one of the earliest and most influential labor drama programs in the workers' education movement. However, as MacKaye synthesized her newfound interest in labor dramatics with her pageantry expertise, she wrestled with approaches that would provide a pedagogically and aesthetically sound experience for her students. MacKaye's tenure at Brookwood foreshadowed a prolific period for labor drama in educational settings throughout the United States, and her work as a bridging figure between pageants and the proletariat highlights challenges inherent to the evolving political performance genre during the mid-1920s.

Chapter 4 demonstrates the interconnectedness and professionalization of labor drama in workers' education programs—particularly for women—during the early 1930s. Specifically, I consider Hollace Ransdell, a teacher, librarian, activist, and journalist most noted for her 1931 ACLU report about the Scottsboro trials in Alabama, who taught labor dramatics at the Southern Summer School from 1928 until 1936. Ransdell's educational and activist background, while connected to radical political circles, included no formal dramatics training. Ransdell's amateur background serves as a testament to the ways in which the budding experiments in labor drama allowed for an increasingly diverse group of artists and educators to take up performance as a method for teaching likewise diverse student populations. Chapters 5 and 6 consider how labor drama operated in a budding southern labor movement in two equally compelling experiments in southern workers' education. First, I examine the work of Zilphia Horton at Highlander Folk School in Tennessee. Horton, an interdisciplinary artist most noted for penning several civil rights anthems, including "We Shall Overcome," also taught drama during her first years at the Highlander Folk School. Her students included numerous activists and artists, including Lee Hays and Pete Seeger of the political folk group the Weavers, whom she instructed in the areas of arts and activism. As a result of this labor dramatics training, Hays spent two years as drama instructor at Commonwealth Labor College, located on the outskirts of rural Mena, Arkansas. There, he experimented with drama as pedagogy. Despite his prolific period of dramatic production during his Commonwealth tenure, he never again worked with dramatic forms. Looking at Hays's brief detour into dramatics helps contextualize not only how and why labor drama programs drifted into obscurity but also how they were transformed into new, largely unrecognizable forms after the 1940s. In concluding this study, I suggest how and why labor drama has largely been forgotten, but also how it was subsequently transformed. In particular, I describe several performance sites and genres where contemporary artists and historians might find remnants and legacies of work by figures like Doris Smith, Hazel MacKaye, Hollace Ransdell, Zilphia Horton, and Lee Hays.

Given my focus on drama as a form of pedagogy, I consider class plans, directors' reports, course material, and other process-oriented materials alongside performances, playscripts, reviews, and other formal product-oriented items produced by these programs. These process- and product-related documents help to reconstruct, but not fully rehabilitate, these programs, particularly in regard to their artistic and aesthetic quality. I do not set out to illuminate these productions' unsung artistic brilliance, and I acknowledge both discrete failures in various programs and the perceptions of failure surrounding labor drama as whole. Conceiving of labor drama as a kind of failure, albeit a productive one, also presents a series of fascinating historiographical quandaries: What are the limits of rehabilitative studies? What is the value of looking at performance that existed firmly in the margins? What do historians make of amateur art? These questions rise to the surface again and again through these chapters. For instance, many criteria theatregoers use to evaluate performance rightly suggest that labor drama was, at best, artistically mediocre. From poorly devised and melodramatically simplistic narratives influenced by Frank Capra movies and Tin Pan Alley tunes to low-budget performances with unsophisticated production values, as exemplified by Brookwood's production of *Man and the Masses*, labor drama's lasting artifacts, from scripts to production photos to reviews, often imply that labor drama was too poorly crafted to warrant much aesthetic attention. Therefore, I have worked diligently to avoid placing these artists and their work on a pedestal. My resistance to excessive praise of labor drama aesthetics allows this form the space to exist as specific to a time, place, and people that was community-oriented, focused on process, and primarily pedagogical. This work looks much like the day-to-day teaching and art practice created in classrooms and learning contexts that creates change and impacts lives, even on a small scale. By discussing what happened within the process of creation as much as I analyze enduring products like reviews and scripts, I draw attention to the meaningful experiences for participants in both learning and theatre-making, even as I acknowledge that some of these productions were probably dismal to watch.

Given the amateur and pedagogical orientation of labor drama, this theatrical work was valuable and sustaining for the school communities that supported it. Instructors and worker-students explored process-oriented techniques for devising new dramatic works, represented real people in real-life situations, and engaged with collective approaches to art-making. These labor drama participants also endured great danger and took serious risks in making political art. Indeed, the labor drama experiments discussed in this book are frequently complicated, if not sad stories. They are defined by too little money, too few resources, and too little time. They are, as Louis Schaffer reminded his colleagues at the 1936 Workers' Theatre Conference, stories of artists searching desperately for audiences, purpose, and meaning. They are delimited by world wars, shaped by the Great Depression, and even scrutinized by the FBI. Each case study is rife with defeat, naïveté, misunderstandings, injunctions, criminal investigations, and a host of relatively awful plays. Nevertheless, these experiments, even with their sad endings and enduring what-ifs, mark the important work and messy nature of artistic experimentation. They speak to the possibilities of transdisciplinarity and of pushing oneself beyond a comfort zone. They serve as testaments to the belief that drama, when tailored to the needs of a specific population, possesses the potential to transform consciousness. They also remind readers that performance-based learning holds the potential to teach people about their lives and about their world in ways that other forms of pedagogy simply cannot, and this transformation can be traced through the archive. This is also a humbling study that demonstrates how committed groups of individuals, regardless of their background or training, created performance that was important to the audiences and the participants who engaged with it. It is the story of students and teachers, of workers and intellectuals, of amateurs and professionals, of artists and skeptics, and of radicalism and legitimation. These experiments in labor drama further reveal the margins of performance as radical spaces of risk where laborers, women, workers of color, and immigrants engaged in art, education, and activism as part of the vast cultural phenomenon that was and is the U.S. labor movement.

CHAPTER 2

Performance from the Ranks

The Advent of Labor Drama
at Portland Labor College, 1922–25

> *In our effort to reach these young people we have got to make it worth their while to come. The stage will not only be an attraction, but it will be a fine means of education.*
>
> James H. Maurer, president of the Workers' Education Bureau

The Unique Portland Experiment

Both labor drama and workers' education grew out of labor activism boosted by a booming war-fueled manufacturing sector and an artificially contracted labor force given the number of men fighting in the Great War. Activism on the part of this invigorated labor movement resulted in several workers' rights victories and union membership growth, particularly in the mid- to late 1910s. As union membership grew, labor activists and unionists looked toward new initiatives, including both art and education, to support workers and sustain the labor movement's momentum, particularly after the war's conclusion. As part of these new programs, experiments with drama-based methods in similarly experimental workers' education initiatives appeared in a variety of institutions throughout the nation. Many of these smaller, geographically diverse programs pioneered techniques, both in drama and beyond, that other workers' education programs adapted for their own use as the movement expanded, grew more interconnected, and professionalized. However, early experiments with labor drama in workers' education did not reflect a robust contemporaneous workers' theatre movement. In fact, labor drama experiments in the late 1910s and early 1920s preceded the founding of the short-lived Workers' Drama League and the New Playwrights' Theatre, some of the earliest

U.S. workers' theatre organizations, by more than five years.[1] Instead, these early programs reflected a period of rapid change for upper-middle-class white women's political activism as part of evolving first-wave feminisms after the Nineteenth Amendment's passage in 1919 and an expanding interest in amateur dramatics. Accordingly, my first case study focuses on a small, short-lived labor college in Portland, Oregon, and the work of actor and educator Doris Smith. Smith, a recent transplant to Portland from the Midwest, and the Portland Labor Players demonstrate how evolving feminisms, an emboldened labor movement, and shifting understandings of national identity shaped the labor drama phenomenon of the 1920s and 1930s.[2] Through Smith's leadership, a "unique experiment" in "the staging of plays by its own members" took place in the early 1920s, providing some of the first methodological approaches incorporating dramatics pedagogy as part of a young workers' education program.[3] Smith's work also demonstrates the earliest experimentation in adapting performance methods for workers' education that were previously isolated to theatre training programs. Portland Labor College's experiment with drama as a method for education, an outlet for creative expression and cultural life, and a tool for activism shapes the earliest lineages of both labor drama and workers' theatre, calling attention to many and varied ways in which politically engaged artists in far-flung areas of the country, including places like Portland, Oregon, participated in this new performance phenomenon.

Riots, Raids, and Reform: Labor Education After WWI

First, the context for early labor drama experiments frames my discussion of the Portland Labor Players. While Portland itself was deeply immersed in a period of self-examination around race, politics, and culture, this moment of collective introspection was just one instance of the nationwide reexamination and redefinition of the United States' post–World War I identity. The labor drama phenomenon occurred alongside a larger trend to democratize and decommercialize dramatic forms in regards to not only the structures and content of theatre-making, but also geography. Even though the workers' theatre movement was still incipient during the 1910s and early 1920s, these experiments were part of an expanding and diversifying popular and mass performance culture and coincided with the advent of film. Most theatre that either engaged workers or dramatized workers' lives during this period was associated with Russian, Yiddish, and German immigrant theatres. Other workers' theatre experiments included a smattering of socially oriented plays in the Little Theatre movement, productions on the pedagogically focused Chautauqua circuit, and political pageantry.[4] Other influences, from trends in progressive education to the increased popularity of drama as a leisure activity to the collective shift among suffragists in search of a new cause, shaped nascent labor drama as well. Furthermore, the turn toward internationalism, a reality made possible through technological developments in radio, film, and a booming print and periodical culture, introduced techniques and tools from a variety of labor movements abroad. Also, both domestic and global travel grew more efficient thanks to advances in the automobile, ocean liner, and steamship industries. This circulation of both ideas and individuals meant that artists, thinkers, and politicians, including those from places like the newly formed Soviet Union, shared their ideas with wider audiences. As a result, ideas and techniques out of international workers' movements seeped into the consciousness of U.S. labor organizations.

Then there was the war. After a long period of isolationism, neutrality, and independence from larger global conflicts, the Great War forced the United States into a new and exceptionally high-profile role in this global conflict. The country's late-stage entry into the European war arena, coupled with President Woodrow Wilson's leadership in brokering the controversial Treaty of Versailles at the contentious and lengthy 1919 Paris Peace Conference, positioned the United States, a country less than fifty years removed from its own bloody civil war with wounds still quite raw, in a more prominent role in the stewardship of global peace. This moment resulted in a rapid and radical realignment not only of global power, but also of the U.S. identity: Did U.S. citizenship now require a different responsibility to a greater good? How did the country's political and cultural identities flow out beyond the nation's borders? What did it mean to be a U.S. citizen *now*?

This period of national introspection arrived alongside the wrenching task of sorting through postwar global trauma. As communities and countries involved in World War I attempted to reconcile the catastrophic loss of life and the calamitous effects of protracted combat, working toward both personal and collective philosophical, spiritual, or political mooring to make sense of the prior decade, the outcomes of wrestling with these anxieties came to define the immediate postwar period. Workers' education, socially engaged art, and radical and progressive politics all reflected a refocused commitment to examining the moral and philosophical structures grounding a nation, helping carve a space for experiments like labor drama. Nonetheless, this same introspection also bore out apprehensions that contributed to newly awakened movements around nationalism, nativism, populism, protectionism, and racism. These ideas would provide fecund soil in which to nurture hysterias that would mature into the horrors of World War II and, later, the Cold War.

These troubling forces would damage left-leaning political groups affiliated with the labor movement for the better part of the 1920s. The negative influences on the postwar labor movement were manifold. First, U.S. entry into World War I had been a deeply divisive issue in the country, and many on the left, including the increasingly powerful Socialist Party of America led by Eugene V. Debs and the more radical communist factions affiliated with the IWW Wobblies, vehemently condemned U.S. military involvement. Unsurprisingly, many war supporters, including several members of Congress and President Wilson, viewed opposing the war as unpatriotic. The labor movement's steadfast objection to the war placed it in a precarious position, particularly after public opinion shifted on involvement by 1917, the result of a concerted government effort to bolster support that included efforts by Wilson's controversial new government agency, the Committee on Public Information (or the Creel committee, named for George Creel, the journalist who chaired it), one of the first state-sanctioned propaganda machines in the modern era. The Creel committee was responsible for now-iconic World War I propaganda images, including the James Montgomery Flagg portrait of an emphatic Uncle Sam, pointing his finger and demanding, "I want YOU for the U.S. Army." Second, Russia's instability added fuel to pro-war efforts and skepticism toward the left. As Russia pulled out of World War I to deal with its own revolution and civil war, conflating the labor movement with dangerous red politics became much more prevalent. Anti-left, pro-war groups capitalized on the U.S. fear of Russian unrest by playing up the threat of a potential stateside Bolshevik revolution at the hands of covert operatives embedded in the labor movement and hiding out in immigrant communities. This campaign was disturbingly effective. The anti-red campaigns led to passage of the Espionage Act in 1917, followed by a series of Immigration Acts in 1918 and 1919 that limited certain groups' entry into the United States, including, but certainly not limited to, political radicals from Russia.[5] The labor movement's alignment with left-leaning political philosophies during this unprecedented geopolitical instability would prove a dire liability.

As the labor movement attempted to sort out concerns about these connections to Russia, a series of recessions (mild in 1918–19 and much more severe in 1920–21) exacerbated tensions regarding the red threat. Although war manufacturing had galvanized the labor movement during World War I and allowed for several positive developments—including the recognition of many new unions, the decline of child labor, and increasing support for the eight-hour workday—once soldiers returned home and the need for war products declined, the economy rapidly slowed. Furthermore, misguided contractionary monetary policy from the newly formed Federal Reserve Bank raised interest rates during this period of economic decline, allowing inflation not only to persist, but to intensify. As a result, unemployment surged, goods were scarce, and the emboldened labor movement, reticent to back away from gains achieved during the prior decade's war effort, opted to mobilize. In 1919, millions of workers from practically every industry participated in thousands of strikes from coast to coast.

This massive mobilization of workers paralyzed entire industries, as in the case of the 1919 Steel Strike, spooking many business leaders and pro-business politicians. In response, these pro-business allies set out to develop strategy to further diminish labor's influence. The choice to undermine labor activism was also politically wise, as publicly renouncing supposedly radical leftists most often associated with the labor movement provided a fruitful platform for Republicans to define themselves against an increasingly unpopular Wilson administration. These tensions erupted when a series of anarchist mail bombings, set to arrive on May Day, targeted anti-labor leaders including the mayors of Seattle and New York City, prominent business leaders like J. P. Morgan and John D. Rockefeller, and numerous politicians including U.S. Attorney General A. Mitchell Palmer. The reaction to the bombings was a swift and sweeping anti-red crackdown known as the first Red Scare. The Palmer raids in 1919–20, named for the same attorney general, set out to completely remove the influence of the radical left, including anarchists and communists, in the United States.[6] A particularly dark chapter in U.S. history, the raids resulted in the unlawful arrest of tens of thousands of people and the deportation of hundreds of immigrants, mostly from Russia and Germany. The U.S. labor movement's more radical arms, including the IWW, the anarchist movement, and Socialist Party, saw their influence diminished, if not obliterated.

If the anti-red crackdown brought on by the first Red Scare was not worrisome enough for more moderate labor leadership, the 1920 presidential election firmly reinforced changing public opinion regarding labor activism. The landslide presidential election of dark horse pro-business Republican Warren G. Harding served as a clear rejection both of Wilson's postwar idealism and of the progressive political movement, metaphorically rendered obsolete upon the sudden and unexpected passing of Teddy Roosevelt, rumored to be planning a run as a Progressive Republican candidate, in 1919. Roosevelt's death left a vacuum for the Republican presidential ticket, and Harding, with promises of normalcy and a commitment to "sustainment in triumphant nationality," coupled with "less government in business and more business in government," filled it.[7] With Harding's sweeping victory, the labor movement entered a period of contraction and redefinition. In the significant albeit short-lived Harding administration, several workers' organizations set out to depoliticize their membership and activist agenda, eliminating concerns about radical infiltration in both their rank membership and their leadership. These tidied-up workers' organizations would allow the labor movement to present itself as a beacon of rationality. Members would be willing to sit at the bargaining table instead of staging massive protests or throwing bombs through their adversaries' windows. These efforts produced much infighting and factionalism among the movement's diminished radical reaches and contributed to labor's decline during the Roaring Twenties, and many leaders viewed cleaning up the labor movement's act as the most reasonable path forward.

The key labor organization spearheading these deradicalization efforts was the American Federation of Labor. AFL president Samuel Gompers had initially opposed U.S. involvement in the war, like most labor leaders, but by 1916 he shifted toward supporting Wilson's preparedness efforts. Gompers's war support, both a practical and ideological decision, was an incredibly divisive but strategic move. While other labor organizations viewed participation in the wartime effort a Faustian bargain, the AFL saw war support as an opportunity to secure a voice in the federal government at a time when labor would be integral to the United States' first major war effort on a global scale. Despite setting the AFL directly in opposition to many organizations associated with the groundswell of labor activism during the war, Gompers's gamble paid off. Wilson named Gompers to the Council of National Defense as the secretary of labor in 1916. This advisory position gave AFL-affiliated unions representation in discussions of war preparedness and directly supported the labor movement during World War I. By stridently committing itself to working within the system, the AFL was key in orchestrating several wartime labor advancements, like increased wages and shorter workdays. More significantly, the AFL set itself apart from other organizations targeted in the anti-red crackdown. By the war's end, as the first Red Scare and the Palmer raids decimated other labor organizations and factions, the AFL was positioned to lead the labor movement forward from a largely apolitical reformist platform focused on anti-radical business unionism that focused explicitly on the rights of workers in the workplace and excluded union efforts regarding workers' cultural lives and broader political activism beyond workplace protections. Under this supposedly innocuous guise, the AFL successfully recruited new membership between 1915 and 1920, their numbers growing to unprecedented levels.[8] While the AFL's role in the postwar economy falls outside of this chapter's scope, its role in the postwar labor movement directly influenced the approach to workers' education and labor drama programs in the early 1920s, including those at the new Portland Labor College.

The Beginnings of Art and Education in the AFL

Although the AFL had included general support for education in its organizational platform since at least 1892, it had never prioritized formal education programs specifically for workers. Instead, AFL leadership advocated for increased state investment in more widespread and comprehensive public education that would allow children to attend school for longer periods of time, delaying their entry into the workforce. This effort to support child labor laws was a direct reflection of the organization's business unionism agenda.[9] Thus, the AFL neither formally endorsed nor funded

education programs for workers, for several reasons. First, education specifically for workers was too closely associated with the social unionism
ideologies associated with the labor movement's more radical reaches. Second, the AFL determined the financial investment into large programs like
workers' education would not best serve their constituencies. However, by
the mid-1910s, conversations about workers' education and proletariat culture as part of the social unionism rhetoric that had arrived from Russia
and Europe had circulated through a variety of labor organizations, including the AFL. These ideas, representing a variety of international perspectives—including the Bolshevik-aligned workers' culture ideas from figures
like Anatoly Lunacharsky and Pavel Lebedev-Polyansky, the British Plebs'
League and the worker-focused Ruskin College, and other workers' college programs such as the German Trade Union School, the Belgian Labor
College, the Czech Labor Institute, and the People's High Schools and Folk
Schools in Scandinavia—could not be contained.[10] Additionally, education institutions in the United States, including the Rand School for Social
Science and programs for women associated with both the Young Wom-
en's Christian Association (YWCA) and Women's Trade Union League
(WTUL) contributed to informal labor education courses in an ad hoc
fashion, creating new opportunities for workers to learn about the labor
movement.[11] Last, labor leaders viewed the new public school movement,
an experiment in its own right, as lacking in its commitment to workers by
teaching elitist knowledge and skills divorced from the lived experiences of
students who would soon work in industry. In total, the conditions were
ripe for pushing education specifically tailored to workers.

In response to these factors, during the wartime labor movement boom
in the 1910s, several AFL-affiliated unions quietly started educational programs without informing the national organization.[12] The most significant
of these proposals came from Seattle unionists in 1915.[13] The Seattle plan
required only local funding, completely sidestepping the national organization's oversight and leading to the formation of one of the first U.S.
workers' education programs affiliated with the AFL, the Seattle Labor
College. The Seattle program served as a model for additional local grassroots organizing for workers' education. Union leaders throughout the
country adopted the Seattle approach and founded the Philadelphia Labor
College, the Chicago Labor College, and the Boston Trade Union College,

all in 1919. Non-AFL unions also picked up on Seattle's framework, including the non-AFL International Ladies' Garment Workers' Union (ILGWU) labor education committee in 1917. Their program would go on to be one of the most prominent workers' education programs in the nation by the mid-1930s and would lead in the workers' theatre movement as well. These workers' education institutions piloted the earliest formal programs in the United States even as they troubled national AFL leadership. The grassroots nature and politicized social unionism philosophies grounding these programs threatened to undo the reformist agenda Gompers had carefully cultivated during the war and immediately after the Red Scare. In essence, formal workers' education was simply too politically divisive for the AFL to formally endorse. Still, the national organization could do little to stop these programs from sprouting up throughout the nation. Portland followed this trend, founding its prominent labor education center for the Pacific Northwest in 1921.

By the time Portland labor leaders founded Portland Labor College (PLC) in 1921, the AFL had given up on trying to stop the formation of labor education programs and instead opted for regulation. The first tactic in getting a grasp on these programs was supporting and endorsing the newly formed Workers' Education Bureau (WEB). The WEB, also founded in 1921 and initially led by socialist leader James H. Maurer, was the first U.S. organization that served as a national clearinghouse for these new workers' education programs. The organization, which built close ties to the AFL over time, published training materials, hosted regional and national conferences, supported networking opportunities between institutions, and served as a national home for the disparate organizations making a go at the new workers' education experiment. The WEB was also one of the first organizations to document the goings-on of the new workers' education movement and hosted national conferences for members of the increasing number of labor colleges scattered throughout the United States. Thus, the AFL's decision to support labor education experiments proved another sound strategic choice. Soon national leadership once again drove the agenda for their affiliated unions' education departments and monitored these organizations for hints of radicalism. The WEB likewise paved a way for drama-based pedagogies in workers' education, notably marked by a formal address presented at the second national conference by PLC president Ernest Schwarztrauber, in 1923. The address, entitled "Educational Value of Dramatic Work in Labor Colleges," gave a "brief account of the history and humble achievements" of the Portland Labor College labor drama experiment. With this presentation, school leadership established their role as pioneers of drama in workers' education, and the WEB network helped to circulate their ideas to affiliated workers' education programs throughout the nation.

Pioneering Labor Drama in the City of Roses

Schwarztrauber's speech about labor drama, which will be discussed later in this chapter, suggested exciting possibilities for this innovative form of arts-based pedagogy. Turning toward the cultural milieu of the Rose City, a Portland moniker that not only captures the mild and desirable climate ideal for growing delicate flowers, but also the unique utopic vision guiding the city's origins, reveals the tangled forces of progress, nationalism, and activism that gave rise to the PLC's labor drama programs. Portland, Oregon, at the turn of the 1920s was a complicated place. In one regard, the city was developing as a West Coast progressive epicenter with complex, if not radical, ideas about politics and culture. These conditions existed thanks to economic and population booms due in part to the Lewis and Clark Centennial Exposition in 1905 and the lingering "Go West!" zeitgeist. In the mid-1800s, Oregon was still viewed as wild and rugged territory, suitable only for the most intrepid explorers and first-wave settlers, but between 1900 and 1920, the city's population more than doubled, to well over 250,000 people by the war's end. In another regard, the city also established exclusionary laws and policies that would shape race relations in the city into the contemporary era. As the state and city grew, leaders enacted undeniably racist and white supremacist laws that excluded black Americans, native and indigenous populations, and other people of color from the city's makeup, resulting in a "peculiar paradise" of whites-only progressivism.[14] For example, even as the population of white citizens soared and hundreds of thousands of black Americans fled the South as part of the Great Migration, by 1920 fewer than two thousand black residents lived in the entire state of Oregon.[15] During this time, the state also had a strong Ku Klux Klan (KKK) presence and infamously elected a KKK sympathizer to the governorship in 1922. The lingering effects of Oregon's racist roots have persisted, resulting in the city receiving a dubious honor from some critics as "the whitest city in America."[16] These tensions between progressive values and racist policies directly shaped the Portland labor movement, a project that almost exclusively engaged with white workers. This complicated reality in Portland directly reflected the progressive movement of the immediate postwar period, a time when new forms of political activism surfaced out of otherwise privileged groups, like the upper-class white women associated with first-wave feminism. Doris Smith, a direct beneficiary of Portland's complicated cultural and political reality, capitalized on these conditions that privileged opportunities for progressive white women in order to advance the labor drama experiment. Her work as a white woman who blurred lines between activism and charity served as a model for the paradigms that would shape early labor drama, as they would shape much of amateur dramatics, in the 1920s.

Smith, a thirty-seven-year-old divorcee with two children, arrived in Portland to find a permanent home after a peripatetic professional life in the theatre. Prior to her work with the PLC, Smith attended Chicago's Columbia College of Expression (now Columbia College Chicago), trained at both the American Academy of Dramatic Art in New York City and the Central School of Speech in London (now the Royal Central School of Speech and Drama), worked with Little Theatre pioneers the Washington Square Players, trained in pageantry with Percy MacKaye (brother of Brookwood's Hazel MacKaye) and pantomime with Madame Alberti, and performed on the vaudeville circuit in the Ben Greet Shakespeare repertory company. As a continuation of this diverse performance pedigree, she directed the PLC's Labor College Players between 1921 and 1925. In this role, Smith was among the first artists to develop courses in labor drama as part of workers' education.[17] After the Portland Labor College closed, the details of which are discussed later, she continued to work in the Portland theatre scene, going on to form the Portland Civic Theatre School for young performers. By the time of her retirement in 1956, "Mama Dorrie," as she had come to be known by her students, earned the title of Portland's "Great Lady of Theatre," a testament to her lifelong commitment to the local theatre community and amateur dramatics programs.[18] Taking inspiration from her work with pageants, vaudeville, Chautauqua, lyceum performances, and the work of Little Theatres during the late 1910s and early 1920s, Smith utilized her labor drama classes as a laboratory for transforming Portland's Labor Temple into the first workers' theatre in the United States.

In addition to her comprehensive performance pedigree, Smith, like many other young female labor drama instructors mentioned in this book, transitioned into this performance experiment by way of ancillary political and performance interests. Despite having worked extensively in several touring theatre companies, known for their grueling schedules and challenging working conditions, she had little connection to the organized labor movement and no experience with worker organizing.[19] Instead, her decision to serve as an instructor in this new and wholly experimental drama program exemplifies the evolution of amateur, variety, and pedagogical dramatics programs from the early 1910s and 1920s. These diverse performance practices, from the Little Theatres to community theatres to children's theatre, fell outside more conventional and commercial theatre efforts during this period and expanded during the first half of the twentieth century. Upper-middle-class white women led many of these new theatre experiments. These shifting paradigms reflected gains achieved by first-wave feminism, as these women pursued both education and political activism between the turn of the century and World War I, but, due to cultural forces defining roles available for women, they were largely unable to participate in the workforce. Social programs, philanthropic pursuits, and cultural endeavors, like amateur dramatics, functioned as transitional opportunities for women emerging from the domestic sphere into public and political life. However, the politicized and gendered underpinnings of these performance forms initially tethered labor drama to the aesthetics, ideologies, and cultural preferences of these women, many of whom were largely detached from the labor movement they hoped to serve. Tensions produced by the imperfect fit between labor drama instructors' vision for their programs and the lived experiences of worker-students play out through many labor drama programs included in this book.

The Origins of the Portland Labor Players

Smith arrived in Portland at a particularly exciting time for both art and activism. As previously mentioned, Portland was in a challenging moment of transition when local labor leaders and educators founded PLC in 1921. Most notably, the Nineteenth Amendment had recently been ratified thanks in large part to the first-wave feminists who marched, picketed, and, of note for this study, created parades and pageants in support of enfranchisement. Suffragist pageants, discussed in greater detail in the next chapter, provided one vehicle for arts-based activism that expanded possibilities for women's public roles in political art. Smith was a direct beneficiary of these developments, having trained with Percy MacKaye in pageantry and settled in a city that more readily supported the first-wave feminist underpinnings of the progressive movement that included the increasing visibility of politically engaged white women. Smith, an unapologetically independent figure with a strong background in a variety of theatre forms, was an ideal candidate to pilot dramatics programs as part of the new workers' college curriculum in Portland.

The PLC formed in 1921 through cooperation among the Oregon State Federation of Labor, the AFL's state arm; the Portland Central Labor Council; and the Teachers' Union of Portland. The decision to investigate workers' education was both a direct response to concerns about public schooling's limitations in regards to educating working-class Portlanders and a reflection of larger interest in educational programs after several one-off workers' education events in the previous year.[20] In order to determine the feasibility of a workers' education program, the three organizations convened a committee in May 1921 with representatives from each organization researching workers' education models and developing a plan for programming. Ernest Schwarztrauber, a high school teacher in the area who would later serve as PLC president, represented the teachers' union. After roughly six months, the committee presented a report and plan for a workers' college to the Portland Central Labor Council in September 1921, which was published in the local labor paper, the *Oregon Labor Press*.[21] In its article, the committee asserted that the new Portland program would "prepare the individual worker, as well as the organization, for a share in the responsibilities of democratic control of industry, such preparation requiring a knowledge of the history, practices, problems and policies of the labor movement and of the fundamental principles of the production and distribution of wealth."[22] In addition to a series of recommendations for courses in economics, history, sociology, and political science, the group made a recommendation for courses in "General Culture" and listed drama as a possible topic.[23] The Portland Central Labor Council unanimously accepted the proposal, and the college held its first classes in December 1921.[24] Courses were arranged with volunteer instructors from area colleges, high schools, and religious institutions.[25] The PLC's launch was auspiciously timed, as it coincided with the opening of the city's new downtown Labor Temple, a gathering site for area workers that included meeting rooms, offices for local labor representatives, and a large auditorium as well, and where all classes were held. The first session was small, with only four courses planned and just over forty students participating. Nonetheless, workers' education was now central to the new wave of visible and well-organized labor activity in early 1920s Portland.

Although dramatics courses were not offered during the first two school sessions, a growing interest in dramatics developed out of the English literature and public speaking courses offered in the second term.[26] As a result of this interest, Smith was engaged as the new dramatics instructor in October 1922.[27] Smith had recently arrived in Portland, joining the faculty of the Ellison-White Conservatory of Music in the Speech Arts department as an assistant instructor in dramatic art.[28] There, she led programs in pageantry, pantomime, play producing, and stagecraft. While it is not clear what drew her to the newly formed PLC, a brief biography featured in the *Oregon Labor Press* described her as having "wide experience in teaching dramatics" and "an interest in the labor movement."[29] Smith began her programs in fall of 1922, the third term in the school's history. She petitioned the Portland Labor College's Executive Board for her new experimental class in dramatic art from the worker's point of view that would "aim artistically to produce good plays."[30] The board approved Smith's course plan, and she started her program in the winter 1922 term. Soon after, a course announcement appeared in the *Oregon Labor Press* in the "Labor College Notes and Comments" column describing it as "a new and unusually interesting" opportunity that "gives working men and women a chance to break away from the monotony of daily toil and give expression to the spirit of play that our machine age tends to suppress."[31] The first class would be limited to only twelve students and would meet one evening a week in the college room at the Labor Temple.[32] The experiment in labor drama was on its way.

Throughout its duration, the course focused largely on production. This choice reflected not only the popular product-focused paradigms in most amateur dramatics programs during this time, but also the need to retain students in the young PLC. In the previous two terms, student attendance was a recurring concern. Programs were held in the evening and tuition was minimal, with union member students paying $2.50 and nonunion students paying $3.50, less than a weekly budget for groceries, for as many classes as desired. The classes' timing, their recreational orientation, the volunteer instructors, and inexpensive tuition that required minimal financial investment resulted in up to two-thirds of students dropping out in the early sessions.[33] Accordingly, in the crucial first phase of the school's existence, leadership was concerned with making sure programs were well attended. The pressure of production would provide accountability for students who signed on to participate in the dramatics program. This strategy for recruitment and retention was successful. Dramatics classes had some of the highest consistent attendance rates of all the classes offered by the college in the initial three years.[34] Smith recruited the first class of thirteen students (ten men, three women) from the previous term's public speaking course, and they immediately began their work, meeting each Tuesday night for two and half hours. They established an ambitious early production schedule with a plan for performances in December, only two months after the class commenced.

Early indicators suggested the new course was a hit. In November, the *Oregon Labor Press* announced, "there is no doubt regarding the popularity of the Dramatic Arts class nor for its instructor."[35] Details of the course, which regularly appeared in the labor press's labor college column, described makeup classes, rehearsals, and the formal establishment of the Labor College Players as a "permanent organization" with a chairman, business manager, stage manager, and "property man."[36] By mid-November, Smith had cast her performers for three one-act plays.[37] The Labor Temple management was also in the process of converting one of its halls into a theatre, retrofitting the space "gradually with all the equipment necessary for little theatre requirements."[38] All these developments were testaments to Smith's work with the Washington Square Players and her familiarity with paradigms common in the Little Theatre movement whereby organizations not only produced art with amateur performers but also managed the theatres themselves in similar fashion. Moreover, her commitment to producing short one-act plays, a relatively new phenomenon at this time, also reflected Little Theatre influences. The Little Theatre movement sparked the popularity of shorter works, which had previously been produced as afterpieces for longer plays, in their production seasons. The logic behind producing one-acts reflected an acknowledgment of more diverse audiences and theatre-makers who were increasingly accustomed to shorter vaudeville and variety paradigms, not to mention film, and who were unable to make the longer-term commitment to producing full-length works.[39] Smith's commitment to these shorter works in her new labor drama program was part of her larger experiment in making theatre more accessible for audiences and artists alike.

With the rehearsal process for the first one-act plays under way, the Labor College Players set out to establish themselves as a presence both in the new Labor Temple and in the larger worker community. Documentation about the rehearsal process for the December performances continued in the *Oregon Labor Press*, with one article noting that the Players had scattered throughout the building to rehearse, including some participants "acting their parts" and "studying their lines" in the women's restroom.[40] As scheduled, the first performances occurred on December fifteenth, only two months after Smith started the course. They began with Richard Harding Davis's *Miss Civilization*, a melodrama "full of life and laughs" about the daughter of a railroad president, "a true delineator of her sex," who confronts a band of robbers in madcap fashion.[41] The group also performed William Butler Yeats's midsummer's eve fairy drama, *The Land of Heart's Desire*, and Marjorie Benton Cooke's *When Love Is Young*, a frothy comedy about two mothers scheming to marry off their children to one another.[42] Worker-student participants performed all these plays; professions included in the cast list included a barber, a teacher, a streetcar man, a building laborer, and two cooks. Additionally, the entire labor college supported the production, with the drawing class making show posters and the teachers' union promoting the productions and managing ticket sales. The well-attended and positively received performances occurred in Hall J of the Labor Temple with admission being twenty-five cents (roughly the cost of movie ticket), officially inaugurating the Labor College Players.

In evaluating these first production choices, Smith's skill as a teacher, artist, and program advocate is evident. First, as a teacher, she activated interest in a new theatre program among potentially unlikely participants with light-hearted, approachable texts that still maintained a slight political orientation, as in the case of *Miss Civilization's* first-wave feminist themes. Second, she produced works that would cultivate new audiences for her performance experiment. While these plays were not political like the better-known workers' theatre pieces of the 1930s—in fact, they were anything but—they were still diverse and accessible, a mix of approachable literary heft, playful farce, and exciting melodrama. With titles like *Miss Civilization* and *The Land of Heart's Desire*, Smith selected plays that would appeal to new participants while also cultivating a particular kind of capital with both larger labor and arts communities. This attention to titles paid off, and the first one-acts were a hit. As the school's director, Ernest Schwarztrauber, noted, "It was indeed an experiment, but the faith of the instructor and the earnestness and enthusiasm of the performers won out. The first performance more than justified expectations."[43] Though no other record or review persists in the archive of these early productions, the subsequent production schedule suggested that labor drama was developing momentum.

The Labor College Players presented two additional one-act plays, Eugene Pillot's popular crime farce *Two Crooks and a Lady* and Booth Tarkington's comedy of errors *The Trysting Place,* on January 19, only a month after the first plays were performed. Once again, Smith chose titles popular in the Little Theatre movement that were light-hearted and approachable for both performers and their Labor Temple audiences. Once again, no reviews or production photographs of these early productions survive, likely due to the fact that the nascent labor journalism efforts behind the *Oregon Labor Press* included few, if any, reviews or criticism of arts and culture programs, let alone images, in the paper. Additionally, the focus on dramatics as a pedagogical effort by amateurs who would not benefit from formal published criticism also likely influenced the lack of documentation about productions.

Nonetheless, program momentum was palpable. In February, the *Press* featured a lengthy article about the new "Workers' College Players," explaining how dramatics fit into the larger Portland labor scene.[44] The article's author reminded readers that none of the performers had "any stage experience before the class" and articulated a need for more women participants, as "women workers are not organized as the men" and thus, "actresses are not so common as actors."[45] Given this shortage of women performers, the article suggests that female relatives and wives of male union members might join the dramatics classes, helping fill out the courses and balance the gender distribution for the plays. The article also articulates how the Labor Temple reinvested money raised from ticket sales back into the Players, helping the group purchase materials for sets, lights, costumes, and props in order to create "more elegant" future productions.[46] Finally, the paper also described an additional performance at the Painters and Decorators' Union social gathering, encouraging other unions to book the Players for performances. Overall, this article provided valuable context for the new labor audiences drawn to Smith's productions, helping them to understand how this experimental program connected with workers' lives and the goings-on in the larger Portland labor scene. If this article is taken as an indicator, the Labor College Players integrated their art not only into the Labor Temple's cultural life, but also into broader Portland labor communities.

With this second set of performances (the best thus far according to both the *Oregon Labor Press* and the school's director, Ernest Schwarztrauber), the nation's first labor theatre was born. Soon, word of the Portland Labor Players spread to New York.[47] Spencer Miller, secretary of the newly formed Workers' Education Bureau, received a program from the second performance and was so intrigued by Smith and her students' labor drama experiment that he wrote to Schwarztrauber to inquire about the program. In the letter, Miller asserted, "I am sure that those of us who are following this movement of workers' education with the deepest interest will watch particularly the success of this dramatic work in Portland."[48] His inquiry about the program was followed by an invitation for the Players to perform at the WEB spring conference in New York City.[49] With this invitation, a fast and furious campaign erupted to secure funding to send the Players across the country with bookings at schools and labor centers along the way to help defray the costs. The WEB also committed to subsidizing the cost of travel and time off of work for the performers.

Even as the campaign began to send Smith and five of the Players to New York City, the labor dramatics' performance schedule continued at breakneck speed. In March, the troupe, now comprised of twenty registered members and the second largest course in the PLC, produced three one-acts: *The Clod* by Lewis Beach, Lady Gregory's *Spreading the News*, and Winthrop Parkhurst's *The Beggar and the King*.[50] Once again, audiences were plentiful, and coverage in the labor newspaper about this production was substantial and positive, likely in the hopes of bolstering the fundraising campaign to send the Players to New York City: "If anyone wishes to get an idea of the hard work being done by the Labor college players, let him attend a rehearsal . . . such persistence is born of a love of the thing they do."[51] The conversion of Hall J into the labor theatre was also progressing, with the *Oregon Labor Press* announcing, "new stage settings of a most effective type" that would "greatly enhance the work of the players," making possible more complex scenery and stage effects.[52] In addition to growing audiences, the labor drama students were also improving production values through their development of skills in performance, resulting in "the most finished production ever put on by the players."[53] The Labor College Players also increased their number of performances in the community, including traveling to nearby Reed College to present a selection of plays.[54] Smith made a name for her program throughout the area in short order.

The March plays also marked a shift in tone and topic from the previous light-hearted fare. Smith lifted *The Clod*, a dark crime drama set in the Civil War with clear political commentary on politics in the South, directly from the Washington Square Players' repertoire. Similarly, both *The Beggar and the King*, a short allegorical work about class difference, and *Spreading the News*, a comedic one-act included in the Abbey Theatre's first slate of plays in 1904, also addressed political issues more directly than previous productions. These more politically engaged plays suggest Smith was comfortable taking new risks with her work, a testament to the growing audiences for the Players' shows and to a commitment to experimentation regarding theatre specifically for a labor audience.

Even though the dramatics program continued to churn out new and better productions, the three-month turnaround time for securing enough

FIGURE I. Production photograph of *Spreading the News* by the Portland Labor College Players, 1923. Photographer unknown. PH1613, Ernest E. Schwarztrauber Papers, 1894–1953, Wisconsin Historical Society, University of Wisconsin–Madison. Courtesy of Wisconsin Historical Society.

FIGURE 2. Cast photograph of three one-act plays (*The Clod, Spreading the News, The Beggar and the King*) produced by the Portland Labor College Players, 1923. Photographer unknown. PH1613, Ernest E. Schwarztrauber Papers, 1894–1953, Wisconsin Historical Society, University of Wisconsin–Madison. Courtesy of Wisconsin Historical Society.

funds to support a trip to the spring WEB conference proved daunting. Schwarztrauber reached out to numerous contacts at other labor education programs, union organizations, and universities along the potential route in hopes of finding sponsorship in exchange for talks on the program and performances, but few, if any, could help given the lean budgets of most workers' education programs.[55] In truth, the sum of money needed to support even a subset of the students to travel east was largely outside the realm of possibility for PLC. In its first years, the school operated all their programming on roughly $1,500.[56] The Players only spent what they earned, roughly $250 in the first years.[57] Individual rail tickets would have well exceeded $50 a person and required several days, if not weeks, of travel. Still, the labor college community persevered. In an attempt to quickly raise additional funds, the Players raised ticket prices to thirty-five cents.[58] More important, the college also had photographs made of the Players for purchase, a testament to their increasing popularity and one of the few extant visual records of the PLC productions.

Two photographs capture the amateur technical elements of these PLC productions. In the first photograph, a close-up of the *Spreading the News* cast (Figures 1 and 2), hastily sewn, wrinkled fabric stands in for masking, legs, and borders. The fabric backdrop is hand-painted with crude attempts to create the perspective of an interior room, complete with simple line paintings of hanging lamps. The main set pieces include nondescript chairs and a pair of small matching wood desks. Costumes are also unexceptional and, in some cases, ill fitting, as if pulled from performers' home closets. A second photograph featuring all three shows' casts captures all of Hall J, including the sizable audience and the small rectangular proscenium in which the fourteen performers barely fit. One of the desks from the previous image has been covered with a white tablecloth and a lamp has been placed atop it, likely a scene from *The Clod*. Inexpensive and probably handmade curtains adorned with geometric drawings reminiscent of stained-glass windows frame the stage. An upright piano sits downstage and house right of the performers, just in front of the audience. Simple globe lighting fixtures, only a few feet higher than the proscenium, dangle throughout the audience space and appear to be the only stage illumination. The house is packed, with approximately one hundred audience members, men in suits and women in dressy attire, filling every wooden folding chair. The production details are charmingly reminiscent of many amateur productions even in contemporary contexts, showcasing how theatre on a shoestring budget has retained many aesthetic frameworks over time whether performed in a church basement, a school cafeteria, or the Portland Labor Temple.

Despite the PLC's best efforts with picture sales, increased ticket prices, and fundraising, leadership could not secure sufficient funds to send the players to New York.[59] Instead, plans were set in place to try again the following year. This outcome was disappointing, but a ray of hope persisted. While the WEB could not support the full complement of labor dramatics students, they supported the travel of one delegate to attend who could "be present to give the assembled delegates the benefit of such experimentation."[60] The PLC sent Schwarztrauber, who gave a speech entitled "Educational Value of Dramatic Work in Labor Colleges" to the bureau membership about the Players' first year. This decision is worth additional analysis given the prior discussion of women's roles within these labor drama experiments. Schwarztrauber's position as PLC director made him an obvious choice to make a presentation about labor dramatics, but leaving out Smith, the driving force behind the Portland labor drama experiment, obscured her contributions. Although Schwarztrauber was careful to credit Smith in his address to the WEB national leadership, the exchange exemplifies the transitional nature of women engaged in activism during this period. Even though Smith tirelessly worked without compensation for the labor dramatics program, she was not empowered to serve as the public face of these efforts. Despite her efforts, Smith's contributions to early labor dramatics programs have largely gone unacknowledged in larger discussions of political performance.

Nonetheless, Schwarztrauber's speech made an impact on WEB leadership. In the address, he outlined the program's history and strongly advocated for drama as part of workers' education. Schwarztrauber considered the philosophical significance of this new project:

> But what is it that holds players so steadily to this particular activity? An answer to this question in large degree reveals the nature of the educational value of dramatic work in the labor college. . . . The worker has the very human desire to be counted as an individual. This desire he has little hope of realizing. Our machine-age destroys the opportunity for self-expression in the worker and

deadens the creative instinct which makes self-expression possible when given the opportunity. . . . If it is true that we are what we think, then it is true that we are what we act—at least for the time being.[61]

Schwarztrauber's discussion of the role art and culture might play in developing self-expression and creativity in workers' lives serves as one of the first articulated philosophies guiding the labor drama experiment. These ideas about labor drama's significance to workers' education, grounded in the belief that creating performance provided workers an opportunity for an aesthetic, creative dimension to a life otherwise defined by the depersonalizing effects of industrial labor, would serve as a philosophical model for all subsequent programs.

However inspiring, these ideas would also present challenges both for the Labor College Players and for subsequent labor drama programs. Given the reality that theatre-making was and is grounded in a sense of collectivism whereby participants defer their personas in pursuit of a fictional narrative, how would these programs support creativity and engagement with the aesthetic dimensions of life? How would playing fictional melodrama heroines or comic Irish villagers provide an opportunity for self-expression to Portland barbers and teachers? Did these plays directly connect to workers' lives, and moreover, did they need to? Was workers' theatre supposed to represent the real toil of exploited labor and create change? And who would be the arbiters of taste and aesthetic value in these programs run by volunteers like Smith that produced amateur works like those depicted in the aforementioned production photographs? What kind of change could labor drama inspire, especially in peculiar and overwhelmingly white Portland? Subsequent labor drama experiments, many of which began in part due to Schwarztrauber's 1923 speech to the WEB, would wrestle with these questions both in classrooms and on stages throughout the 1920s and 1930s.

These enduring questions notwithstanding, Schwarztrauber's address stands as the first known formal discussion of the possibilities for combining workers' education and dramatics. Even more, Schwarztrauber offered these initial ideas about labor drama in a public forum whereby various delegates from a host of workers' education programs had an opportunity to think about integrating drama into their programs. At the end of Schwarztrauber's speech about the experiment of labor drama in his workers' education program in Portland, James Maurer, president of the WEB, offered the following somewhat humorous commentary on the possibilities of drama: "As I was listening to his address I felt that, perhaps, it would open the way to another thought in our work. The average student that we get into the classes becomes very serious minded. And most of us in the labor movement take ourselves entirely too seriously. . . . Some think it is all wrong to enjoy yourself. . . . In our effort to reach these young people we have got to make it worth their while to come. The stage will not only be an attraction, but it will be a fine means of education."[62] This statement from the WEB president, a staunchly Socialist politician deeply invested in the labor movement, is compelling, particularly in the context of thinking about art, education, and activism during this period. Maurer's interest in considering the role of pleasure in labor activism directly connects with interwar period's turn toward popular entertainment. This phenomenon was a reasonable adaptation for new audiences who both embraced middle-class leisure and looked for outlets to escape fatigue brought on by incessant and often violent growing pains associated with making a go of society in a new and rapidly changing post–World War I nation. Considering the role of entertainment as pleasure in the larger project of the labor movement was prescient. However, lauding this labor drama experiment for its association with leisure and pleasure simultaneously opened it to further questions. For instance, given the titles produced by the Portland Labor Players, was there anything that defined it as labor drama other than the performers who participated in the courses and the audiences who witnessed their productions? Even more, how could these performances, echoing back to Maurer's quote, both entertain *and* teach about the labor movement? Could tough truths and challenging concepts be transmitted through an artistic vehicle like a one-act play? Future labor drama programs would likewise engage with these questions and challenges. As these remarks demonstrate, Smith's Labor College Players posed compelling and challenging questions that would drive the movement forward for the next twenty years.

The Final Years of Portland Labor Drama

In May 1923, the paper announced that the Players would present works at the forty-third AFL convention to be held in Portland in October.[63] As Schwarztrauber planted the seeds for the larger labor drama experiment in New York City, back in Portland, Smith and her students stayed the course with their programs. They performed a final set of one-act plays to close the PLC school year in May 1923, including Lord Dunsany's 1914 abstract and fantastical allegory *The Glittering Gate*, George Bernard Shaw's one-act comedy *How He Lied to Her Husband*, and small-town comedy *The Neighbors* by Zona Gale, who had been the first female recipient of the Pulitzer Prize for drama two years earlier. Commentary in the *Oregon Labor Press* described the Shaw and Gale pieces as once again well-received and well-attended, "captivat[ing] the largest audience which has yet attended a presentation in the Labor Temple."[64] However, the paper also offered the first critical feedback on the Dunsany play, describing it as a "difficult piece . . . of a class which probably does not have as strong appeal to the average audience as do the more homely plays dealing with actualities."[65] This particular commentary articulates the first tensions regarding aesthetic preferences among Smith, the Players, and their audiences. The fantastical Dunsany piece, a more experimental, poetic, and darkly toned sardonic work about a pair of burglars attempting to pry open the gates of heaven, did not carry the same appeal for labor audiences as melodramas and farces for several reasons. First, the play was more of a think piece with an unresolved ending wherein the gates are flung open, revealing only stars.[66] While not overtly atheistic, the play treads a fine line in its commentary on spirituality and morality. Second, the work's expressionistic and fantastical style required audiences to make a larger leap in their interpretation of the play. Given these critical reactions, Smith had found the limits of experimentation that audiences would tolerate. Despite many of the Players' pieces moving into repertory production, Smith quickly abandoned *The Glittering Gate*.

Despite *The Glittering Gate*'s lackluster review, the general mood toward the labor drama program was otherwise remarkably positive. A series of summer performances remounting the previous year's productions, including productions at the Multnomah County Fair and a YWCA benefit, and rehearsals for the fall programs kept alive energy for the drama programs during the PLC summer recess.[67] By June, the group was rehearsing new works in preparation for the October AFL convention performance.[68] Additionally, the program had grown so popular that PLC planned a second "beginning class" for dramatics and engaged a second instructor, Agnes Cover, to lead the new course. Cover, a graduate of the Cumnock School of Oratory at Northwestern University, was a Portlander and had worked with the Players in previous school sessions.[69]

By fall 1923, PLC was abuzz with energy as leadership prepared for the busiest term for the school thus far, with thirteen classes on offer.[70] In October, the advanced dramatics class performed their first full-length play, *The Inheritors* by Susan Glaspell. This work marked another important shift in the PLC labor dramatics program. *The Inheritors* was the first explicitly political work produced by the Players that dealt with issues related to free speech, immigration, and nationalism.[71] More specifically, Glaspell's play responded directly to the anti-communist sentiments rippling through the United States writ large, and its production at PLC was likely a direct critique on Samuel Gompers's anti-communist crackdown in the AFL. Even though the experimental *The Glittering Gate* had fallen flat, Smith approached program innovation from a new perspective, directly tying the Players' production to contemporaneous political goings-on regarding the anti-communist hysteria taking hold in the early 1920s.

As planned, the group also performed *The Inheritors* at the AFL convention, but this accomplishment was overshadowed by the convention's contentious proceedings about issues directly relevant to the play's themes. Earlier in 1923, Gompers had laid out a plan to rid the AFL of any communist influence after hints of labor radicalism appeared once again among union membership.[72] Many labor organizations that had piloted workers' education, including those in Seattle and Chicago, were the subject of investigations by the AFL and had their local leaders forced out by the national federation. By the October 1923 convention, the expulsion of supposedly radical members from the AFL was well under way, a reality exemplified by the public impeachment of Marxist politician and organizer William F. Dunne from the organization during the conference.[73] The dramatic developments at the AFL convention would both eclipse the endeavors of the PLC Players and foreshadow challenges for both the PLC and the labor movement more broadly.

Despite the sense of foreboding brought on by the 1923 AFL communist crackdown, the labor dramatics program continued, but moved away from political fare. In January 1924, the elementary class presented the innocuous one-act comedy about rural Wisconsin life *The Feast of the Holy Innocents* by S. Marshall Ilsley, directed by the new instructor Agnes Cover. Smith chose equally anodyne texts for the advanced course, producing Alexander Dean's New England comedy *Just Neighborly* and Alice Gerstenberg's satire *The Pot Boiler,* which mostly poked fun at theatrical production in general.[74] Later in May, the students concluded the rocky 1923–24 PLC session with productions of *The Way the Noise Began* by Don and Beatrice Knowlton, *Fourteen* by Alice Gerstenberg, *Rights of the Soul* by Giuseppi Giacosa, and an uncredited piece entitled *The Florist Shop.*[75] All four resembled the preceding works in their tame themes and lighthearted nature. These productions were well received, but the lack of political import in all of them suggested that labor drama in the style of Glaspell's *Inheritors* was a short-lived experiment at Portland Labor College.

The optimism and energy that defined the beginning of PLC's 1923–24 school year was likewise short-lived. By 1925, the labor college entered a period of instability related to the school's relationship with the increasingly conservative AFL. In critiquing the national organization's new policies, Schwarztrauber committed a series of public political gaffes, ultimately resigning after the spring 1925 session.[76] Afterward, the school faced a series of setbacks and leadership crises, challenges only exacerbated by the diminished influence of labor after the brief controversy-drenched Harding administration ended with Harding's death in 1923. Harding's vice president and successor, Calvin Coolidge, ushered in a more stable but still staunchly pro-business administration that would take a hard line against the labor movement with significant public support. The effects of a larger anti-labor sentiment directly contributed to instability in the labor movement throughout the nation that would persist through PLC's decline and de facto closing in 1928. Despite this turmoil, the Labor College Players continued to be popular. They produced several full-length works with whispers of class consciousness: Oscar Wilde's *The Importance of Being Earnest* and *Lady Windermere's Fan,* Theodore Dreiser's *The Girl in the Coffin,* and Henrik Ibsen's *An Enemy of the People.* However, they also increasingly moved away from the embattled labor college and workers' education more broadly. The Portland Labor Players quietly evolved into the Portland Playmakers, an amateur production group ultimately absorbed into Portland Civic Theatre under Smith's directorship. Smith went on to be a prominent figure in the Portland theatre scene, directing pageants and productions with a variety of community groups.[77] She also served as a pioneer in the youth theatre programs as part of the Junior Civic Theatre School, one of the first theatre training programs specifically for school-age children.[78] After her transition to the Portland Civic Theatre, her work in labor drama was downplayed. Subsequent biographical profiles list her involvement in "normal schools" and "day schools" but largely omit the work with the Labor College Players.[79] Smith probably avoided discussion of her work in the labor movement in response to shifting attitudes about leftist politics that would conflate any involvement in labor activism with radical political ideologies, a potentially dangerous affiliation for the ladies of Portland amateur dramatics in the 1950s. Likewise, in the histories of the Portland Civic Theatre, the Labor College Players are entirely left out of the lineage of amateur dramatics. Even in progressive Portland, by the end of the 1920s, workers were an increasingly dangerous group with which to claim affiliation.

Despite the attempts to evade, if not elide, this part of her theatrical career later in life, Smith's investment in labor drama moved the genre forward as both a pedagogical practice and an art form. Ultimately, the movement metamorphosed, thanks largely to the political conditions surrounding labor activism in this period, and Smith, along with many young instructors documented through these pages, faced a difficult choice: stay with the increasingly dangerous work of the labor movement or move into more acceptable forms of creative and political expression. Smith, a single woman with two children to support, chose the latter, turning her attention to the safer work of amateur dramatics and children's theatre programs at the Portland Civic Theatre. Other artists would make different choices, but all would face the repercussions, for good and ill. Nonetheless, Smith's experiment inspired other labor drama programs, which I examine in the following chapters. These programs, scattered throughout the country, picked up labor drama as part of workers' education thanks to Doris Smith's pioneering efforts and Ernest Schwarztrauber's willingness to speak about them. In particular, the early efforts of the Workers' Education Bureau to circulate ideas about the experiments in labor drama fed into both the New York labor theatre scene of the 1920s and 1930s and the increasingly diverse workers' education movement throughout the country, especially as the labor movement evolved and expanded as part of the 1930s New Deal agenda. While largely obscured upon first glance, this small experiment with arts and activism in Portland has a far-reaching legacy.

Above all, Smith's experimental program demonstrates one example of risky performance that synthesized educational trends, political movements, and theatrical innovations of the time. Smith's work not only established the precedent for labor drama as a mode of pedagogy, but also opened up myriad questions about how best to approach the use of drama within labor education. Her story also captures the complex interplay between the Progressive Era's influence on an evolving labor movement and the challenges faced by women, even highly privileged women, who deigned to go public with their activist pursuits. Finally, Smith's dramatics experiment not only reveals an early lineage of her lifelong work in amateur dramatics but also adds nuance to understandings of amateur drama and politically engaged art during the early 1920s. Smith and the Labor College Players highlight the stakes and challenges associated with mapping histories of politically engaged performance like labor drama, and her pioneering efforts frame the other case studies presented in this book.

CHAPTER 3

The Variegated Shoots

Hazel MacKaye and the Development of Labor Dramatics at Brookwood Labor College, 1925–26

Every cemetery has a number of Shakespeares buried in it for want of opportunity to develop their talent.
Hazel MacKaye

Say, if I have to die many more times tonight, I'll be black and blue all over!
A "Very Dead Corpse" in rehearsal for *Miners*

In 1925, Brookwood's student-run newspaper published an article about the school's new dramatics program written by the program's new director, Hazel MacKaye. In the essay, MacKaye, a New York City suffragist who served as a charter member of the radical Congressional Union and possessed an impressive theatrical pedigree, included the assertion about cemeteries filled with would-be Shakespeares as a glimpse into the philosophies guiding her new and largely experimental course. This provocation highlighted MacKaye's strident belief that all students, regardless of aptitude or experience in the performing arts, needed only an "opportunity to develop their talent" in order to liberate their potential for creating art. The egalitarian philosophies at the core of MacKaye's teaching and artistry, as evinced by the aforementioned quotation, spoke to the artist's interest in labor drama as an experimental performance genre that would allow her to evolve suffragist performance forms with recently reawakened interest in labor activism in much the same spirit as Doris Smith. MacKaye arrived at Brookwood, located north of New York City in Katonah, prepared to combine her expertise in political mass spectacle performance with an experimental curriculum in workers' education that would include labor drama at the most prominent workers' college in the United States.

Given MacKaye's early experimentation with labor dramatics at Brook-wood, her time at the school between 1925 and 1926 marks a moment of transition whereby early experiments by Doris Smith at Portland Labor College and in other workers' education programs evolved into more robust and long-lasting labor drama programs, particularly at residential institutions. MacKaye's tenure at Brookwood speaks to increasing inter-connectedness between these early programs and frames labor drama's propagation throughout residential labor colleges who looked to Brook-wood as a guide. Hazel MacKaye's Brookwood tenure also illuminates the rapid evolution of arts-based activism during the tumult between 1920 and 1926 and showcases how one artist, once at the theatrical and political van-guard with her women's suffrage pageants, became suddenly and inexpli-cably irrelevant, never producing much in the way of theatre after her time at the school. Her work at Brookwood exemplifies not only the rapidly changing forms incorporated into propagandistic and politically minded performance during the early 1920s, but also the leaving behind of artists, once at the front line of radical art practice, who could not keep pace.

As MacKaye attempted to synthesize her newfound interest in labor dramatics with her experiences in suffragist pageantry, she hoped to find an approach that was pedagogically sound and aligned with the progres-sive philosophies shaping workers' education. During her time at Brook-wood, MacKaye experimented with different methodologies and settled on a process-oriented, student-focused approach. These experiments, which MacKaye documented in a series of essays toward the end of her time at Brookwood, guided other instructors who followed her, both at the school and beyond. However, as her ideas about labor drama developed, MacKaye met with challenges. Brookwood administration hired MacKaye with the idea that she would develop polished labor pageants that might serve as publicity tools for the new school much in the way pageants served the women's suffrage movement. Instead, many of MacKaye's productions challenged and, at times, defied the administration's expectations. Ten-sions over what labor drama should be, both to the Brookwood commu-nity and to the larger labor movement, proved a constant struggle for the participants in labor dramatics programs, and many artists, students, and instructors simply fell to the wayside as the movement rapidly changed. As one instructor left behind, MacKaye might be read as kind of a canary in the increasingly organized and politicized coal mine of labor activism during the period.

From Pageants to the Proletariat

When Brookwood opened in 1921 as a small residential workers' college in Katonah, New York, it was a groundbreaking institution in the workers' education movement. The school was the first residential workers' education program in the United States and the first workers' education program to receive widespread support from unions throughout the country. As historian James Robinson notes, the institution "remained the leading residential co-educational school for persons preparing for a labour movement career in the United States" for most of its eighteen-year existence.[1] Even today, the institution is regarded as one of the most successful experiments in the history of U.S. workers' education. In its early years, it maintained connections with the AFL-aligned Workers' Education Bureau (WEB), the federation's educational arm, securing its place as a sanctioned institution for studying about labor issues. The school also engaged in aggressive fundraising campaigns, soliciting monies from unions, wealthy donors, and the Garland fund, and these fundraising efforts drew attention from other influential organizations due to the high-profile financial investment in the school. Its location only a few hours north of New York City also positioned it to participate in the labor activism in the Northeast. However, the school's existence was not without strife. In the early 1920s, the same post–World War I recessions and pro-business Harding and Coolidge administrations influencing Portland Labor College also affected Brookwood, shaping the school's reputation as a training ground for future labor leaders and an institution potentially harboring members of the radical left. In fact, like many workers' education programs discussed in this book, the school also came under attack by the AFL in 1927 for its sympathies with communism, and the organization urged affiliate unions to defund the program and sever ties. In 1929, the school was expelled from the WEB under accusations of "disloyalty."[2] Nonetheless, many figures in the workers' education movement were curious to see what would come of this new workers' education laboratory and supported it vigorously throughout its existence.

Under the leadership of Christian Socialist A. J. Muste, an alliance of pacifist and socialist leaders founded Brookwood as a response to criticisms regarding public schooling's inability to educate workers. Points of discussion included the lack of opportunity for basic education for immigrants and unskilled workers, the unique educational needs of the working class in areas around New York City, and the political and social climate that increasingly demanded a practical approach to labor activism courtesy of increasingly salient business unionism agendas of organizations like the AFL after 1919.[3] Despite its highly visible profile, Brookwood was a small institution, with an average of 40 students attending at any given time. Only 186 students graduated in its first ten years. Students as young as eighteen and as old as fifty studied at the school, but the average student age was twenty-six. Most students had only a basic education, having started work in their early to mid-teens.[4] Students came from a variety of trades, with the garment industry, mining, and metal, building, and transportation trades representing the largest portion of the student body.[5] Ethnic, racial, and cultural diversity was a central value at the school, and students from over twenty different ethnic and immigrant groups, including black and international students, attended Brookwood in its first ten years, though most students came from highly industrialized areas in the Northeast. The school's curriculum, a mix of offerings in labor theory, labor histories, economics, and other courses that directly related to labor, set out to prepare workers to lead in the movement. After the 1929 AFL expulsion, Brookwood attracted an increasingly radical student population, and due to financial difficulties tied to the pre–World War II anti-red hysteria, it closed for good in 1937.

Larger political and cultural developments during the early 1920s did not help Brookwood's commitment to studying diverse perspectives and theoretical underpinnings supporting the labor movement. An unprecedented confluence of events—in addition to the worldwide anxiety associated with World War I's end, the unification of Soviet republics into the USSR in 1922; the power vacuum after Lenin's death in 1924; and increasingly volatile race relations epitomized by riots, instances of lynching, and burgeoning Ku Klux Klan membership throughout the country in the first half of the 1920s—resulted in a period of increasing radicalism and reactionary antiradicalism in the United States. With Republican power now steadied under Calvin Coolidge and strengthened with Republican majorities in

Congress that would endure until 1932, business leaders and conservative government officials were emboldened to paint the entire labor movement as a radical Soviet-aligned force that threatened to destroy U.S. society.

While these accusations were untrue, the massive strikes between 1917 and 1921 had resulted in food and coal shortages throughout the country, shifting public opinion regarding labor's power. The Palmer raids and the first Red Scare effectively shut down the U.S. labor movement's momentum by the mid-1920s, and economic prosperity associated with the Roaring Twenties only hastened the growth of antilabor sentiments. As business boomed, working conditions improved, and wages increased, the labor movement had a hard time making a case for itself among rank-and-file workers. These events profoundly impacted the ways artists, educators, and activists engaged with labor issues, including those interested in workers' education. During this period of experimentation and innovation, drama arrived on the scene as both an arts-based strategy for activism and as a mode of progressive pedagogy, thanks to the writings of John Dewey and other contemporaries and the influence of labor propaganda from the USSR and Europe. Also, Ernest Schwarztrauber's 1923 speech to the Workers' Education Bureau provided a frame with which leaders could conceptualize drama as more than entertainment. Labor drama could also teach about the labor movement, provide a space to rehearse activism, and enliven key ideas about worker exploitation. Brookwood, having come into existence at the right time and in the right place, evolved into a training ground for learning and disseminating knowledge about labor dramatics.

While the advent of Brookwood labor dramatics was somewhat haphazard, the program grew under the leadership of Hazel MacKaye. A radical suffragist whose women's rights pageants prominently featured in the suffrage movement's activist art, MacKaye served as the first instructor during the fall of 1925 and spring of 1926. During her brief tenure, MacKaye's experimental and innovative approaches to drama as a teaching method advanced the early experiments of Doris Smith and established new pedagogical frameworks for instructors who would follow her. As a result of these efforts, Brookwood dramatics programs flourished after MacKaye's departure. Jasper Deeter, best known for his founding of the politically progressive Hedgerow Theatre outside Philadelphia and for his work with the Provincetown Players, replaced MacKaye, bolstering dramatic production through Brookwood's performance ensemble, the Brookwood Labor Players (BLP). The labor drama pedagogies and productions pioneered at Brookwood inspired practically all subsequent courses both in labor colleges and in other forms of workers' education programs.[6]

Although documentation of MacKaye's time at Brookwood has largely drifted into obscurity within studies of U.S. theatre history, her family's significance as theatrical innovators and her theatrical production in the women's suffrage movement are still well known. As the youngest child of famous actor, playwright, and theatrical artist Steele MacKaye and his wife, amateur dramatist and actress Mary Keith Medbury MacKaye, Hazel was part of a theatrical dynasty. The only daughter in a family of five boys, Hazel was her father's "mascot of high fortune," and "the happiest moment" of Steele MacKaye's life was her birth.[7] She was named for the protagonist in her father's play *Hazel Kirke,* and she grew up participating in a variety of her family's theatrical endeavors, as well as acting in and assisting with her brother Percy MacKaye's pageants and plays when she was older. Her relationship with her father, mother, and Percy directly influenced her work in theatre.[8] However, Hazel's position as the youngest and only female of the MacKaye children situated her in the shadows of her highly accomplished older brothers despite her prolific theatrical career and prominent political activism.[9]

As a young woman, MacKaye combined her theatrical upbringing with an interest in political causes, committing a large portion of her life to creating theatre that dismantled barriers for women in a politically complicated time for feminist causes. MacKaye pursued a college education at Radcliffe, Harvard's coordinate school for women, where she studied theatre with George Pierce Baker. She left the program after a short time to gain experience in the field, seeking out opportunities to expand her knowledge and develop skills in all facets of theatrical production. In documenting MacKaye's early work in theatre, Karen Blair, scholar of women's volunteer organizations, notes the diversity of MacKaye's apprenticeships during this period, from assistant director of several political pageant productions to a charter member of the American Pageant Association in 1913.[10] MacKaye also worked as a professional actress, performing in and assisting with several of her brother's productions, including the *Caliban* and *Sanctuary* pageants. In his 1916 text of *Caliban,* Percy cites Hazel's contribution to

the field, lists her as staff assistant, and includes her "community organization chart" as a reference tool.[11] She also honed her youth drama skills via
her work as drama instructor and director at the Children's Educational
Theatre founded by Alice Minnie Hertz, where she connected with pioneers in children's theatre and educational drama like Constance D'Arcy
Mackay.[12] Mackay offers commentary on Hazel's theatrical work in Percy's
biography of their father, stating, "The debt American pageantry owes to
Hazel MacKaye can never be fully evaluated in its true significance because
the results of her work have been so wide-spread, and so far-reaching."[13]
These experiences facilitated MacKaye's involvement with a network of
women interested in the pedagogical and political potential found in amateur dramatics.

This interest in amateur dramatics directly influenced MacKaye's political pageantry between 1915 and 1924. Her pageants were massive affairs,
largely focused on reimagining U.S. history from women's perspectives.
Amateur dramatics circles took up pageantry in the United States during
the 1910s and 1920s, and the form was particularly popular among women's
groups.[14] In his study of early twentieth-century pageants, scholar David
Glassberg notes that communities and artists employed pageantry to synthesize traditional performance forms with U.S. histories in order to create a new and uniquely U.S.-based folk art performance that envisioned "a
new American civilization as it was being born."[15] The pageant's accessibility, large-scale production values, and historical significance as art for
the masses positioned it as an ideal genre for representing a more unified
post–World War I U.S. identity, particularly among groups who sought
inclusion in the cultural narratives of U.S. society. Notably, first-wave feminists and other groups of white women were central to the development
and propagation of this particular brand of pageantry. The phenomenon of
mass spectacle performances that included women's bodies, women's perspectives, and women's histories functioned as an important innovation of
this genre. From the inaugural Miss America pageant in 1921 to activist pageantry associated with the radical suffragist organization, the Congressional Union, pageants with, by, for, and about women formed a performance
domain in which women were visible in large scale in a performance and
cultural landscape otherwise dominated and defined by men. Specific to
the discussion of Hazel MacKaye's political art, artist-activists involved in

the suffrage movement sought out pageantry as a new and uniquely American artistic vehicle to engage in political discourse through performative means. The inclusion of performance within the suffragists' activist agenda was a necessary strategy given their exclusion from dominant avenues of political dialogue and enfranchisement.

Prior to developing interests in workers' dramatics, MacKaye produced pageants for a host of organizations and community groups focused on women's issues, including *A Masque of Industry*, produced in Buffalo, New York, in 1911; *Pageant of Education* for the U.S. Education Bureau in 1913; *Pageant of Athena* about great women in history that involved more than four hundred college students and was performed at Vassar College's fiftieth anniversary in 1915; and a collection of pageant productions for the Congressional Union including *The Allegory* (1913) performed on the steps of the U.S. Treasury, *The American Woman: Six Periods of American Life* (1914), *Susan B. Anthony* (1915), and the post–Nineteenth-Amendment *Equal Rights Pageant* (1923).[16] In each of these pageants, MacKaye innovated on the popular mass spectacle format, using techniques like large numbers of women performers, music, historical reenactment, tableaux, dance, and choral speaking to represent and rehabilitate histories of women as part of suffragist propaganda. MacKaye's work in suffragist performance carefully balanced the need for activist art within the context of the movement's rather conservative ideologies. As historian Jean H. Baker writes, MacKaye "appreciated the need for a 'galaxy' of grassroots female supporters" but also "understood the necessity of an unassailable hierarchy in the early stages of the women's movement," and she carefully crafted her pageants to performatively reimagine a society that understood women as fully enfranchised citizens.[17]

These massive spectacles included hundreds of amateur performers from a variety of ethnic, racial, and cultural backgrounds, took place at prominent sites, and attracted huge crowds. For example, as Blair notes in her chronicle of MacKaye's pageantry, the artist's second pageant, *The American Woman: Six Periods of American Life* (1914) included over five hundred women performers, singers, and musicians, including prominent political activists, and took place in New York City's cavernous 71st Regiment Armory, which contained almost 200,000 square feet of performance space.[18] In her most popular pageant, *Susan B. Anthony* (1915), over four hundred women and more than two dozen singers and live musicians performed for almost three hours before an audience of three thousand at the original red-brick Convention Hall in Washington, D.C.[19] MacKaye also made innovations, connecting pageantry with parades and marches and adding spectacular technical elements, the most thrilling example being her use of illuminated barges filled with performers floating in choreographed unison on Seneca Lake below a flashing electric sign that read "Declaration of Principles" in her 1923 thousand-woman *Equal Rights* pageant commemorating the Nineteenth Amendment's passage.[20] By both reimagining and representing female contributions to U.S. history, MacKaye's pageants performatively and theatrically inserted women into larger narratives of the United States' past, present, and future. MacKaye's work during this period was so significant that Blair asserts the young artist "was singular in pushing the pageant form still harder, seizing it to voice controversial questions about the depth of sexism in American society. Her work represents an ambitious endeavor to invest mainstream rituals with social change messages."[21] To this day, MacKaye's pageants are among the few documented instances of U.S. performance specifically about women's histories written and performed by women for largely female audiences, and they exemplify the innovative, arguably radical, political motivations and artistic ideologies at the core of the artist's work.

MacKaye at Brookwood: Fall 1925

MacKaye's pageantry career probably influenced Brookwood leadership's decision to hire her as dramatics instructor in 1925. Moreover, her arrival at the college marked a shift in focus toward drama as an integral component of the school's larger pedagogical goals. Prior to MacKaye's tenure, limited albeit significant dramatics programming occurred on campus. While no mention of dramatics appeared in school literature before 1924, the December edition of the school paper, the *Brookwood Review*, announced the formation of the "Brookwood Workers' College Players" and described an upcoming production of scenes from Gerhart Hauptmann's *The Weavers*. Students, campus secretary Lillian Schachat, and English instructor Josephine "Polly" Colby facilitated the production, and it toured to the Workers' Education Bureau convention and the Manumit School, a boarding school for workers' children best known for its summer programs with the Pioneer Youth, in the spring of 1925.[22] In conjunction with the production, Schachat published an article about the process, illustrating nascent ideas about labor dramatics bubbling at the school after *The Weavers*'s success. In the essay, Schachat discussed possibilities for synthesizing the political agenda of the workers' movement with amateur dramatics, stating: "The work of play-acting at Brookwood will more than stand the students in good stead when they return to the task of organizing their fellows, attracting them to union meetings, and implanting the germ of class consciousness."[23] These early experiments sowed the seeds for drama as a tool for activism at Brookwood.

Schachat's discussion built upon several developing ideas at the core of Brookwood's new dramatics program that extended the early experiment at Portland Labor College. First, Schachat's suggestion that "play-acting" would "stand students in good stead" for attracting workers to union meetings reveals an early bias toward dramatics' chief value as a form of recreation designed to hook otherwise disengaged workers. Second, Schachat's articulation of drama's main value as entertainment designed to "implant a germ of class consciousness" both echoes tensions Doris Smith encountered in producing art that was too political and foreshadows tensions among teachers, students, and school administrations regarding appropriateness in labor drama programs at Brookwood and beyond. While MacKaye viewed drama as a means to wrestle with abstract principles associated with the U.S. labor movement in the same spirit as her unapologetic and often controversial suffragist pageants, school administrators saw drama as a public relations tool that would help with advocacy for the larger workers' education experiment. As Schachat's article hints, Brookwood's leadership first thought of drama as a largely anodyne tool for keeping the larger labor agenda on workers' minds; overt or militant labor activism was not part of their goal for labor drama. Meanwhile, MacKaye thought more critically about the form's political significance to worker/artists and set out to create productions that used popular performance to communicate political ideas.

Regardless of the program's early philosophical underpinnings, drama was a hit on campus. By spring of 1925, *The Weavers*'s success inspired faculty leadership to consult with other experts in the field in order to enlarge the program. Hazel MacKaye was among the first experts to whom the school reached out. While records do not clearly indicate how Brookwood faculty knew of MacKaye, she was likely well known for her pageantry work in the area. Faculty meeting minutes from April state that plans were made to "consult with Miss McKye [sic]" on "pageantry work" at the school.[24] By the sixth of May, school president A. J. Muste reported on a "conference with Miss McKye [sic]" that included a motion to "engage her for pageantry work at Brookwood and in other centers located near Brookwood."[25] Soon after, the school's executive committee moved to request a "statement of what her work would consist of" and her salary requirements.[26] This request was submitted shortly thereafter, and MacKaye began preparing for her new role as the college's dramatics instructor and pageantry director. As part of this preparation, MacKaye visited Brookwood Labor College later in the month of May as a "noted expert in pageantry and general dramatics" and "conferred with the Brookwood faculty on the subject of dramatization of labor interests."[27] Afterward, Brookwood faculty moved to retain MacKaye at a rate of $2,450 for the academic year, $450 more than any other Brookwood faculty member outside the school administration.[28] She immediately formed a committee on dramatics with Polly Colby, the school's English instructor; A. J. Muste, the school's president; and Howard Young, a student interested in the technical side of dramatics who was hired as a "student tutor" to assist her. As this set of developments indicates, Brookwood leadership rapidly set in motion the necessary steps to support MacKaye's arrival on campus for the 1925–26 academic year.

MacKaye immediately committed herself to this new role. Shortly after her visit, she wrote a lengthy essay explaining her theoretical and practical approaches to labor drama for the newly formed dramatics committee. I linger on this essay to demonstrate how comprehensively MacKaye conceptualized her labor drama program. She opens by asserting that the document serves only as a "skeleton" and a "crude skimming" to which the rest of the committee would issue "various statements or bulleting or whatever you wish to call them, off occasionally during the summer."[29] Despite the caveat, the essay gives an extremely comprehensive analysis of the pedagogical, social, and political goals and inherent challenges regarding labor drama. She opens by posing an important question: "We who are interested in the Drama and the Labor Movement have in mind what ultimate goal?"[30] This question about the ultimate purpose for synthesizing drama and labor activism in an educational setting was an important inquiry to make, particularly from a teacher/artist facing a new environment where the chief motivation for drama seemed to be its draw as entertainment and potential to support community-building, advocacy, and, most critically, fundraising. She continues with her thoughts on the answer:

> Is it not the quickening of the spirit animating the labor Movement by the inter-preting and illuminating of the ideals back of the movement through the means of great and beautiful plays, greatly and beautifully interpreted?
>
> And have we not a very distinct picture of the form this quickening process would take throughout the Movements? Do we not picture countless groups of people absorbed in the creation of increasingly beautiful and noble works of art—in their own theatres with their own leaders and actors and onlookers? In brief, is not the ultimate goal of the Drama and the Labor Movement "a labor theatre in every community"?[31]

Her suggestion that theatre might serve as vehicle for bringing to life "grand, beautiful, and noble" narratives that absorb "countless groups of people" speaks to her ambition, especially when contrasted with Schachat's ear-lier suggestion that labor dramatics' primary value rested with its ability to attract workers to union meetings. This motivation probably sprang from MacKaye's experience in theatrical production and her success with pageantry. Unlike Schachat, who had not worked professionally in theatre and very likely first participated in dramatics at Brookwood, MacKaye had already spent decades thinking about the political dimension of art in tandem with her consideration of its aesthetic, poetic, and rhetorical function.

MacKaye's sophisticated engagement with the principles guiding her art practice also presented problems in regards to her transition from suffrage to labor. For example, her theoretical discussion of labor drama's potential to open up "noble" and "beautiful" plays reveals several inherent incom-patibilities with the more practically oriented curriculum at Brookwood and other workers' education programs like it. By focusing on the noble and beautiful, MacKaye's essay suggests a certain naïveté regarding the grit and grime associated with the ugly, small-scale struggles inherent to the workers' movement, a reality that other Brookwood faculty felt was vitally important to illuminate and examine as part of the school's curriculum.

This disconnect is not surprising given MacKaye's connection with the upper-class white feminism at the suffrage movement's core and the aesthetics she adopted in her earlier pageants, which often echoed neoclassical and quasi-religious forms with women appearing in white togas and as winged angels. Furthermore, by asserting a goal of "a labor theatre in every community" as the ultimate goal of this new initiative, MacKaye established high expectations for Brookwood's fledgling theatre program and, by proxy, her leadership. The goals outlined by MacKaye would be ambitious for any new theatre program, let alone one made up of amateur worker/performers who maintained interests in drama mostly as recreation. Nevertheless, this opening essay, complete with its aspirational, if somewhat grandiose, discussion, serves as a testament both to MacKaye's enthusiasm for her new program and to the excitement about labor dramatics' possibilities in the early 1920s.

While this essay foreshadowed some of the challenges MacKaye would ultimately face in marrying Brookwood's expectations with her unique artistic and ideological proclivities and experience, it also demonstrated her competency in developing a new program. Unlike many other theatre artists who worked in labor drama, MacKaye was not naive in her approach to theatre. She had extensive production experience and publications about the topic of drama with a social purpose. Even if her ideas initially appear cavalier and discordant with Brookwood's larger values, she most certainly felt them to be achievable under her leadership. This fact is clearly supported by the detailed analysis she makes in her "skeletal" outline for the program. For example, in discussing challenges associated with promoting labor drama, she asks the following progression of questions concerning the present role of dramatics in the larger workers' movement:

- ► Can it be said that there exists among workers any conscious interest in the Drama as a means of interpreting the Labor Movement?
- ► If so, how widespread is this interest?
- ► If not, what policy should be pursued in arousing an interest?
- ► Should an earnest demand be created before an adequate "supply" exists to satisfy this demand?
- ► And when we say supply, what do we mean?
- ► Do we mean plays, etc. on social questions, directors and actors who understand existing limitations in resources among the workers or audiences receptive to this "Proletarian" drama?

► Would it be the part of wisdom to agitate the question of the Drama and Labor before adequate experiments had been made which might serve to guide the workers as a while in this intricate problem?

► Could experimentation and "promotion" of some aspects, at least, of the problem, go on at the same time?[32]

Here, MacKaye, an experienced artist, asks astute questions about what exactly labor dramatics should look like, what goals it should prioritize, how experimental theatre practice would augment existing programs, and how to best manage promotion of these new works. This list exemplifies the thoroughness with which MacKaye approached her new appointment.

She further demonstrated her competence by addressing the practical aspects of the program's design and equating the dramatics committee members to architects who "must see the design as a whole, in its essentials, at any rate, before we can decide what step is best to take at first."[33] In this discussion of essentials, she articulates the following hierarchy: "1. a play 2. a director 3. actors 4. a stage and auditorium 5. setting—scenery, costumes, lights, etc. 6. an audience."[34] MacKaye's poetics of performance demonstrate her knowledge about the practicalities of making theatre. This fairly rigid, top-down structure for dramatic production appeared alongside her discussions of possible experimentation in more democratic, student-centered dramatic productions. She asserts that "no honest effort should be discouraged in the very beginnings of our experiment" and that creating new material should be given "earnest consideration."[35] Instead of stridently adhering to her pageantry roots or relying on extant dramatic scripts, she was open to new strategies that would support student ownership of the work. MacKaye's willingness to consider student-centered artistic production as part of her curricular design was an important development in the life of Brookwood dramatics since it marked the first moment where original work was considered alongside published works in labor drama.

MacKaye also included thorough analysis of all aspects of the new dramatics program, such as the "Spirit Back," or metaphysical/spiritual dimension ("Through the moans of the drama, i.e., plays and other dramatic forms, this Great Wish to Live can be interpreted better than in any other way").[36] In addition, she offered considerations for selecting dramatic material for production, stating, "Evidently an audience will accept any illusion of setting, from the crassest realism to the most post-impressionist symbolism, provided the performance as a whole be consistent and dramatically moving."[37] Possible play titles she suggested were Eugene O'Neill's expressionist drama *The Hairy Ape*; George Bernard Shaw's now-obscure one-act *Annajanska, The Bolshevik Princess*; and *The Little Women of the Slums*, a lost title of unknown authorship. Beyond these discussions, she also recommends potential avenues for additional research for new labor drama titles, and even offers a warning against the committee bogging down in too much theoretical discussion: "Unless the committee starts thinking together from the first on the reasons for undertaking a piece of work, a great deal of confusion arises and much time is wasted by the necessity for repeating many points which should have been established in the beginning."[38] Her final comment requests feedback from her new colleagues.[39] These first ideas shaped an intense period of experimentation in which student playwriting, directing, and performing would establish the foundation for the Brookwood Labor Players' success in the late 1920s and 1930s.

Despite her request for additional input, no members of the dramatics committee responded to MacKaye's essay. Given MacKaye's detailed thoughts on labor drama, perhaps the rest of the committee had little else to contribute in terms of a formal response. Determined, MacKaye pushed against the silence from her new colleagues. In early August, she again wrote to Muste under the guise of updating the president on a potential collaboration with Harry Dana, a former Columbia University comparative literature professor and socialist sympathizer with ties to labor drama.[40] In addition to describing her recent meeting with Dana, she articulated a desire to have a clear outline for the dramatics program by early October, the start of the semester. This subtle nudge for feedback on her earlier document finally elicited a response. A few days later, Muste wrote to MacKaye that he had "read over with much interest" her suggestions for the course, but "I believe I have no specific comments."[41] He also suggested that Colby and Young would send her a response, but it does not appear either of them wrote to her. Nonetheless, Muste seemed excited about the program despite his laissez-faire response. He cited his enthusiasm about the partnership with Harry Dana and suggested a possible collaboration with miners' groups in central Pennsylvania. He also promised to more thoroughly read MacKaye's course outline and essay, stating, "I may write you after that," but it does not appear he had any other comments.[42] In a

September letter, a seemingly frustrated MacKaye wrote again to Muste, asserting, "practical details are only a part of making a 'go' of a dramatic venture, as you know," and suggesting, "one has to have a keen sense of what is wanted and what is possible within any given group."[43] Again, she received no reply. In all, these exchanges suggest that despite the school's financial investment, early drama programs were not a central concern of the school's administration. Brookwood leadership's lack of response to her extensive planning very likely came as a surprise to the celebrated and clearly dedicated MacKaye.

Notwithstanding the communication difficulties during the planning process, MacKaye arrived at Brookwood prepared for the fall semester, and a prolific period for labor dramatics began. In October, just after the start of the fall academic term, the *Brookwood Review* announced: "Miss Hazel MacKaye will be in residence at Brookwood at intervals throughout the year, to stimulate the study and the production of labor plays and pageants and to help develop the whole field of dramatizing the labor movement."[44] MacKaye's class notes reveal an ambitious plan for her first year at the school, and the first-year program demonstrated her expertise in developing an appropriate progression of dramatics pedagogy that would best meet the needs of students new to drama:

Possible "Booking" of Programs (Scheduling)
1. Late November or early December: 3 or 4 one-act plays
2. Late January—3 scenes from labor plays
3. Middle of March—1 long labor or socially significant play
4. Late May—Workers' Dramatics Festival (This to be written by the Brookwood players and performed . . . of the Dramatic Conference / Workers Players.)[45]

While ambitious, this blueprint indicates thoughtful consideration of opportunities and limitations associated with a new program. MacKaye planned an appropriate progression of curricula for strengthening her students' skills, considering their existing abilities and previous experiences with drama. For example, instead of tackling a full-length production from the outset and very likely encountering some degree of morale-busting exhaustion from taking on too much too soon, she started her program with lower-stakes scene studies in an appropriate extension of the previous year's work on *The Weavers*. Then, she progressed to short one-act plays and a subsequent full-length production, closing the year with a student-led dramatics festival that would travel to the conference for workers' theatres. This schedule also positioned MacKaye for success by ensuring that the first visible products of her new program, the touring show and dramatics festival, would have a full year to develop.

Although MacKaye was not unique in her ability to plan a substantive dramatics program, she was one of the few instructors considered in this book who managed to execute the plan largely as designed. This ability probably resulted from her extensive experience making theatre, setting her apart from many other labor drama teacher-artists, who were mostly energetic but inexperienced amateurs. MacKaye even exceeded Doris Smith's expertise. Right on schedule, the *Brookwood Review*'s December edition announced, "Three One-Act Plays To Be Given Dec. 12" and introduced the newly formed "Brookwood Labor Players," a subtle name shift from the previous "Brookwood Workers' College Players" that would last throughout the group's existence until the late 1930s.[46] The new Brookwood Labor Players opened with two works from the inaugural New York City season of Little Theatre pioneers, the Provincetown Players: *A Dollar*, a symbolist allegory of capitalism written by noted Yiddish dramatist David Pinski, and *The People*, a satirical comedy about a labor press by feminist writer and Provincetown Players cofounder Susan Glaspell.[47] *Peggy*, a drama about southern tenant farmers written by the Carolina Playmakers out of the University of North Carolina–Chapel Hill under the direction of Friedrich Koch, southern drama pioneer and southern regional director for the Federal Theatre Project, rounded out the performance. All three plays included casts described as "truly representative of the people" with students from "English, Hebrew, Finnish, American, Negro, and Italian" backgrounds representing "seven trades—textile workers, Finnish cooperatives, teachers, plumbers, miners, clerks, and garment workers," a testament to Brookwood's commitment to inclusivity and diversity in its student body.[48] An article by MacKaye entitled "To Dramatize Workers' Lives" accompanied the performance announcement. In it, many of the same questions and concerns raised by MacKaye in her initial course outline appeared: "Can the most dramatic movement in the world, the Labor Movement, be dramatized? Can they, in effect, create a form of drama characteristic of the new proletarian spirit in production?"[49] Once again,

MacKaye demonstrated her commitment to experimentation, but she also exposed her precarious position as a director, producer, and playwright in this nascent field. If the answers to these questions were yes, and labor drama evolved to value authentic experiences of workers over the theatrical expertise of those who might lead, then MacKaye would have little role to play in the work. If the answers were no, MacKaye would have similarly failed by not making inroads into labor drama as a new genre of amateur dramatics.

While MacKaye's comments support the suggestion that the school community was opening its mind to the possibilities for labor dramatics, they also incited conversations and experiments that would ultimately undermine the value of her theatrical expertise. As the workers took ownership of their art, the leading director grew increasingly irrelevant to the process. MacKaye would feel the impact of this development as the program grew. MacKaye closed her essay by asserting that Brookwood would take "an experimental step" in setting out goals to "not only present plays already existing . . . but to develop if possible the writings of plays and pageants by the workers themselves."[50] By suggesting that drama functioned as an invaluable tool for worker/student/artists to "create a form of drama characteristic of the new proletarian spirit," MacKaye intended for her program to play a more central role in Brookwood's curriculum, even if it meant jeopardizing her position within the school community.[51]

The newspaper's announcement of Brookwood's first one-act plays created buzz for labor dramatics on campus. Alongside MacKaye's article and descriptions of the one-acts, the December edition of the paper also announced that the next play was already in production and would be "written and largely produced by the students."[52] Even more exciting than allusions to MacKaye's course plan working out on schedule was increased evidence of support from Brookwood leadership. President Muste, who had previously articulated "no specific comments" regarding the program only a few months before, published an article entitled "Dramatizing the Labor Movement" in the same December issue of the paper.[53] The article's significance is twofold: it highlights the external developments in the workers' movement while contextualizing Brookwood's place within them, and it serves as a symbol of shifting attitudes on campus toward MacKaye's program from amicable indifference to true investment. In regard to the larger labor movement, Muste's essay alludes to the complicated negotiations in which leftist political groups, like the socialists who founded Brookwood, engaged during the interwar period. He offers the following passage: "When labor strikes, it says to its master: I shall no longer work at your command. When it votes for a party of its own it says: I shall no longer vote at your command. When it creates its own colleges and courses, it says: I shall no longer think at your command. Labor's challenge to education is the most fundamental of the three."[54] Here, Muste provocatively invokes the writings of Henri de Man, exemplifying this push toward new conceptions of activist labor education that empowered workers to "no longer permit others to dictate its thinking."[55] Muste's citation of de Man is also a powerful reminder of the rapidity with which labor-oriented philosophies and ideologies were transformed into new, unpredictable forms in the face of geopolitical instability. This reference begs a moment of additional analysis.

De Man, president of the Belgian Labor Party, endeared himself to many members of the U.S. leftist contingency by combining his commitment to socialist principles with strident support of the Allies during World War I. More specifically for this discussion, his writings reexamined Marxism's cultural dimensions during the interwar period and had a significant influence on socialist education, which directly influenced Brookwood's curriculum.[56] This uncommon combination of values also allowed de Man's writings to serve as a blueprint for U.S.-based socialism that adeptly navigated the forces of industry and capitalism. However, de Man's complex synthesis of socialist principles and ideas sympathetic to the Allies' larger agendas regarding nationalism, colonialism, and military development under the guise of antibourgeois discourses produced a path toward Nazism. As historian Zeev Sternhell notes in his investigation of de Man and his peers' post–World War I political ideologies, many of these artists, thinkers, and activists found themselves a part of a "dissident left" that "forged that brilliant and seductive ideology of revolt that the historian now recognizes as fascism."[57] De Man, a professed anti-Semite, briefly collaborated with the Nazi regime, earning him war crimes charges of which he was convicted, and leaving him "curiously absent" from histories of twentieth-century socialist political thought.[58] De Man's rapid evolution from an influential socialist thinker to shunned fascist traitor and war criminal exemplified how quickly good ideas could become terrifying ideology. Muste's evocation of de Man in the opening of his essay reminds contemporary readers of the promise still found in leftist thought in the early 1920s while also inadvertently alluding to the unsettling future on the horizon for radical art, radical left politics, and experimental learning institutions that allowed room for politically complicated ideas to percolate.

The remainder of Muste's essay articulates support for the "experiment" of labor dramatics classes, asserting their importance to the larger labor movement. Muste states that Brookwood would be a "pioneer" in techniques for labor dramatics pedagogies, a first attempt at a coherent vision for the program. Muste drew on larger trends in arts-based activism, particularly in regards to issues around the function of propagandistic art, and he described labor dramatics' evolution at Brookwood from a "very small scale" to an "extending phase."[59] He also identified the labor dramatics program as a form of propaganda, suggesting, "If Labor is to have some part in determining the dreams and visions of the American people it will have to utilize the great modern agencies of propaganda with which this may be done."[60] Muste's use of the term in this context was informed by developments in propaganda for the war effort during World War I and in other international workers' movements, like those in Russia and Germany. Similarly, his examples of earlier propaganda forms to which Brookwood might look included the AFL-produced silent movie *Labor's Reward*; a radio station on which organizations hoped to play programs centered on "labor, progressive, and radical causes"; labor Chautauquas; and the work of labor players' groups in workers' education centers.[61] Additionally, these different examples of potential arts-based initiatives contextualize Muste's view of labor dramatics' utility on the Brookwood campus. By his design, plays produced by Brookwooders should be much like *Labor's Reward*, a rehabilitating and legitimating film produced by the controversy-averse AFL that set out to illuminate the union's value as part of "the development of literature that is not only of the workers and for the workers but by the workers."[62] In total, Muste supported a belief that labor drama should be politically oriented, but also safely accessible in regards to content or form—not in any way avant-garde and certainly not radical.

Muste's views on labor drama also reflected the labor movement's struggles during the new postwar prosperity of the Roaring Twenties.

With Coolidge's steady-handed leadership now in place, business boomed. In addition to managing the lingering effects from the first Red Scare and Palmer raids (discussed in the previous chapter), the labor movement also found itself managing challenges associated with the profitable business sector's implementation of welfare capitalism practices that essentially circumvented labor agendas. Instead of complying with labor requests, businesses simply offered workers concessions—less expensive housing, shorter workdays, increased pay, and the like—on their own, undermining many unions' core platforms. These factors probably influenced Muste's rather conservative position on labor drama as a force that would help show workers the labor movement's relevance while also avoiding controversy that had plagued the labor movement in prior years.

Muste probably did not realize that his supposedly conservative views also contained seeds of radicalism that would ultimately present problems for the school. Although he suggested drama should function as a legitimating force, Muste also appears to have wrestled with this framing. He may have felt unsatisfied with a conception of labor drama as merely propaganda designed to quell anxieties over labor's potentially dangerous dimension, but his school's relationship to the AFL gave him little choice. These tensions are captured in the essay's closing, whereby Muste evokes a militaristic, activist-oriented trope: "It is the movement that marches and sings and flings banners to the breeze, that know how to dramatize itself, that gets work done and wins battles."[63] While Muste's conceptualization stops short of advocating for theatre as a weapon, a deliberate choice to keep radical interpretations of the work at bay, he foreshadows the increasingly politicized if not radical turn labor drama would eventually take. These ideas considered alongside his earlier evocation of Henri de Man also demonstrate Muste's struggle, like many labor educators and activists during this period, to make sense of competing philosophies in his early ideas about labor drama, workers' education, and progressivism. Despite Muste's struggle to situate the new drama program in the workers' education experiment at Brookwood, his essay demonstrates increased buy-in from the school president accompanied by a more explicit turn toward drama as method for advocacy, if not activism. MacKaye had found legitimacy in the Brookwood administration's eyes.

The first one-act performances further legitimated MacKaye's role on campus. On December 12 and 13, 1925, a cast of thirty-four Brookwood students and faculty performed *Peggy, A Dollar,* and *The People* for the campus and community. In January, the *Brookwood Review* published a review with the headline "Labor Drama Has Initial Success," and declared, "this performance represents the initial step in an experimental course in labor drama at Brookwood."[64] Students and faculty collaborated and performed the plays in the social room of the campus commonhouse, and great pains were taken to outfit the space for production. The school administration authorized $200 for the purchase of materials, with students installing wiring to power a new floodlight and spotlight.[65] Howard Young and his crew designed and built sturdy new scenery that "contrived to get the effect of depth and shadow in very limited space" and that the school could reuse in subsequent productions.[66] The costume crew sewed and installed both a new proscenium curtain and a fabric cyclorama and made all the costumes. These innovations reflected campus-wide investment in the programs, with practically every student and faculty member being involved in the plays' success. These efforts also revealed the limitations of outfitting a student lounge as a temporary theatre. In the *Brookwood Review*'s words, the "low ceilings and cramped space provided many perplexing problems."[67] Sets had to be brought in and out from the porch, creating excruciatingly long wait times for the audience between plays. The plays' large casts were cramped and unable to move about on the stage, and seating for the audience was extremely limited, necessitating an additional performance to fit in all the out-of-town guests.[68] Despite these challenges, Brookwooders were very proud of their first dramatic accomplishments. The school paper's review glossed over shortcomings ("Too rapid speech was carefully toned down, and blurred enunciations overcome") and lauded the "finish and self possession" of the performers, going as far as to suggest they "would have done credit to a much more experienced group."[69] Slowly, labor drama carved out a space for its role on campus.

MacKaye and the players capitalized on energy surrounding their first performance and traveled to New York in March to perform the three one-acts at New York City's Labor Temple. The performance, sponsored by alumni "interested in the development of courses in labor drama at Brookwood," was a fundraising event and received attention from the *New York Times*.[70] Muste spoke on behalf of the school, citing drama as a tool to "quicken the spirit of the workers and to illumine the purposes and ideals back of the Labor Movement."[71] However, the performances fell flat. The swelling pride felt by the Brookwood community about their first one-acts did not extend beyond the school. In great contrast to the celebratory review in the school paper, an accompanying set of reviews reinforced both the truly amateur nature of these first performances and the difference in evaluation from those inside and those outside the Brookwood community. For example, a review from the *New York World-Telegram* offered the following critique: "The performance was amateurish in situations that had been taught to the students . . . there were other situations which they understood from their own experiences, and these they delivered with convincing effect simply by being themselves."[72] Similarly, the *New York Times* weighed in on Brookwood's first performances, treating the work delicately, but with a clear sense of critique. While the review avoided specific evaluative language, it clearly indicated that the one-acts were an "initial step" in an "experimental course" and reinforced Muste's commentary about drama's primary role as "an agency for self-expression."[73] These early external reviews, while not celebratory, helped steer conversations among MacKaye, the dramatics students, and the school community about the purpose of labor drama. Namely, this feedback demonstrated the value of workers crafting theatrical pieces based on their lived experiences, even if the results failed to resonate with audiences outside the Brookwood community. As a result, Brookwood continued to explore drama in workers' education, focusing more closely on the lived experiences of student performers.

Miners, Shades, and Bootleggers: Spring 1926

After the trip to New York City, MacKaye proposed a new curriculum to the faculty for "original work of students" and announced plans to take performances to New York and Philadelphia.[74] The *New York Times* coverage, albeit somewhat negative, also attracted attention, and requests from community groups for help with dramatics programs poured in from around the country. MacKaye was placed "at the disposal" of these new programs for supporting and advising.[75] With MacKaye now a resource to the larger community, she began to move out of her traditional position as a director and producer and into an experimental role as a facilitator.

The Brookwood dramatics program further reflected this shift as students generated more original works. In February 1926, the group produced their first student-written play, *Miners,* by Russian immigrant and textile worker-student Bonchi Friedman. As discussed in the Introduction, Friedman developed the piece in collaboration with coal miners who visited the campus in December 1925, and the play premiered before workers' education leaders who gathered for a conference at Brookwood over the weekend of Washington's Birthday. The production of *Miners* marked an important transition for the school. As the first instance where the BLP produced student-written work, the performance demonstrated the pedagogical progression of the labor dramatics program as a learning medium.

Miners illustrated the increasingly ambitious but collective nature of dramatic production under MacKaye's guidance. The three-act play included a two-act prologue, twenty-five characters, numerous scenic shifts, several large crowd scenes, and an exceptionally melodramatic bent—ambitious for the first student-written work produced by the school. The narrative followed the life and untimely death of Martha, a labor organizer and wife of a striking miner. The play opens, as described in the Introduction, with a crowd of "the Masses" crying out for bread, begging for sunshine, and threatening to "come out of our grave." It closes with Martha's murder followed by the same Masses screaming "Revenge!" as Peter, her widower, wrenches himself on the stage with grief, "the agony that Peter, Martha's husband, goes thru [sic] to remember his obligation to the working class."[76] Between Martha's untimely demise, the exaggerated characterization of the mining boss titled in the script as "The All-Devouring Capitalist," corrupt priests, the antics of grief-stricken Peter, the portrayal of pathetic child urchins groveling for food, and hordes of miners afflicted with miner's flu who cough and wheeze their lines in a dramatic display of their toil, it is safe to say that *Miners* abandoned subtlety. Despite the play's lack of nuance, *Miners* undoubtedly provided plenty of action for its audience.

The *Brookwood Review* praised *Miners,* with the reviewer asserting, "It is difficult to say which of the players in the three acts deserve special mention, for they were all admirably suited for their parts."[77] The reviewer follows with a description of every person who participated, and even mentioned the cameos by faculty children who played their ragamuffin roles with "spirited and natural action."[78] Within the celebratory review of Friedman's play, a subtle turn toward critical evaluation also appears for the first time. In contrast to previous reviews' glossing over the plays' shortcomings, this more level-headed assessment noted: "The performance was not perfect . . . there was some fumbling of lines . . . one or two characters were not quite convincing. . . . The delays necessitated by the cramped spaces for scene shifting rather broke the continuity of the play."[79] This willingness to think more critically about the aesthetic dimension of Miners suggests that students were learning about the qualities of performance and developing an evaluative vocabulary for talking about their work beyond a congratulatory pat on the back. This subtle shift suggests a step forward in the pedagogical dimension of the labor drama experiment. MacKaye's commitment to student-written work, even if replete with melodramatic narratives about wheezing undead miners, indicated her willingness to evolve and innovate her pedagogical artistic philosophies.

Miners also marked the first moment of discord between the school's leadership and the dramatics participants regarding content. Minutes from a January faculty meeting discussed the play's depiction of a corrupt Catholic priest with his hand in the All-Devouring Capitalist's pocket, suggesting that "it would be more realistic to make religious functionary be of a more general nature."[80] Faculty charged Muste and Arthur Calhoun, the director of academics, to take up the matter "with all parties involved."[81] The suggestion of editing Friedman's drama to remove the corrupt priest in exchange for a supposedly more "realistic" construction of a more ideologically neutral religious figure, particularly given the school's alliances with sympathetic religious groups, serves as one of the first examples where the struggle to place drama within the Brookwood set of values appears in conjunction with the practicality of producing a show. The potential threat to the school's image via controversial representations of workers' religious communities tested the limits of constructing labor dramatics as morally upstanding recreational curricula designed to keep workers out of pool halls. The faculty minutes make no further commentary on the outcome of Muste and Calhoun's talk with the dramatics participants, but if the extant script and reviews of the play are to be taken as documentation of the outcome, the Priest was, at most, toned down—not eliminated. A school review cites the student actor who played "the hypocritical Priest" as one of the performances deserving special mention, and the script paints the Priest in a rather negative light.[82] Furthermore, despite this attempt to censor *Miners*, the school administration's decision to premiere the work before leaders of the workers' education movement with the hypocritical Priest intact served as a testament to Brookwood's commitment to dramatics, even as cracks appeared in Muste's carefully crafted drama-as-labor-legitimator artifice.

Following tensions associated with the content of *Miners*, the Brookwood Labor Players refused to shy away from controversial themes in subsequent works. A month after *Miners* premiered, drama students produced another original work entitled *Shades of Passaic*. This self-designated "dramatic study of Expressionism" about textile strikes taking place in Passaic and Paterson, New Jersey, in 1926 borrowed the three-act prologue from *Miners* and added a short piece, developed as part of a unit on writing dialogues, entitled "Listening in on Limbo" by student Stanley Guest. The scene depicted deceased labor activists as ghosts, or shades, in labor purgatory, and it premiered at the Conference of Teachers in Workers' Education in April.[83] In their commitment to developing work that reflected dramatics students' values, the Players prepared their fictional drama just as the actual textile strike grew increasingly volatile.

The Brookwood dramatics group not only took up current events with *Shades*, but they also toured the production to the striking workers in Passaic, New Jersey. By the time the Players visited Passaic with the show, the strike was entering its third month. The sheer number of striking workers and their aggressive picketing resulted in the Passaic City Council invoking a Riot Act, empowering police to act with force against the crowds. Using tear gas, hoses, clubs, and armed mounted officers, police seriously injured hundreds of workers, with at least fifty strikers hurt by police the night before the *Shades* performance alone.[84] In the midst of this chaos, twenty-five Brookwooders packed up their sets, props, and costumes and traveled over fifty miles on a ninety-dollar budget into a near-war zone to share their performance with angry, disenfranchised workers still reeling from the previous day's violence and the effects of a lingering and largely unproductive strike.[85]

A detailed account of the performance entitled "Passaic Strikers Like 'Shades of Passaic'" appeared in the school paper's May issue. According to the article, a transformative experience transpired for the Players during their trip to New Jersey. *Shades* appeared alongside a remount of *Peggy*, and during the show, angry workers in the crowd responded passionately to the plays, aggressively jeering the "silk-headed capitalist" Mill Owner and cheering for the disenfranchised workers. In fact, the audience was so loud that "the enthusiasm made their presentation rather difficult."[86] The agitated audience added only one level of complexity to this performance. In the midst of the raucous group, "the sheriff and plain clothes dicks" circulated, taking "copious notes . . . divided between horror and amusement at such temerity" regarding the audience response.[87] The presence of police officers in the labor hall in conjunction with the striking textile workers undoubtedly transformed the performance space, imbuing it with the air of agitation. The tension was apparently palpable. Between workers displaying collective, angry, and impassioned audience interaction with the performers and police scrambling to keep the peace while taking notes on the raucous response, the moment solidified drama as tool for activism in the eyes of many Brookwooders. Perhaps this move toward activist art derived from the phenomenological, ephemeral moment generated in the Passaic Labor Temple, with members of the Brookwood Labor Players experiencing the possibility of labor dramatics as an activating method among real workers in real-life situations. While the potential for such moments appears in the writings of Muste and MacKaye, they were always presented in hypothetical terms. In Passaic, drama had a direct effect on the workers in the hall, and for the first time, Brookwood drama was on the front lines of labor activism.

After the excitement around *Shades*, MacKaye and her students continued with an impressive period of theatrical production. In her course notes, MacKaye described twelve different performance opportunities in April and May alone, from monologue performances to circus acts to social hymn singalongs to undoubtedly racist minstrel shows.[88] Each of these new works and performances moved forward labor dramatics' pedagogical experimentation. For example, only a few weeks before *Shades* traveled to Passaic, the BLP also premiered *Moonshine* by Arthur Hopkins on "The 13th day of March in the year 1926 A.P. (After Prohibition)," a pun reminding audiences about the play's engagement with the vice of alcohol.[89] Although *Moonshine* was not an original work by the Brookwood Labor Players, the play marked yet another experiment in student-directed works. Announcements in the school paper indicated *Moonshine* was a laboratory piece produced by students for students. In late April the show's production teamed up with other students working on *The Price of Coal* by Harold Brighouse for a combined performance of the first two student-directed one-acts.[90]

Students also busied themselves with exploring other dramatic techniques, including playwriting exercises. Although MacKaye's course planning notes included several possible scenes for study, it appears she abandoned these plans and instead supported student-written work.[91] The most notable of these included the aforementioned "Listening in on Limbo," a rough draft dialogue upon which the students based their short play, *Shades*. Other scenes, mostly entr'acte bits, were comedic interpretations of pertinent labor issues. Titles included "If A Straw-Hat Salesman Told the Truth," a short satire about a hat shop owner honestly hawking his subpar wares: "They're a lot of old junk no other stores would by [*sic*]. Most of 'em were left over from last year, but the boss told us to go ahead and work 'em off on the poor fish who come in here."[92] Another scene entitled "What They're All Doing Back Home" documented an interaction between a "Former Resident" of "most any town or city" with a "Current Resident" revealing an entire town's leadership has turned to bootlegging alcohol in order to get rich: "Yep. Lem made quite a bit with the lawn sprinklers, but he allus was smart and he got into the bootlegging game and is worth a half million now!"[93] They even wrote "Henry Ford Applies for a Job at the Edison Plant," a dialogue in which Edison quizzes Ford with a series of academic questions during a job interview. Ford responds with a humorous series of answers indicative of his disregard for the learned sects. A few examples: "Edison: What's the capital of Sudan? Ford: I dunno; I came in a coupe"; and "Edison: What does the Monroe Doctrine guarantee? Ford: Ninety days' service at any of our service stations."[94] While labor drama students never performed these scenes in a formal context, they appeared to have been workshopped extensively, given the notes on staging and the number of edits included on the prompt copies. Moreover, the scenes' topics, from getting rich off illegal liquor to poking fun at the irrelevance of academe in the world of industry, spoke to workers' engagement with themes germane to their lives. These sketches' quite successful satirical style, particularly when compared with the heavy-handed melodrama of many of

Brookwood's other plays, showcases the increasing diversity of and sophistication in the original dramatic forms with which students experimented during the first year.

Yes, We Are the Tailors! The End of MacKaye's Brookwood Tenure

Much like the entire 1925–26 school year, the final months at Brookwood in 1926 were busy with performances. As planned, MacKaye and the Brookwood Labor Players ended the first year of labor dramatics with a "Labor Revue" after commencement exercises in May. The revue, performed in the new outdoor Sylvan Theatre, included choral performances, an interpretive dance piece called *Liberation*, a remount of *Shades of Passaic*, and a new work, "a series of songs and dances representing the workers and boss of a union shop, written and devised by the cast," entitled *The Tailor Shop*.[95] At first glance, this devised six-page work seems lacking in sophistication, much like many of the works produced by BLP in 1925–26. However, knowing the trajectory of labor drama's evolution during its first year, it is hard to deny the significance of *The Tailor Shop* as a final artifact documenting the progression of MacKaye and her students' work. The play's narrative is quite simple: a brutish boss catches a group of female tailor shop workers dawdling on the job and threatens to fire them. In an act of solidarity, the female workers rush the boss off the stage while singing "The Owner of a Union Shop," a proletarian spoof of "My Gallant Crew" from *HMS Pinafore*. The play's description suggests amateur details, from a set design including a pale blue fabric cyclorama decorated with bright colored construction paper for "heightened effect" and simplistic choreography where performers "sway their legs to the music," "wave their hands above their heads," and "join hands and circle around the boss."[96] Given this description, no one would call *The Tailor Shop* an exemplar of high art.

Nonetheless, *The Tailor Shop* reflects the synthesis of MacKaye's pageant expertise, the innovative pedagogical practice with which the Brookwood Labor Players engaged during 1925–26, a direct connection to workers' struggles via the focus on exploited tailor shop workers, and the use of popular culture elements that helped connect workers to the material. It also demonstrates the application of techniques taught by MacKaye throughout the year and the evolution of labor drama into an activist art for the workers who helped create it. Moreover, *The Tailor Shop* integrated key issues that affected not only the everyday lives of workers, but also the viability of parent labor organizations by engaging with union in-fighting. Finally, the play marks the first moment where the Players generated a text that conceived of and represented a solution to these workers' real-life problems.

First, the play reveals increasingly radical approaches to the creation and production of theatre at Brookwood even within its superficially simple plot structure and dramaturgy. For example, the description of the piece as "A Free Interpretation, Through Dances and Songs, of the Spirit of the Shop" with "Words Written and Dances Devised by Students of Brookwood Labor College, Under the Direction of Miss Hazel MacKaye" demonstrates the collective development of the production through experimentation and consensus.[97] This collective art-making produced the most cohesive synthesis between drama and the socialist ideologies at the core of Brookwood's values. The forward-thinking nature of this work becomes clear when considered in contrast with MacKaye's earlier writings advocating for a top-down director-and-text-focused poetics of dramatic production. In less than a year, MacKaye had adjusted her philosophy in practice. Thus, by innovating on forms by which students created theatre, *The Tailor Shop* marked another moment of evolution whereby MacKaye released her authoritative power, allowing students to dictate the terms of dramatic production. By doing so, she further opened the dramatics classroom, empowering students to take full ownership of their dramatic art.

Given this shift, *The Tailor Shop*'s content reflects concerns specific to female garment workers from the Northeast, a large percentage of the student population at Brookwood. The decision to set one of Brookwood's culminating works in a tailor shop was not arbitrary and directly relates to Brookwood's affiliation with the International Ladies' Garment Workers' Union. The ILGWU, one of the first unions to attract large numbers of women, rose to prominence after the Triangle Shirtwaist Factory fire in 1911. The ILGWU's role in changing conditions for women workers after the fire provides important context for *The Tailor Shop*. The Triangle Shirtwaist fire resulted in the deaths of over 120 young garment workers—mostly young immigrant women between the ages of fourteen and twenty-two—after their bosses locked doors from the outside and disabled fire escapes in order to prevent workers from taking unauthorized breaks or stealing from the factory, thereby trapping the women inside the burning building. Despite the management's clear culpability in failing to protect their young female workers' basic safety, the owners were acquitted of all manslaughter charges brought against them. In an outcry against this gross negligence, the ILGWU was born.

In broad strokes, The Tailor Shop's theme, in which young female tailor shop workers rush their mean boss off the stage after he attempts to cut their hours, steal their wages, and then fire them, pays homage to and reimagines possible empowerment of the young women silenced by the fires roughly a decade prior. More specifically, the play also comments on the current goings-on of organizations like ILGWU. During the mid-1920s, the ILGWU negotiated a trying set of political and ideological challenges as leadership struggled to unify its diverse membership around a common platform. In 1923, the organization entered a moment of crisis. A disparate constituency of socialists, communists, anarchists, progressives, and "conservative pure-and-simplers" began fighting one another for positions of power within the ILGWU leadership, a reality made even more fraught given the AFL's purging of radical members.[98] New ILGWU president and "guerilla" for labor activism Morris Sigman "applied the iron" to the organizational factionalism and began a process to remove openly communist members, much to the chagrin of more left-leaning members.[99] Given this unrest, The Tailor Shop's simple plot offers a gentle critique of the infighting among the ILGWU. For example, the play opens with characters singing "The Song of the Workers," a tune championing the achievements of unionization set to the tune of a popular ballad, "The Lilac Tree." The song's final stanza demonstrates the ILGWU feud:

> In the sweatshop days, we'd not dare to play
> But we'd slave from dawn to dark
> For the eight-hour day which our union gained
> Makes us ready for a lark,
> Still we get too tired if we work eight hours
> Without pause for rest and play
> But if you watch us here and now
> To join work and play we will show you how.[100]

The lyrics reflect the gains of an eight-hour day, but also lament the lack of breaks within the tailor shop's grueling work schedule. Here, the play draws a distinction between the gains brought about by the conservative business unionism agendas (the eight-hour day) and the desire for a more left-oriented social unionism agenda (higher quality of life via breaks and time for play) at the core of the ILGWU's factionalism. The song even makes a strong claim to the demand for a more social unionist agenda, stating, "But we want our fun while our work goes on," suggesting that workers will rebel if not given time for rest and recreation.[101] By setting these issues to the tune of a popular ballad, this opening song makes accessible for workers the otherwise obscure issues in the unions' ongoing debates.

In addition to specific political commentary, *The Tailor Shop* also showcased students' preferred style of recreational entertainment via inclusion of pop culture tunes, dance numbers, and vaudeville structures. The play references *HMS Pinafore* in the show's final number, and all the other songs are new renditions of popular 1920s melodies, swapping Fred Waring and the Pennsylvanians' "Collegiates! Collegiates! Yes, we are collegiates!" for "Tailors! Tailors! Yes, we are the tailors!" and "Ain't My Baby Grand" for "My Big Handsome Boss." Each song is a solo, and a simple plot works in service of these musical bits. The Cutter performs the first number, revealing her love for the Boss in her rendition of "My Big Handsome Boss." Machine-Operator follows with a powerful ballad, "Union I Swear by You," based on "Pal of My Cradle Days," and Needle-Hand offers a rousing call-to-action number in "I've Grown Sharp and Pointed" to the tune of Irving Berlin's "Yes, Sir, That's My Baby."[102] Finally, Button-Sewer performs "All Kinds a Buttons," a melody that equates workers to buttons to the tune of "I'll See You in My Dreams," a popular hit from the prior year.

Each solo's popular culture roots augment the pointed commentary on the union struggles, making critiques palatable for a wider audience. The Cutter's revelation of love for her boss, while comical, warns against lusting after the boss's "motor car and lots of dough."[103] Similarly, Needle-Hand's "Sharp and Pointed" tune of empowerment calls on workers to be mobilized, engaged, "undaunted when an issue is on hand," and at "no loss when the boss tries to tell me where I get off."[104] Finally, Button-Sewer's song about different buttons warns audiences, "But do not count on me, To stay eternally, Unless you anchor me, I roll off and leave," reminding workers not only of their union's power, but also of the union's responsibilities to their workers. However, the most powerful commentary appears in the show's final moments, shedding light on the corruption present even within unionized spaces. At the end of "All Kinds of Buttons," the Boss storms in and sings "Get Back to Work" while he "struts about the stage looking very important."[105] The workers quickly mobilize, circling up to form a plan to kick out the boss, and the show concludes with "The Owner of a Union Shop," the "Gallant Crew" spoof. At the song's beginning, the Boss compliments the workers for being "very very good" and states, "His wage complaints are few."[106] The lyrics quickly reveal that the Boss is corrupt and uses double-speak to appease unions while exploiting the workers. Verses like, "Though my ties are bright, And my car a Willys-Knight, I never ape the Bourgeoisie" pave the way for "I used to work my girls twelve hours / until the union made you stop / But remember if you can / I am a proletarian," exposing the Boss's thinly veiled hypocrisy.[107] Even though he proclaims to be a union sympathizer, he wears high-end clothes and drives an expensive car, not embodying the proletarian spirit at all. As a response to the Boss's corruption, the workers challenge his assertions, ultimately forcing him to admit that he will cut their pay "hardly ever."[108] With the Boss's admission that he will, in fact, cut the workers' pay, all the workers including the Cutter, who originally sang about how much she loves the Boss, "circle about the boss" and "rush him off the stage." This final moment provides a concluding image of synergistic rebellion, and the play ends abruptly.

The Tailor Shop demonstrates that the variety drama with proletarian adaptations of chart-topping popular songs was a worthwhile theatrical and pedagogical form suitable for learning about issues of the workers' movement. As MacKaye asked in her first article about labor drama, could workers create a "form of drama characteristic of the new proletarian spirit"? *The Tailor Shop* suggests the answer is yes. Even with its characters named after sewing accouterments, pop tune parodies, and construction-paper set decoration, *The Tailor Shop* stands as one of the more engaging pieces of extant dramatic literature from these labor college initiatives. It adeptly represents a moment where workers reclaim their union-guaranteed rights, demand change in their workplace, and comment on larger union policies. The play also presents an accessible dramatization of young women speaking out against corruption and unifying against oppression. Finally, the music is catchy. *The Tailor Shop*'s success had a great deal to do with MacKaye's commitment to a pedagogy that empowered her students as both workers with a political point of view and as artists with valuable aesthetic ideas. In facilitating students' creation of performances that captured their personal connections to larger-scale debates, like those happening within the ILGWU, MacKaye indeed taught her students about making art representative of a new proletarian culture. While *The Tailor Shop* is a far cry from the Shaw and O'Neill plays that MacKaye initially hoped to teach at Brookwood, it nonetheless demonstrates her commitment to experimentation that met her students' needs. *The Tailor Shop* represents one the most powerful enduring artifacts of the pedagogical experimentation in arts-based learning found in Brookwood's early years.

There Is a Lark! Making Sense of MacKaye

MacKaye clearly created opportunities for students to generate performances that reflected their lives as workers. Under her leadership, Brookwood students used drama to critique corrupt pro-union bosses and Catholic clergy, to intervene in current events like the Passaic strikes, and to dramatize women garment workers' real-life struggles. MacKaye opened her mind to pop culture forms, melodrama, and humor to gain students' support of labor drama. However, MacKaye's evolution of ideas also appeared to alienate her from Brookwood leadership. After *The Tailor Shop*'s final performance at the 1926 Brookwood commencement, Muste offered a rather disconcerting final evaluation of the first year of dramatics in the *Brookwood Review*, observing that labor dramatics' chief value rested with its ability to "quicken the spirit of the workers and to illumine the purposes and ideas of the Labor Movement."[109] In this statement, Muste reverted to his conservative conception of drama as a publicity tool. Gone was the radical rhetoric with which he experimented earlier in the year when he suggested labor drama would help "get work done and win battles." Instead, he decided labor drama should inculcate workers into the labor movement through entertainment. This was a far cry from the radical reimagining of arts-based activism to which Muste hinted in other writings later in his career, a fact to which I will return in this book's conclusion. These comments are not far off from Lillian Schachat's early assertion that drama was best used to enliven union meetings. In the end, Brookwood wanted a program that generated pleasant, informative plays and pageants that showcased the positive aspects of labor activism without controversy. MacKaye gave Brookwood the opposite.

MacKaye was not reengaged for the 1926–27 school year. Faculty suggested they needed an instructor who could combine efforts in dramatics with a public speaking course.[110] MacKaye's high salary was likely a burden on the Brookwood budget, but no effort was made to renegotiate her compensation, and the vote against reengagement was unanimous.[111] In any case, she seemed motivated to continue the work, at least in the immediate period after she departed Brookwood. After leaving, she traveled to Taylorsville, Illinois, to direct labor dramatics classes for miners at the invitation of Tom Tippett.[112] Tippett, a Columbia economics student who grew up in an Illinois mining town, led workers' education in the Taylorsville area in 1926 and would later pen a popular labor drama script, *Mill Shadows*.[113] Accounts of MacKaye's work appeared in newspapers around the country after the Associated Press picked up an article written about the collaboration with the miners. By November, the miners had performed "a half dozen one-act plays" and plans were in the works for a tour to other Illinois mining towns. A goal of this work included "spreading, if possible, the idea of labor drama."[114] While MacKaye was no longer part of the Brookwood community, she continued to experiment with labor drama in part-time workers' education programs.

MacKaye kept in touch with A. J. Muste for a brief period of time after her departure from Brookwood. In one letter, she describes her busy schedule, the ornate stage on which the miners would perform, and her overly "conspicuous" picture included in the "impressive affair" of a playbill.[115] Despite her lighthearted and self-laudatory tone, MacKaye's parting words reveal her continued struggle to evolve labor drama into a performance genre that met her artistic standards, various institutional expectations, disparate goals for activism, and, above all, workers' needs. She jokes: "If this 'high brow' fare is too 'high' we shall have to find some other fare which will be acceptable to the lark of our public and to our own standards! *There is a lark!* Well, I shall let you know. . . . 'The best' let us hope."[116] MacKaye's insistence about labor drama as a lark can be read two ways. One interpretation suggests that MacKaye hunted for an elusive aesthetic frame that would result in labor drama productions that were both resonant with worker audiences and recognizable as high-quality art among professional theatre artists. This fun would eventually lead to something more meaningful. Another interpretation insinuates that MacKaye grew tired of this work and its challenges. Some form of labor drama that she and her worker-students would enjoy that would also meet the standards of the audiences to which they performed? That lark is a fool's errand. MacKaye's subsequent involvement in labor drama suggests that she was similarly unsure if she felt emboldened for action or worn out from experimentation after she departed Brookwood.

In May 1926 and February 1927, MacKaye published two articles in *Workers' Education,* the main periodical associated with the Workers' Education Bureau: "Plays for Workers" and "A Labor Drama Council."[117] The first essay outlines several appropriate published texts, many of which she produced at Brookwood in the previous year, and offers suggestions for producing plays with amateur workers' groups. The article makes no mention of devising new works, but it closes with a critical comment about the lack of high-quality labor dramas: "So many of the plays on the Worker or on Labor and Capital depict the lives of exceedingly sophisticated people, with drawing rooms and butlers and a lot of small talk . . . such plays are rather difficult to act convincingly by those not accustomed to drawing-rooms and butlers."[118] This critique addresses the same concern about the quest for accessible material that she mentioned in her last letter to Muste. Her later article, "A Labor Drama Council," articulates a solution to this problem: a leadership council for the movement.[119] In discussing this possible development, she employs an extended metaphor to document the "variegated shoots . . . governed by the kind of soil in which these seeds of labor drama have been planted," to explain her view of the field's development.[120] She also describes different projects that had begun to sprout up: "plays that please" in which workers participate for the sole purpose of self-expression; new studies of drama as literature with a slant toward labor; and finally, the "ambitious" and "more creative expression," of creating new plays that "interpret the lives and ideals of the workers and help to clarify the whole Labor Movement."[121] She also makes sound recommendations to expand labor drama, like the publication of a labor drama bulletin, a "Jitney Tour" of labor plays, labor drama conferences, and the formation of players' groups within unions.[122] After this publication, she largely disappeared, producing little, if anything, in the way of new theatre. Her 1944 obituary makes no mention of her time at Brookwood or her work with labor drama, describing her only as a "consultant for community drama."[123] It also asserts that her last dramatic work was *A Quest for Youth*, a pageant she wrote for children and published in 1924.[124]

Given her insightful *Workers' Education* articles on labor drama councils and next steps for the movement, MacKaye's abrupt departure from the field is odd. In fact, her entire tenure at Brookwood is difficult to evaluate. In one respect, her experimentation in these first classes helped establish and define the field of labor drama as a curriculum in labor colleges. For example, shortly after MacKaye's departure, Helen Norton, Brookwood's journalism instructor, published a compelling report about Brookwood's labor drama program in *Labor Age*, asking, "What does it mean, this sudden interest in circus clothes and the art of dying gracefully? Only that there is being launched at Brookwood an experiment in the evolution of labor drama."[125] In the essay, Norton humorously cites the "Extremely Dead Corpse" who "suffered in the process of falling dead six times in succession" as part of his participation in *Miners*, a testament to the commitment and community MacKaye built during her Brookwood tenure.[126] Similarly, Arthur Calhoun, the aforementioned director of academics, also published "The Social Significance of Labor Drama" in *Workers' Education* in 1926, commenting, "It is through these services of release, recreation, review and rehearsal that Labor Drama, not in the hands of professionals, but liked as a part of the common life, may claim an honored place in the movement."[127] Given Brookwood's prominence in workers' education circles, these articles undoubtedly influenced other dramatics instructors and programs. Furthermore, labor drama groups took up every suggestion MacKaye offered in her article: *Workers' Theatre* magazine appeared in 1931, the Brookwood Labor Players toured in their own jitney during the mid-1930s, and workers' theatre conferences were vital networking and knowledge-sharing events through much of the 1930s. At Brookwood, MacKaye's successor, Jasper Deeter, led the program with fervor, and the Players are among the best-known workers' theatre groups from this period.

At the same time, no one, least of all MacKaye, seemed inclined to give her credit for these ideas; she is all but forgotten despite her instrumental role in the movement. These contradictions are difficult to reconcile. Perhaps, as mentioned in the opening of this chapter, MacKaye's abrupt and unexpected obscurity derives from her role as a transitional figure between one phase of activist performance and another. Brookwood leadership expected elegant, polished pageants they could truck to New York City for fundraising events. MacKaye gave them pop tune parodies and construction paper sets in *The Tailor Shop*. While Doris Smith made a smooth transition into amateur dramatics, MacKaye was not as lucky. Only later did the labor drama movement realize that MacKaye's experimentation would serve as a model for other forms of workers' theatre produced by groups like the ILGWU and the New Theatre League. Her lack of commentary about Brookwood and relative obscurity after the mid-1920s make any larger claims about MacKaye's contribution to labor drama difficult. However, her early plays and essays and the art she produced in her short tenure shaped the field through the 1920s and 1930s. Even though MacKaye germinated the seeds of labor drama at Brookwood, her work as a bridging figure between pageants and the proletariat obscures her larger contribution to field, leaving her dramatic legacy and lineage notably incomplete.

CHAPTER 4

Of Untold Possibilities

Hollace Ransdell and the Ladies of Southern Labor Dramatics, 1928–36

> Mary Frederickson: *She was really sort of interested in basic social change, in a major social change more, perhaps, than a lot of the women who were involved in the school. Was that true?*
>
> Miriam Bonner Camp: *Perhaps . . . she was probably more conscious of the basic roots than the rest of us were.*

In 1976, when historian Mary Frederickson interviewed Miriam Bonner Camp, former English instructor at the Southern Summer School for Women Workers in Industry (SSS), their conversation eventually drifted to labor drama instructor Hollace Ransdell. Ransdell, a teacher, librarian, activist, and muckraking journalist most noted for her 1931 ACLU report about the Scottsboro trials in Alabama, taught labor dramatics at the SSS from 1928 until 1936.[1] Despite this long tenure, Ransdell is one of the most enigmatic figures in this study of labor drama. She seems to have come from nowhere, having shown no interest in drama before arriving at the SSS, and she virtually disappeared after eight years of work in the field, never working in drama again. The aforementioned comment from Miriam Camp exemplifies her obscurity; even her close colleague could not make a definitive statement about Ransdell's beliefs in regards to social change. Beyond her mysterious biography, Ransdell's work at the SSS is compelling for many reasons. First, her eight-year tenure marks one of the longest examples of continuous instruction by one labor drama teacher in a residential program. Second, Ransdell's educational and activist background, while well connected to radical circles, included no formal dramatics training. Ransdell's lack of experience with drama, particularly when compared to figures like Smith and MacKaye, who both worked professionally in theatre prior to their collaboration with labor drama programs, indicates increasing diversification of the labor drama movement. Last, the evolution of Ransdell's work with the SSS shows the increasing interconnectedness and professionalization of labor drama in workers' education programs during the early 1930s and its evolution toward a more political form that responded to contemporary politics and the larger workers' theatre movement, particularly in the 1930s.

Summer workers' education programs like SSS were important sites where women workers carved out spaces to teach and advocate for one another amidst larger cultural tumult. Since these programs focused exclusively on women, they created an environment safe for pedagogical experimentation from uniquely female perspectives. These programs also regularly included dramatics programs as part of their curriculum. In addition to their pioneering work in women-focused workers' education, summer programs for women workers also adeptly managed networking and documentation of their programs via connections with women's organizations like the YMCA, the Affiliated Schools for Workers, and women's college alumnae groups. These path-breaking programs, born at places like Portland Labor College and Brookwood and through Workers' Education Bureau (WEB) networks in the early 1920s, rapidly evolved and propagated throughout the labor movement by the early 1930s. These programs reflected both the growing popularity of workers' education initiatives and a concurrently booming workers' theatre movement, particularly after the stock market crash of 1929. The Group Theatre's founding in 1931; the ILGWU dramatics program between 1931 and 1937; Hallie Flanagan's Vassar Experimental Theatre, her 1928 book, *Shifting Scenes in the European Theatre*, and her 1931 work, *Can You Hear Their Voices?*; the founding of the Workers' Laboratory Theatre in 1932; the formation of the League of Workers' Theatres and the Theatre Union in 1933; and the first publication of *Workers' Theatre* magazine in 1931 all serve as examples of the growth in the workers' theatre movement during this period. Through this expansion of programs and performance initiatives, labor drama as a pedagogical method found traction, and several groups interested in women-only workers' education embraced drama as part of educational experimentation. While there are no examples of long-term women-only residential workers' education like the coeducational programs at Brookwood, Highlander Folk School (Chapter 5), or Commonwealth College (Chapter 6), myriad summer residential programs for women appeared throughout the country in the 1920s. These summer programs' use of dramatics demonstrates pedagogical experimentation for engaging new groups of women workers as the labor movement expanded and diversified.

Women-Centered Labor Activism After WWI

Given the unique and experimental nature of programs like the SSS, analysis of Hollace Ransdell's labor drama programs requires a contextualizing discussion about the SSS's relationship to developments in women-focused labor activism. The industrial era saw increasing numbers of women workers in the United States, particularly in female-oriented industries like textiles and hosiery, service/domestic labor, and clerical/administrative professions.[2] Additionally, while substantial numbers of women joined a variety of unskilled and skilled trades to replace men fighting in World War I, even after the war the numbers of women workers increased through the Depression as men's rate of employment declined. However, women's trades and professions were and continue to be undercompensated as compared with traditionally male-dominated industries. Since women often worked in the lowest positions in worker hierarchies, their needs often fell outside the agendas of organizations like the AFL. For example, in 1920, women made up less than 7 percent of the AFL's membership despite making up roughly 10 percent of the national workforce.[3] Even as more women entered the workplace after World War I, labor organizations like the AFL did little to encourage their affiliated unions to lift exclusionary tactics like gender-restricted membership or holding meetings in bars where women were not permitted.[4]

The few coed organizations that took up women's causes, like the IWW and ILGWU, were often more radical in their goals and agendas. Although the radical arms of the labor movement supported women's rise in leadership, including figures like Lucy Parsons, Mabel Dodge, Rose Schneiderman, Mother Jones, and Elizabeth Gurley Flynn, to name only a few, these women's political outspokenness often directly conflicted with their suffragist peers. As discussed in Chapters 2 and 3, Progressive Era feminist leaders at the core of the suffrage movement supported an agenda focused on the dissolution of very specific de facto inequalities. They looked for the presentation of upper-class, educated, and largely well-behaved white femininities to prove their right to a place within male-dominated political enfranchisement. In contrast, the women of radical labor challenged these ideas, looking instead to agitate against first-wave feminist understandings regarding which women should contribute to activism and how they might best accomplish their political goals. For example, the IWW attempted to organize prostitutes in the late nineteenth century, and Lucy Parsons, a founder of the IWW and one of the few women leaders of a mixed-gender workers' organization, prioritized access to birth control and the legalization of divorce.[5] Unsurprisingly, these groups failed to find significant common ground and largely worked independently of one another, if not in direct opposition. In the midst of these negotiations, women workers who fell somewhere on the spectrum between these two extremes negotiated their place within a rapidly changing cultural landscape regarding women's roles in labor. That is, if they had time for an explicit political affiliation. As women entered the workforce, they balanced their newfound need to work with continued expectations that they would also manage domestic spheres.

Given this controversy, moderate organizations like the AFL made few efforts to explicitly support women workers within its political platforms until the early 1930s. This decision was both practical and ideological. Despite the achievement of large-scale policy and legal advances for women's rights, including the Nineteenth Amendment's ratification in 1920, the formation of the Women's Bureau within the Department of Labor, and the work of the Women's Trade Union League, challenges associated with advocating and organizing for all workers meant larger agendas necessarily eclipsed issues specific to women in labor. While practical in light of the larger political attacks against labor, and reinforced by a third Republican landslide election in 1928, the streamlining of labor advocacy by groups like the AFL during this period meant that the most vulnerable workers—young immigrant women workers, women workers of color, and southern women in agricultural and textile trades—simply fell off the radar of many of the most powerful labor organizations. Additionally, the rise in xenophobic and racist attitudes toward new immigrants, of which women and children were the most at risk, and the continued strength of the pro-business Republican government placed many women in precarious positions with no labor protections.[6] Just as women entered the workforce, support systems advocating for their rights rapidly contracted.

The Great Depression magnified these concerns, particularly in the South. The United States interwar period can be bifurcated into two distinct periods: before and after October 24, 1929. In a matter of a week, the stock market plummeted 36 percent, foreshadowing a free fall that would not end until 1932. The effects, which included unemployment, bank failures, starvation, and a global recession, were catastrophic. Likewise, the weakened labor movement had little recourse, particularly in the earliest stages and most certainly for women workers. By the early 1930s, state legislatures introduced bills that required businesses to hire men over married women or to fire women who had employed husbands. Many companies chose to independently enact this policy by asking women to resign, refusing to hire married women, or firing women simply because of their gender. Simultaneously, job opportunities in low-skill professions that employed mostly women disappeared.[7] The AFL was of little help since leadership, in addition to turning a blind eye toward women workers, also strategically prioritized their longstanding "family wage" agenda as a working-class right to an "ideal family" where women worked without compensation in the home and men earned money in industry. Even though the AFL introduced their family wage platform in the late 1890s as a progressive critique of industrialization's impact on traditional family structures, the policy "legitimated the division of labor by gender" by assigning higher value to male wage earners in society.[8] Accordingly, AFL-affiliated unions advocated for men to receive higher paying jobs to support families and encouraged women to drop out of the workforce. Single, divorced, and widowed women were literally and figuratively left out in the cold. Unsurprisingly, with the most influential labor federation turning toward the family wage, the few jobs that still existed for women largely abandoned work standards that labor advocates had worked so diligently to obtain in previous decades.[9] If employed, women workers between 1929 and the mid-1930s worked longer hours for less money in harsher conditions than both their male counterparts and many of their female predecessors.

Both white women workers and black workers in the South fell victim to these developments more than any other group in any other place in the United States. The anti-union, racist, and conservative religious attitudes that pervaded southern culture further contributed to women workers' oppressive working conditions. Much of this tension related to the political agendas of the conservative southern Democrats, a group who maintained practically unshakable power for twenty years and enacted countless pieces of legislation designed to disenfranchise both black and, to a lesser degree, poor white voters. The fallout from these manipulations often pitted poor white people against black people and left both sets of unskilled workers without resources, further strengthening racist attitudes among these white communities and allowing racist policies to decimate southern black communities. Unsurprisingly, the economically depressed southern states were also ground zero for the nadir of race relations in the United States during the interwar period. In the early 1920s, incidents of lynching increased, the Ku Klux Klan grew increasingly powerful, and racialized violence, once thought to be isolated to states below the Mason-Dixon line, appeared in northern cities and in places like overwhelmingly white Portland as the effects of the Great Migration threatened white supremacist policies outside the South. By the early 1930s, nearly half of all black Americans were out of work, with even higher rates in the South. Violence against black Americans was also in a noteworthy national uptick in 1932 and 1933. The problem of the South, with all of its violent and racist implications, was becoming a national concern.

At the same time, the South, with its rich agricultural resources and cheap labor, was poised for rapid industrial expansion, and many enterprising northern industrialists looked to invest in the region. Many labor leaders, including those who started the SSS, saw the region as a space ripe for innovation whereby labor education experimentation as part of a new southern labor movement might take shape.[10] While the subsequent chapters on Highlander Folk School and Commonwealth College will engage in greater detail with labor organizing among workers of color, namely black American workers, the southern labor movement and related labor education experiments focused on both workers of color and women workers, navigating the complicated segregationist politics and Jim Crow laws that often prevented activists from working simultaneously with both groups.

Although women's concerns and political interests failed to find a great deal of traction within larger agendas of labor advocacy throughout most of the 1920s, gains made by first-wave feminism and the increase in women workers after World War I, coupled with progressivism's influence on education (which included increasing numbers of high school and college-educated women), paved a way for explorations of women's unique educational needs in regards to workers' education. Programs like the SSS exemplify how inchoate ideas regarding labor drama pedagogy developed sophistication as new groups experimented with the genre. They also reframe preexisting understandings of women's roles in the labor movement and recover the ways in which women-led and women-focused arts initiatives helped shape labor drama and workers' education, particularly in the South.

From Bryn Mawr to Black Mountain: The Road to Workers' Education for Southern Women

The SSS directly benefited from the networking infrastructure built by women-only organizations like the Affiliated Schools for Workers (ASW) and the Young Women's Christian Association (YWCA).[11] Workers' education pioneer Eleanor Coit, a Smith graduate who worked with the YWCA and later supervised workers' education programs as part of her job with the Works Progress Administration in the 1930s, led the New York City–based ASW. She helped publish resources, facilitated educational programs throughout the country, and organized conferences and symposia around the issues of women workers and education. The ASW also aided connections between different organizations interested in short-term residential education for working women by founding the Affiliated Summer Schools for Women Workers in Industry in 1927. Under this initiative, various summer programs, including the SSS, the Bryn Mawr School for Women Workers, the School for Workers in Industry at the University of Wisconsin, the Summer School for Office Workers in New York, the Barnard College Summer School for Women Workers in Industry, the Occidental School, and the Vineyard Shore Schools, networked under the ASW umbrella, sharing resources, fundraising information, and professional contacts.[12] The SSS, a unique institution that maintained ties to the ASW but operated largely independently of this organization until later years, served as the southern outpost of this network.[13] The SSS was unique in its efforts to provide southern women workers opportunities to study southern labor issues.

Former YWCA National Industrial Secretary for the South Louise Leonard (MacLaren) drove the organizational plan for the SSS's founding and remained its leader throughout the organization's existence. A Columbia economics graduate, Leonard set out to organize a residential program for southern women after experiencing difficulty planning programs about labor for southern women workers under the auspices of the YWCA. Due to the influence of male mill owners, husbands, ministers, and fathers and local business leaders' practically impenetrable authoritarian rule, Leonard found that women workers were either too scared to consider issues surrounding labor activism or too conditioned to view labor activism as antithetical to southern identity. In response, she organized a residential program in workers' education in the hope of distancing women from overbearing male influences in their communities and bringing them into a more open homosocial learning community. She secured a grant from the American Fund for Public Service (the Garland Fund) and built coalitions and funding streams via women's organizations like the League of Women Voters, other southern YWCAs, the American Association of University Women, and the National Women's Trade Union League.[14] To plan the curriculum, Leonard met with trade unionists, progressive educators, and other workers' education leaders including noted economics professor Broadus Mitchell.[15] The high-profile faculty Leonard recruited further demonstrated both her tenacity for organizing and her connections to workers' education circles. In addition to Hollace Ransdell, faculty included Lois McDonald, professor of economics at New York University (labor economics); feminist activist and Cornell professor Alice Hanson Cook (public speaking); and North Carolina College for Women in Greensboro English professor Miriam Bonner (English).

The YWCA was also integral to the SSS's existence, and members from the YWCA Industrial Department made up the core of women supporting the SSS's formation. As a religious organization, the YWCA fell under less scrutiny for its activist agendas during the late 1920s and 1930s, particularly in the South, since the YWCA's God-fearing Christian women were considered unlikely to take up radical communist and socialist agendas.

This assumption contrasted with the robust, but largely obfuscated efforts of the southern-based communist and Christian Socialist movements, as well as the desire for the YWCA to "Christianize the social order" during this period.[16] While the conservative ideologies at play in the organization's leadership influenced the level at which students could engage with labor issues, the SSS's affiliation with the YWCA not only provided financial support for the program, but also helped to connect the school with women's organizations throughout the region. This alliance provided networks for recruiting students, securing funds, and supporting the program's longevity by keeping its programs off the radar of those interested in bringing down radical arms of the labor movement.

When SSS leadership formed their southern program, they first looked to similar programs for inspiration—more specifically, the Bryn Mawr Summer School for Women Workers. Practically all other summer schools based their programs on the Summer School for Women Workers (SSW) held each summer on the Bryn Mawr College campus outside Philadelphia. Labor drama at the SSS owes its existence to the SSW. Since the SSW included dramatics classes, other programs did too, including the SSS. The Bryn Mawr SSW began in 1921 as an experimental initiative designed by longtime Bryn Mawr president and suffragist M. Carey Thomas.[17] In an opening speech given to the second class of women attending the Bryn Mawr SSW, Thomas announced that her conception of this new program came to her in a vision while on a 1919 visit to the Sahara Desert, where "Arabs would unpack our camp chairs and we would sit for hours watching the sun set and moon rise."[18] While sitting on her "golden hilltop" in the desert, Thomas envisioned labor education as the next frontier of activism after suffrage. She equated "the peculiar kind of sympathy that binds women together" to the oppression of workers, and she felt labor activism was well suited to women because they could "utilize the deep sex sympathy" as motivation.[19] Thomas's evocation of her Saharan holiday while speaking to a group of working-class women, all of whom received scholarships to attend and many of whom risked losing their jobs by participating, demonstrates the disconnect between the wealthy women who started these programs and the working-class women who attended them as students. Thomas's statements also echo both Doris Smith's and Hazel MacKaye's transitions to arts-based labor activism. Despite Thomas's obvious disconnect from the Bryn Mawr SSW students' socioeconomic backgrounds and life experiences, she nonetheless committed herself to realizing her vision. These lofty aspirations, paired with her well-documented tenacity as an activist, supported creation of a new program that was, according to SSW president Hilda Worthington Smith, "simple in conception" but "far reaching in results."[20]

The SSW utilized Bryn Mawr campus buildings, otherwise vacant during the summer, to "offer young women in industry opportunities to study liberal subjects and to train themselves in clear thinking; to stimulate an active and continued interest in the problem of our economic order; to develop a desire for study as a means of understanding and of enjoyment of life."[21] The summer program was separate from Bryn Mawr College, but alumnae and school leadership aggressively supported the programs in the first years. SSW leadership carefully avoided affiliation with any radical groups like the IWW while still maintaining values of intellectual freedom. Their doctrine stated the program was not "committed to any theory or dogma" and was "conducted in a spirit of impartial inquiry with freedom of discussion and teaching."[22] Between sixty and one hundred students attended the SSW each summer. Students came from diverse backgrounds, geographic regions, religious beliefs, and union affiliations.[23] In 1926, the program set a precedent by also inviting black women to participate in the school. Faculty with an affinity for "experimental teaching," most of whom also taught at colleges and universities throughout the United States, offered various experimental courses.[24] Subjects included combinations of English and economics as the core curriculum with secondary courses in public speaking, history, government, labor movements and problems, industrial organization, physiology and hygiene, and, of course, labor drama.[25] The SSW received accreditation from the AFL as approved workers' education for women, a boon to the program, and it endured for seventeen incident-free years before being asked to leave the Bryn Mawr campus in 1938 after program leaders were falsely accused of supporting a strike and generating scandal for the alumnae and administration. It lived on as the Hudson Shore Labor College in West Park, New York, until 1952, but the 1938 controversy was devastating to the program's history. Despite its demise, the Bryn Mawr program inspired several other similar programs, including the coeducational University of Wisconsin Summer School for

Workers (1925) and the Barnard College Summer School for Women Workers (1927), in addition to the SSS.

Dramatics was an influential component of the SSW curricula. Programs involved performances of plays, mass recitations, and pageants; reading and analysis of extant dramatic texts; and development of new labor plays. During the seventeen years of SSW on Bryn Mawr's campus, students wrote and produced dozens of original labor drama scripts, many of which still remain in archives. In her 2004 study, Karen Hollis documents some of the goings-on with SSW dramatics curricula, noting that the school employed a dramatics instructor as early as 1923, the same year word of Portland's labor drama programs circulated at the WEB conference.[26] By 1932, the program was in full swing with a dedicated instructor, Esther Porter, and 1937 was the "crowning year for Summer School dramatics."[27] The apex of SSW drama occurred under the leadership of Jean Carter (Ogden). Carter, another dramatics instructor and an undeniable advocate for drama in labor colleges during this time, took over directorship of the SSW after Smith departed for a new role within the Works Progress Administration. Carter advocated for the SSW dramatics program to hold a more prominent position within the curriculum.[28] During this period, labor drama flourished with students creating and presenting hosts of skits, pageants, and full-length plays. This experimentation with dramatics at the SSW directly influenced Hollace Ransdell's pedagogy at the SSS.

Beyond labor drama, the SSW influenced practically every aspect of the SSS's inception. The SSS also billed itself as a "non-sectarian, non-political experiment in Workers' education sponsored by an independent committee of southern workers and educators," following the SSW's philosophy that espoused no specific political or ideological doctrine.[29] It also targeted women and followed a similar curriculum. The SSS started in 1927, evolved into a coed program in 1938, and closed for good in 1951. Unlike the SSW, which remained at the Bryn Mawr campus for decades, the SSS was a transient program. Each summer, the program traveled to different locations in the Blue Ridge Mountains of North Carolina and Virginia, spending most summers at different school campuses and camp locations near Asheville, North Carolina. The school's curriculum focused on challenges inherent to preparing southern workers—particularly women influenced by conservative, religious, racially charged, anti-industrialization, anti-North, and anti-labor ideologies that permeated much of working-class southern culture—to advocate for themselves and for their communities.[30]

The location of the college in the Blue Ridge Mountains of North Carolina was also significant given the connection to both southern economic development and the development of southern activist art. The area around Asheville was in a period of economic boom during the early 1900s with Asheville on pace to become one of the largest cities in the South.[31] The promise of economic prosperity in the city coupled with its breathtaking natural beauty attracted a wide variety of visitors, particularly wealthy business owners from the North, West, and Northeast, who looked for an idyllic summer retreat. The Biltmore estate, the massive summer home of George Vanderbilt and now a popular tourist destination, exemplifies this trend. The decision to place the SSS program in this area was a testament to the region's promise in a new southern economy and culture and to the emerging role of North Carolina's Piedmont region as an industrial center in textile production. However, the Great Depression hit hard in the region, and the impact on the economy was cataclysmic. The fallout set back development in the region for decades, as it did for much of Appalachia during the 1920s and 1930s. Still, these conditions proved advantageous for groups interested in experimental initiatives. The region's natural beauty and reputation as a retreat for the rich coupled with a depressed economy kept down the cost of living and attracted artists and education pioneers alike, including the more well-known Black Mountain College contingent starting in 1933, which included Merce Cunningham, John Cage, Buckminster Fuller, Robert Rauschenberg, Josef and Anni Albers, and many other artists.

In 1935, director Louise Leonard earnestly, albeit incorrectly, touted the SSS as the "only school in the South devoted to Workers' Education."[32] Although Commonwealth College formed in 1924 and Highlander Folk School formed in 1932, the SSS was the first and only school exclusively for women workers. The program also rapidly expanded, initiating several outreach programs during the winter months, including programs in drama led by Hollace Ransdell. However, the core programming took place over the summer, with programs lasting roughly six weeks. Unlike all other programs considered in this study, the SSS student makeup was "one hundred per cent American, one hundred per cent Protestant, and about two hundred per cent exploited."[33] All students, without exception, were white southern Christian women employed in textile factories, hosiery mills, and tobacco industries. Women of color and immigrant women were not admitted both due to the controversy-averse culture of these programs and the Jim Crow laws preventing mixed-race institutions. White women ages eighteen to thirty-five were admitted, and the average age of students was twenty-three.[34] Thus, the student body was homogeneous. These sessions provided residential accommodations for students, and the school required a sixth-grade education, two years' less schooling than Bryn Mawr's SSW required and a testament to public education opportunities in the South.[35] Students averaged an eighth-grade education, although some reports suggest some dropped out of primary school as early as the second grade to work in the mills. Less than half of the students were union members when they attended, a reflection of larger anti-union efforts at play within southern industry, and all students attended on scholarship that covered an average tuition expense of $150. Fundraising took care of all additional expenses. Curriculum closely mimicked that of the Bryn Mawr SSW and included courses and educational initiatives designed to "develop social consciousness of the working women" via an "economic approach . . . which leads directly to the heart of the problems of the working class."[36] Classes included labor history, economics, English, public speaking, personal hygiene, physical education, and labor dramatics. Between 1927 and 1937, over 350 women attended, with yearly classes averaging around forty students.[37] Overall, the SSS was a unique institution designed to support labor activism among white women workers in the South.

Tobacco Shops, Yaller Dogs, and Subpenys: Hollace Ransdell's Early Labor Drama Program

Hollace Ransdell started working at the SSS in 1928 and remained at the school until it transitioned into a coeducational program in 1936. While working at the SSS, she penned seven original published dramatic works and led students in dramatics and current events courses. She also served as campus librarian, and at the end of her SSS tenure she pioneered efforts in teacher training. Although Ransdell's path to dramatics instructor is not entirely clear given her apparent lack of formal training in performance disciplines, her experiences with radical circles of labor activism undoubtedly informed her work at the SSS. Ransdell attended Colorado Women's College, a now-defunct institution that aspired to be the Vassar of the West at the time. She received a master's degree in economics at Columbia University where she studied industrial relations and worked as the school's industrial relations librarian.[38] She also probably attended Brookwood Labor College around 1923–24.[39] After her formal education, Ransdell took on a variety of roles with labor organizations, mostly as a journalist.

Between 1926 and 1928, she worked with International Labor Defense (ILD), serving as the organization's secretary and publishing articles in the ILD's official publication, *Labor Defender*.[40] The ILD, a legal defense organization associated with the U.S. arm of the Communist Party, collaborated with organizations like the ACLU and worked aggressively to defend leftist labor activists.[41] It was also placed on Attorney General Tom Clark's first list of subversive organizations on December 4, 1947, as part of the second Red Scare. Its most noted cases included the Sacco and Vanzetti case; the legal defense of strikers in Passaic, New Jersey; and the defense of the Scottsboro Boys.[42] As part of Ransdell's participation in this organization, she published several articles about various labor activists' incarcerations and trials both in the *Labor Defender* and in other labor publications.[43] Her work with the ILD, Sacco-Vanzetti National League, and Prisoners' Relief Fund also led to her inclusion in the antiradical 1936 publication *The Red Network: A "Who's Who" and Handbook of Radicalism for Patriots*.[44] Overall, these muckraking articles documented the human side of labor strikes, commenting on the gross injustices suffered by workers who dared to organize. They paid particular attention to the experiences of immigrant workers, women, and children and were employed, by and large, as propaganda to solicit funds for legal defenses.

Despite their role as moneymakers for the ILD, these articles were also valuable journalistic contributions to the labor press and undoubtedly led to Ransdell's ACLU-sponsored assignment to cover the 1931 Scottsboro trials in Alabama. Although Ransdell had already started teaching dramatics at the SSS by the time she wrote about the Scottsboro case, she is best known for this thorough, detailed, and thought-provoking report. In 1931 in Alabama, two young white women mill workers falsely accused a group of young black men, later known as the Scottsboro Boys, of rape. The case led to heated debates and legal challenges regarding issues of race and the right to a fair trial, and inspired Harper Lee's *To Kill a Mockingbird*. Despite Ransdell's affiliations with these radical activist groups, the leadership of the SSS downplayed her involvement with those organizations and instead drew attention to her work as a librarian.

Ransdell's firsthand knowledge of the labor movement via her work in journalism influenced her approach to dramatics, and notable shifts in programming occurred after her arrival. Before Ransdell's SSS tenure, labor drama was not a course offering, with a class in "the Appreciation of Music" serving as the only extracurricular course beyond physical education.[45] A few students interested in "trying out their dramatic ability" produced several skits, but no formal productions occurred.[46] In 1928, Ransdell arrived on campus, charged with both teaching dramatics and managing the campus library.[47] During the first year SSS students produced several labor-oriented works, including a pageant dramatizing "scenes depicting the ways people have earned their living" as an extension of their economic history course and three one-act plays: *Peggy* from the Carolina Playmakers, a second unidentified script that showed "some of the effects of economic pressure upon the city worker," and a student-written improvisational dramatization about working conditions in a tobacco factory entitled *Tobacco Shop*, which has not survived.[48]

In 1929, Leonard established a year-round directorship and set up program headquarters in Baltimore, Maryland, with the goal of enacting "experiments in the field" as part of "Applied Workers [sic] Education."[49] Ransdell returned for the 1929 summer session and devised two new plays with students: *Work and Wealth: A Modern Morality Play in One Act* and *Oh Mr. Yaller Dog Take Him Away: A One-Act Sketch Taken from Life in a Mill Village*. *Work and Wealth* (Figure 3) reflected the lingering influence of pageantry in amateur labor drama circles. The "modern morality play" included characters fashioned as archetypes: Work and her associates Machinery, Overwork, Disease, and Ignorance engage in a tête-à-tête with Wealth and her crew, Pleasure, Profits, Love, Book-Learning, and Health.[50] Work, who appears in a "worn gingham dress" with "dark lines of weariness" etched into her face, and Wealth, who appears in an evening gown and jewels and rests atop cushy pillows, are the only characters who speak.[51] They meet at a crossroads and then engage in a dialogue about each of the other nonspeaking characters, who dance and move about the stage as

Work and Wealth discuss them. A few stage directions: "Overwork comes hobbling in leaning on a cane; Disease floats like a ghost a few steps behind . . . they approach Work who shrinks but does not move from where she is standing."[52] Naturally, Wealth is terrified of Overwork and Disease, but Work knows them "too well."[53] The five-page play ends with Machinery, wearing a costume of "a cardboard box covered with black paper," gathering up Poverty, Ignorance, Disease, Overwork, Unemployment, and Accident, forming a chain gang, and pushing on Work as they crack whips and cry, "Faster, faster."[54] As Work becomes increasingly exhausted, Wealth sits on a sofa, powdering her nose and ignoring Machinery's new influence on Work. The play abruptly ends, with the explicit themes of labor exploitation clear.

FIGURE 3. Production photograph of *Work and Wealth* produced by students in the Southern Summer School, 1929. This photograph is also one of the only extant images from productions from Ransdell's time at the SSS. Photographer unknown. "Labor Drama" Folder, Box 111, American Labor Education Service Records, 1927–1962, Kheel Center for Labor-Management Documentation and Archives, M. P. Catherwood Library, Cornell University, Ithaca, NY. Courtesy of Kheel Center, Cornell University.

In contrast to *Work and Wealth, Yaller Dog* resists archetypal structures and pageantry influences, instead dramatizing a moment in the lives of women mill workers. Recognizing Ransdell's experience with journalism, the play reads as a documentary theatre piece. Its subject matter derived from the millworker strike in Marion, North Carolina, roughly forty miles from Asheville, during which several women were tried in the nearby Burnsville court for violating an injunction.[55] Members of the SSS community attended the trials and met with the workers, and faculty lectured at the millworker rallies.[56] A dramatic retelling was an appropriate extension of their study about the Marion strikes. The reference to a yellow dog signifies on several levels. In the play, *Yaller Dog* refers to a taunting folksong sung to antiunion activists who refuse to organize. The reference to yellow dogs also reflects the increasing popularity of the pro-business "yellow dog" contract in the South in the 1920s. These controversial employment contracts forced potential employees to sign away their right to join a labor union. While they were outlawed via the Norris–La Guardia Act in 1932, at the time of writing *Yaller Dog* they were still widely in use, especially in female-oriented professions. On another level, yellow dog was also used as a euphemism for southern Democrats (otherwise known as yellow-dog Democrats), evoking southerners' strident beliefs about southern identities and ideologies. Critics believed, as indicated by colloquialisms, "Southerners would rather vote for a yellow dog than a Republican" or "Southerners would vote for a yellow dog if it were a Democrat," and that southern tradition, aided by the Democrats' power, prevented its culture from moving forward.[57] The many degrees of signification in the play's title alone suggest that Ransdell and her students thought carefully about the perceptions of southern culture as they related to labor issues.

Yaller Dog begins with Miss Shaw, a "Government Industrial Investigator" likely fashioned after Ransdell, stopping by the home of Mrs. Bessie Dashwood, a unionized millworker, in the midst of a strike.[58] A comedic exchange starts the play, with Mrs. Dashwood's young son Johnnie screaming for his "Maw" after Miss Shaw greets him. In the play's first half, Miss Shaw interviews Mrs. Dashwood, asking a series of questions like "Tell me what your grievances are. Why did all of you go on strike?" and promising to change the law: "The government wants you workers to be satisfied . . . it can pass some laws to help you."[59] In dialect-laden dialogue, particularly when compared to Miss Shaw's pristine speech, Mrs. Dashwood reveals skepticism toward Miss Shaw's plan: "I don't know's laws will help us out much. Seems laik nobody don' pay much tention to the few little ole laws we got already."[60]

Despite the comical southern characterization of Mrs. Dashwood, as the narrative progresses, she reveals startling and sobering facts about her life. She laments her work schedule, discussing how it regularly exceeds sixty hours per week despite the law, and she remarks on how "it seems laik nobody runs the bossmen but theirselves."[61] In another moment, she also matter-of-factly discusses her relief at losing her husband in a mill accident because the mill "bought the coffin" and besides, she "couldn't bear to be gettin' a new baby every year or so . . . watchin' 'em growin' up peaked and pale around me."[62] She even shows surprising self-awareness when discussing her naive decision to move for a job in the mill: "But law we was green. We thought if we nice and fine . . . . We didn't know then that the bossmen was assayin' to theirselves, 'them mountain people don't need no more'n just 'nuff to keep 'em from starvin' to death.'"[63] In all, Mrs. Dashwood's testimony provides honest, provocative documentation of the experiences of southern working women even as her comically stereotypical characterization makes her statements accessible to the audiences at SSS.

After Mrs. Dashwood's commentary, Mrs. McClain enters. Although the outspoken Mrs. Dashwood proudly joined the union, Mrs. McClain has not. As such, she represents the antiunion ideology at play in many southern workers' resistance to organization. She states, "I ain't goin' let no union tell me what I cain and what I cain't do."[64] The three women debate the pros and cons of unionization until the only male character in the play, the Sheriff, enters and interrupts their exchange. The decision to include the male Sheriff, a buffoonish figure brandishing a "subpeny to appear in court," reads as deliberate commentary about male interventions in labor activism. Prior to his entrance, the three women, all from different walks of life with different perspectives on labor, engage in a dialogue about issues, sharing their thoughts via a heated but respectful exchange. The Sheriff's entrance disrupts all of this collaborative conversation. He demands that Mrs. Dashwood see the judge and not go to the picket line. Mrs. Dashwood responds with indignation: "Here's the sheriff a servin' me with an injunction paper sayin' I cain't go in the union picket line; he'll be servin' me with one sayin' I can't blow my nose next."[65] Upon hearing Mrs. Dashwood's resistance, other women, passing by on their way to the picket line, gather round the boss and begin "jeeringly" singing "Mr. Yaller Dog Take Him Away."[66] The increasingly angry Sheriff uses his club to chase out all of the women in Mrs. Dashwood's yard and menacingly reminds Mrs. Dashwood that she should stay off the picket line "fer your own good."[67] In a surprise response, Mrs. McClain jumps up, requests a copy of the injunction, and ends the play declaring, "I'm a goin' to jine the union. I ain't agoin' to have nobody a tellin' me I cain't picket!"[68]

By imagining a realistic route for activism among these female workers, Ransdell distinguishes her texts from earlier works. *Yaller Dog*'s ending is somewhat surprising, particularly when compared to other similar plays like *The Tailor Shop* produced by Hazel MacKaye, because the play's striking millworkers, unlike *The Tailor Shop*'s garment workers, are not successful in shoving off or silencing the Sheriff in a theatrical act of solidarity. Instead, the Sheriff rushes the women off the stage, leaving the remaining characters, Mrs. Dashwood and Mrs. McClain, to assert their agency in the face of oppression. Mrs. McClain must make a choice: join the union or become complicit in shutting down her fellow women's right to picket. The distinctions between the endings of *The Tailor Shop* and *Yaller Dog* highlight Ransdell's unique approach to labor drama, drawing attention to the way she navigated challenges unique to the SSS. For example, Brookwood students crafted *The Tailor Shop* prior to the AFL antiradical and anticommunist efforts in 1927–28, so the possibilities regarding what could be represented were much more open. Depicting a boss rushed off the stage by women tailor shop workers was playfully subversive, but not dangerous. In contrast, Ransdell, acutely aware of both the aura of skepticism surrounding labor activism in the South and the recent goings-on with the AFL, not to mention the Brookwood controversy that resulted in AFL president William Green condemning the institution, opted for a more conservative solution for her striking women.

The move from outlandish solutions with little practical application in the real world—as in the case of rushing a boss off the stage while singing "Owner of a Union Shop" or shouting down a sheriff brandishing a club and a "subpeny"—to a more realistic approach whereby women represented practical approaches to labor activism also speaks to Ransdell's adeptness in navigating the SSS's expectations for her program. As in other programs, SSS leadership used dramatics as a tool for community building and publicity, and Ransdell struck a careful balance with her plays. Her program needed to represent her southern students' real-life experiences, but the productions could not generate controversy for the new school. These productions' purpose as school publicity also helps explain Ransdell's use of pageantry forms in *Work and Wealth*. The allegorical good-versus-evil plot demonstrates dramatics students' investment in and engagement with different issues contributing to labor exploitation. Similarly, using pageantry paradigms for dramatizing complex economic concepts like the influence of machinery on the experience of workers shows the potential for performance-based pedagogy to help students make sense of abstract concepts in the curricula. However, these broad archetypes, even as they exploited poor, gingham-clad Work, avoided controversy. *Work and Wealth* was a living economics lesson where characters were concepts—not real people. Likewise, the narrative explained an economic process instead of giving voice to specific examples of real-life worker oppression.

Students performed both *Work and Wealth* and *Yaller Dog* for the student body and for the school's first labor conference, held on campus at the end of summer. Forty-three guests, all labor leaders, visited the SSS and saw Ransdell and her students' work.[69] The decision to present these original labor dramas at the SSS's inaugural labor conference demonstrates the increasingly visible role dramatics played in the SSS students' educational experiences. Furthermore, these performances were also important profile-raising efforts that reinforced the SSS's no-doctrine philosophies even as they showcased how the students developed knowledge about the southern labor movement. News reports of the school's goings-on, like an article featured in *Women's Wear Daily,* took note of the innovative but safe dramatics program in which Ransdell took "the themes and many of the lines suggested out of the experiences of the students."[70] Likewise, Eleanor Coit, director of the ASW, published a report of the SSS in a December 1929 edition of *Women's Press,* citing the SSS's work in labor drama when she suggested that the school might become "the classroom of the southern labor movement."[71] If these reports are an indicator, Ransdell balanced the politics of labor drama during her first years with aplomb.

"Well? . . . Whut Air We Agoin to Do About It?":
Depression Strikes the Southern Summer School

SSS labor drama programs expanded in 1929–30 despite the October stock market crash. According to a February 1930 issue of *The News*, the SSS's intermittently published newsletter, English teacher Miriam Bonner and Hollace Ransdell spent the winter of 1929–30 in Europe "visiting workers' schools and other progressive educational centers" in Brussels, Copenhagen, London, Berlin, and Leipzig.[72] During this time, Louise Leonard also started teaching extension courses in Nashville, forming a partnership that would last several years and establishing foundations for a later dramatics extension program. In Leonard's course entitled "Worker's Risks," a culminating assignment was the creation of "a dramatic sketch, written by members," "presented by the class" with "a real trade union message and was itself an example of another form of workers' education."[73] Leonard's incorporation of drama into her larger course demonstrated that Ransdell's work continued to have an impact on the SSS programs. Luckily, the structure of the SSS in the summer of 1930 encountered only a few and mostly positive changes. All staff returned from the previous year, and the school relocated to a more desirable campus in Arden, North Carolina, an Asheville suburb.

Despite positive developments in terms of staff continuity and improved location, the Crash had clearly affected students. The 1930 student body, a more "mature and serious minded" group, was notably smaller than previous years' cohorts: only twenty-five students attended.[74] Leonard's 1930 director's report noted concern regarding the shift in students' darker outlook on labor, remarking that it seemed to be "a reflection of the social situation at the present time."[75] Alongside discussion of the challenges of teaching this smaller, more somber group of students, Leonard also makes note of the growth in "socialized dramatics" programs, citing the "noteworthy" results.[76] In addition to new student-produced scripts, the school also started more significant conversations with visitors to campus regarding labor drama outreach opportunities. Leonard describes Ransdell's skill as dramatics instructor as "a rare combination of ability both to teach through dramatics and to present artistic productions" and discusses the potential extension work planned for five southern cities for the winter of 1930.[77] In

another testament to labor drama's growth, the school also welcomed playwrights William Wolff of the Carolina Playmakers and Dorothy Gardner
as the first guest teaching artists.[78] Leonard surveyed the 1930 dramatics
programs in an essay she published in *Mountain Life and Work* in January 1931.[79] While playtexts from the summer of 1930 are missing from the
archive, glowing assessments from the director about the course remain:

> In dramatics classes they discuss dramatic situations in their common expe-
> rience, situations arising, as a rule, out of their work life either on the farm or
> in the factory. With the dramatics director, who has great skill in editing their
> work, they create plays depicting the most dramatic situations of their group
> life, such as the picket line at Marion, or the employment office in a southern
> city. These plays have both artistic and educational value. Drawn from real life,
> as they are, they are an addition to the folk literature of the South.[80]

Clearly, Ransdell's work made an impact on Leonard, and the labor drama
program continued to grow throughout 1930 and 1931.

After the summer session, Ransdell continued work in labor drama via
extension programs. In the spring of 1931, the same period during which
she traveled to Alabama to report on the Scottsboro trials, she was also "on
tour in the South to encourage the formation of workers' dramatic groups
as a phase of workers' education."[81] For a salary of three hundred dollars a
month, she led programs in Nashville, collaborating with the newly formed
Union Labor Dramatic Group to produce *And They Call Us Civilized!*, a
one-act farce based on real events surrounding the corrupt Duckhead
Overall Company's union-busting efforts the prior year. She also supervised a "second experiment" in Louisville, Kentucky, where she collaborated with the Amalgamated Clothing Workers and Transportation Broth-
erhood on another new production, a farce entitled *What's Wrong with
Business?* about unemployment relief.[82] She led a third program in Jackson,
Tennessee, but details on this initiative are scant.[83] Ransdell submitted a
lengthy report about these programs to the SSS in which she offered insight
about her approach to labor drama and discussed her motivation for working in the discipline. This report provides some of the only documentation
from Ransdell's perspective regarding her intense commitment to labor
dramatics between 1928 and 1936.

When commenting on drama's value to workers' education, Ransdell
boldly suggests that "social recognition and appreciation of the poetic

imaginative qualities, the dramatic instinct found in the working class and the dynamic self-confidence which its recognition would bring, completes an educational force of untold possibilities."[84] Ransdell's suggestion that drama helps to complete a virtually limitless force of educational possibility indicates that she found labor drama compelling because it provided a synergistic, collaborative format in which to synthesize her work as a journalist and her work as an educator. She goes on to describe the pedagogical design of her SSS summer courses: "The dramatic program of the Southern Summer School which has been carried on for four summers during the six weeks' session of the School has served as a laboratory for experimentation in the use of dramatics as a potent education force for workers whose limited schooling and industrial life have given their minds little chance to grasp abstractions."[85] Here, Ransdell articulates drama's value as a pedagogical tool that makes abstract ideas concrete for worker-students. Her evocation of laboratories whereby pedagogical experimentation takes place speaks to the reflective practice in which Ransdell immersed herself as she evolved as a dramatics instructor. Through this reflection, Ransdell determined that labor drama was good for workers' education because it avoided traditional pedagogical formats with which SSS students, a group of nontraditional students with an average eighth-grade education, had little experience. This commitment to meeting the unique needs of her worker-students also appears in Ransdell's assessment of program outcomes. She asserts, "The most important thing that stands out in looking over the results of this first dramatic extension program of the SSS is the corroboration it gives to the idea that dramatics makes a great appeal to those who spend their lives in physical activity and has great value as an educational force."[86] Her references to labor drama as an experiential learning medium that also connected to the lives of her students reflects evolving ideas about dramatics' value as a pedagogical tool in the United States. Unlike Smith and MacKaye, who mostly focused on drama as an aesthetic form of pleasure and self-expression, Ransdell connected more explicitly to the pedagogical significance of creating and performing dramatic works.

By the summer of 1931, dramatics was fully integrated into SSS curriculum. Ransdell, secure in her role as dramatics instructor, took more risks with her productions. SSS's later plays are much darker and more critical of worker injustices, as shown by the course's title change from "Social-ized Dramatics" to "Workers' Dramatics."[87] Students now attended daily classes in drama where they "read together and learned folk plays and character sketches."[88] They also produced five short plays in 1931. Two, *Job Huntin'* and *On the Picket Line*, have survived. *Job Huntin'*, an absurdist "tragi-comedy in one act," depicts a group of downtrodden unemployed millworkers who decide to start a "Starvation Army" in order to use their deaths as a tool for advocacy. It is simultaneously a funny, timely, and even painful piece of folk theatre. The seven-page work opens with two unem-ployed cotton weavers, Jake and Dan, chatting in front of Jip's Employment Agency. They discuss their ten-mile walk to the agency and critique Pres-ident Hoover's recent actions, or more accurately, inaction, on unemploy-ment; workers were outraged when the President's Emergency Committee on Employment refused to designate public funds for workers' relief. As the characters wait in front of the unemployment office hoping for jobs that are unlikely to materialize and lament their hunger (Dan's been sub-sisting on blackberries he foraged from the wooded area near his home), they hatch a plan to be "jist as inconsiderate-like as we could when we wuz goin' kick the bucket" by dying en masse on the front steps of the boss's home.[89] The play concludes with the millworkers electing a captain of their newly formed Starvation Army and singing a dirge-like labor hymn as they march off to die on their boss's porch. *Job Huntin'* presents a modest pro-posal about the ever-increasing problem of unemployment in the South that functions as a sophisticated satire highlighting workers' acute desper-ation. At the same time, the darkly comedic aspects of the play bring levity. In the final moments, a crew of zombie-like workers, "ragged and hungry," stumble across the stage singing a parody to the tune of "In the Sweet By and By": "We will eat, by and by / In that beautiful land beyond the sky / Work and pray, Live on hay / You'll get pie in the sky when you die." The lyrics capture much-needed humor in its representation of these issues. Through its satirical style, *Job Huntin'* avoids the heavy-handed melodrama that predominates in many labor drama scripts.

In contrast to *Job Huntin'*, *Picket Line* offers another slice-of-life narra-tive about labor organizing similar to *Yaller Dog*. While similar to *Yaller Dog* in theme and structure, *Picket Line* conveys darker, more desperate tone in response to the deepening Depression. The play opens with a group of strikers sitting around a bonfire. A high wire fence of the Walden Cotton Mill appears in the background. The strikers are on watch, making sure scabs do not cross the picket line at night. It is cold and late, and the strikers are punchy with exhaustion and hunger. They trade jokes about stealing one of the boss's chickens, huff and puff about beating up scabs who cross the picket line, and sing labor tunes.[90] Various characters drop by the picket line bonfire, including Joe, the union organizer who checks on the men's well-being and brings them coffee, and Miz Howard, a scab who makes ends meet by doing the bosses' laundry.[91] Even Walden Cotton Mill owner Boss Peters stops by, commenting on the strikers' apparent laziness: "You seem to be takin' it easy enough."[92] Ma Simpson, an "old and lively spinner," quips back, "Ye..e...e..h! Jist like a bossman... if'n I had the money."[93] The group suppresses laughter as Boss Peters stares suspiciously at the stewing stolen chicken, and as he exits, one of the strikers walks behind him, comically imitating his pompous gait. The mood is jovial. Later, the play's tone shifts. As in *Yaller Dog*, the Sheriff enters, brandishing injunction subpoenas for the strikers. The strikers' indignant responses hearken back to *Yaller Dog*; they cheekily discuss how they use their other subpoenas to "start th' kitchen fire," how they framed and displayed them on the wall "like I did my marriage license," or how they gave it to the "baby to chow on."[94] After making light of the injunction papers, they threaten to vote against the Sheriff in the upcoming election.

Despite their taunting, the Sheriff is not deterred, as in *Yaller Dog*. He saunters offstage, warning, "I'll see yuh all in co't one these days."[95] The group once again feigns flippancy, but when the Sheriff is out of earshot, the strikers "fall silent and stare thoughtfully into the fire. They are disturbed, uneasy."[96] Only after a lingering silence does Tom, the young and outspoken member of the group, ask, "Well? .... Whut air we agoin to do about it?"[97] Another pause. Finally, Old Man Sally, an otherwise quiet character "who is about 40 but looks 60," simply says, "I dunno, lad. I dunno." The drama ends with the group quietly singing, "We are building a strong union" to the tune of "Jacob's Ladder."[98] Even though the show's stage directions indicate the singing slowly grows "stronger and stronger," the somber tone penetrates the play's final moments. Unlike in *Yaller Dog*, no one acts; instead, the strikers simply sit, unsure of themselves and their purpose with another round of injunction subpoenas in hand. The message is clear. These strikers have been here before and nothing seems ready to change. A quiet desperation lingers among the once-punchy workers, and their marked ambivalence about what comes next trumps their surging chorus. In this simple drama about stolen chickens and boss-ladies' laundry, Ransdell and her students raise important existential questions about the purpose and goals of labor organizing in such a dire time. Both *Job Huntin'* and *Picket Line* provide a sophisticated embodiment of the Depression's impact on workers using absurdist theatrical tropes, and they pay homage to Ransdell's risky but innovative approach to staging her students' narratives.

In addition to creating and producing plays like *Job Huntin'* and *Picket Line*, Ransdell also responded to the impact of the Depression by broadening curricula to help her students plan for outreach in their respective communities. Her new focus on helping students develop dramatics clubs speaks to her increasing prominence and growing commitment to disseminating labor drama techniques as workers' education tools in southern communities. In a planning session held at the end of summer, students and faculty collaborated on workshops and talks about teaching dramatics in home communities.[99] As a response, students from Atlanta, Durham, North Carolina, and Louisville, Kentucky, all presented plans for dramatics courses. They described new classes at local YWCAs and strategies for organizing labor play benefit presentations to raise money for the SSS and to network with local trade unions.[100] A report about the 1931 summer session in *School and Society* took note of these innovations. Elsie Janison, a professor at the Texas State College for Women and a visitor to campus, remarked on labor drama, commenting that the program "demonstrated well the fact that even a small group may show considerable dramatic ability when asked to portray situations which are familiar to its own experience. A run on a bank or a meeting to discuss unemployment remedies can be depicted with both humor and pathos by those who know the bitter irony of such situations."[101] Janison's reference to "bitter irony" speaks to the political complexity included in *Picket Line* and *Job Huntin'*, and her commentary that "even a small group may show considerable dramatic ability" indicates that Ransdell's experimental dramas opened new, more nuanced interpretations of SSS students' life experiences that outsiders found compelling.

The Depression's impact finally hit SSS in 1932. Financial strain, held at bay for a few years by Louise Leonard's expert fundraising skills, threatened to shutter the program by the end of 1932. After the summer session, Leonard wrote to ASW director Eleanor Coit, stating, "There were many times during the past year when we thought the [SSS] would have to be given up because of lack of funds" and expressing concern that the 1932 session might end in a financial deficit.[102] The program also moved again, this time to a less expensive but much smaller campus in Hendersonville, North Carolina, thirty miles south of Asheville, and several faculty members who had been with the SSS since the beginning did not return.[103] Only twenty students attended, and leadership was unable to hire support staff like cooks or maids. "Domestic work" fell to the faculty and students.[104] Visitors to the campus were also in short supply, and the annual labor conference was significantly smaller than in previous years. The summer of 1933 was not much better. A group of thirty students shrunk to twenty-two a week before the session's start due to a "business up-turn" that "brought back their jobs."[105] Thirteen of those who attended were unemployed and attended mostly because they had nothing better to do.[106] These students shared similar concerns about the increasingly dire state of southern economies: cut wages, higher expectations for output, part-time employment, and unexplained and unwarranted termination.[107] Once again, the program moved locations, now forced to share a campus in Weaverville, North Carolina, with another program due to financial pressures.[108]

Still, Ransdell stayed on as dramatics instructor despite other colleagues' departures, and labor drama endured as an undoubtedly bright spot. In the same memo Leonard wrote to Eleanor Coit lamenting the challenges of the 1932 session, she also commented on labor drama as "not only another avenue of expression and a delightful form of recreation, but a method of conveying to fellow workers information and a point of view about industrial problems."[109] Through this work, Ransdell honed her craft and continued to spread the word about labor drama beyond the SSS community. She also made available a few of her plays for twenty-five cents in order to raise funds for the school while generating and publishing new plays with her students. In regards to the summer course, student Emma Smith commented on their "recreational study" in a 1933 course description, one of the few testimonies about Ransdell's instruction:

This group meets just before dark when groups of girls love to sit around and talk. In this class they are given much opportunity for constructive talk. After reading a short play on one labor problem or another, Hollace asks the students to analyze the characters, the play, and the author's ideas in writing it. One of the biggest surprises came when after a group of nine students practiced parodies to several popular songs without the help of music, stage setting or scenery, they produced "The Forgotten Man." It was enthusiastically received by the faculty and guests who spoke of the good work which had been done by the director.[110]

The production of *The Forgotten Man*, a 1933 "musical skit" by Commonwealth College teacher Bill Reich, signaled the increasing interconnectedness of the southern labor schools and the commitment to supporting other initiatives in the southern labor drama community. A description of the production featured in *The News* also demonstrated the challenges Ransdell encountered in producing plays at this new site. The performance space was a "classroom," and the "director worked under hardships of having no stage and very little stage properties."[111] Despite these lackluster conditions, Ransdell continued her courses. Students read and studied seminal labor plays like *The Adding Machine*, *RUR*, and *The Weavers*, and they also created at least three more plays during this period: *Bank Run* (July 1932), *World Economic Nonsense* (August 1933), and *Mother Jones' Tin Pan Army* (August 1933).[112]

Bank Run, another "tragi-comedy sketch in one act," once again showcases Ransdell's perpetual experimentation by asserting its status as the first drama "based on an actual scene."[113] The play also shows Ransdell's increasingly outspoken approach to labor drama. An opening description includes the following information: "This sketch is based on an actual scene that took place during a run on a large eastern bank which failed in the Fall of 1931. Many of the remarks in the dialogue are repeated word for word as they were heard and noted down by a person who stood in the line. The sign about a 'word to the wise' was pasted on the window and was worded exact as given below."[114] The narrative depicts depositors waiting in line at a failed bank hoping to retrieve their money. They wait in a line "stretching from the door of the bank on the right clear across the stage and out into the wing on the left as far as the eye can see," next to a prominent sign that reads, "The thrifty person is one who has started a bank account and regularly makes his deposits ensuring his future with funds that mean so much to him when most needed. A word to the wise is sufficient."[115] The sign is an ominous reminder of the Depression's economic atrocities. Throughout the skit, a Hobo, the play's narrator, shuffles back and forth along the line, stopping to talk with different people: an old man who has lost his entire life savings; a Shopkeeper who suggests the bank "didn't invest the money the way they should"; and a couple of men who discuss the role of elected officials in the bank bust.[116] Finally, "a large unhealthily fat man with a pasty complexion, probably a German baker," announces, in a German accent that he is going to "look into vat these Reds are saying, by Gott if I'm not!"[117] The group debates the pros and cons of communism and talks about the economic state of affairs in Russia. Suddenly, a Cop appears, threatening to arrest anyone who speaks of Russia.[118] By the skit's end, the Cops brandish their clubs, demanding that the group disperse. The Hobo escapes the scuffle by hiding behind people in line and delivers a final monologue:

> See? I told you so. You say anything's that true, they call you a Bolsheviki. They tell you to beat it, I know. I see the same thing everywhere I go. If they throw you out of your job to starve, take it. If they take away your furniture and set you out in the street to freeze, take it. If they fool you into putting money into the bank and then steal it from you, take it. Take what they give you, for if you don't you're a BOLSHEVIKI, one of these here Reds. And why don't you get back where you came from?[119]

This final moment is powerful. Ransdell and her students articulate a scathing critique of banks, law enforcement, government officials, and the wealthy. They also criticize the systematic silencing of any voices of dissent through their characterization of blustering Cops who threaten to arrest anyone who speaks of Russia. A far cry from the demure allegory in *Work and Wealth*, *Bank Run* reveals an increasing radicalization of SSS labor drama.

Two additional works produced during this time period, *Economic World Nonsense* and *Mother Jones' Tin Pan Army* are equally inflammatory. *Nonsense* is a satire of the 1933 London economic conference at which President Franklin D. Roosevelt controversially refused to join an international agreement that would stabilize currency and relieve the worldwide impact of the Great Depression. The text, written in rhyming verse, features a Hog and a Clown as narrators. The cast is made up of a cadre of international delegates, including two buffoonish U.S. representatives who bicker throughout the entire scene and start a raucous fight at the end of the play.[120] The Clown and the Hog manipulate the puppetlike delegates, forcing them all to settle down after the U.S.-instigated fracas.[121] The final moment of the play shows the Clown forcing every delegate to turn and grin at the audience, save the German delegate who grimaces at the French delegate. As the two stare at each other, the Clown yells to the stagehand, "Hey, turn off that light quick! They can't hold that grin much longer!"[122] The effect provides a haunting image foreshadowing the lead-up to World War II.

Mother Jones dramatizes a moment described in Mother Jones's autobiography where she and her tin-pan army, a group of women marching with mops, brooms, and tin pans, butt heads with law enforcement. The Sheriff and Deputy are terrified by the raucous group of women and are barely able to stop their bayonets from shaking as the army approaches.[123] In the middle of this exchange, in which Mother Jones clearly has the upper hand, a scab working in the mines wanders by the group. The women rush him, trip him with their mops, bang their pans in his ears, and leave him completely disoriented.[124] In his bewildered state, the scab agrees to join the union as he "looks fearfully at the women."[125] At that moment, the Union President rushes in "wringing his hands" and gives Mother Jones a talking-to once she announces that the scab joined the union: "Took them into the Union? What do you mean? How could you do that? You didn't have the ritual! . . . That's not according to the by-laws of the Union."[126] The play ends with Mother Jones giving a rousing speech in which she states she is going to "fight like . . . well like my women fought today! And you men had better come and join us!"[127] *Mother Jones* is a radically feminist work in its depiction of incompetent male leaders; images of violent, rowdy women; and critiques of union policy that keep women disempowered for purposes of activism.

If there were any confusion about the shifting tone of Ransdell's plays, *Bank Run, Nonsense,* and *Mother Jones* indicate a clear turn toward a political agitation style of performance. All three of these plays are provocative texts with no-holds-barred commentary about the labor movement's state of affairs. However, these plays did not appear to encounter any controversy with the SSS leadership. No documentation exists suggesting that SSS leadership censored these texts or prevented their publication or production in any way. In fact, they are among the handful of texts published by the SSS and circulated in workers' education circles. Given the lack of controversy surrounding these dramas, they stand as defining examples of an evolving movement, markers of labor drama moving away from politically palatable progressive self-expression to more radical forms designed to agitate on behalf of disenfranchised workers.

The more radical tone that appeared in her plays from 1932 and 1933 also appeared in Ransdell's work with community groups. Between the 1932 and 1933 summer sessions, Ransdell planned to continue her outreach work in Alabama. However, this turn toward activist themes presented problems given Ransdell's new association with the Affiliated Schools for Workers. With the SSS struggling to make ends meet, funds could not be secured to support planned projects in Mobile, Alabama. Instead, Ransdell was forced to continue her work as a teaching artist for the ASW under Eleanor Coit's supervision.[128] Coit dispatched her to the Northeast to devise theatre with women workers through local YWCAs. This initiative was a pilot project, designed to serve as a model for other extension programs, but these other opportunities never materialized.[129] Ransdell committed to projects in Woonsocket and Pawtucket, Rhode Island, northeastern textile centers and sites of recent strikes.[130] There, she encountered several challenges. The women with whom she worked were uninterested in developing dramatics clubs and hoped that Ransdell would simply direct them in a play, much to Ransdell's disappointment.[131] Through much cajoling, Ransdell managed to unify the women and produce "What, No Work?"— a short skit about unemployment relief and sweatshop conditions in the area mills.[132] The tone of Ransdell's letters to Coit reveals her frustration and annoyance with the lack of investment in the political dimension of labor drama from the Rhode Island women: "We are therefore putting on a short, quite simple skit which we may call 'What, No Work?' or some such thing. . . . Our performance will be simple, for I've tried to continually emphasize the question of going on with dramatics, and we have spent quite a bit of time talking over plans for organizing the group. . . . I will go into this more fully when I see you in New York."[133] Her reference to "continually emphasizing" the question of strategies for organizing labor drama clubs, the primary purpose of her visit, highlights the resistance she encountered with the group.

Under the auspices of the ASW, Coit also charged Ransdell with organizing local dramatics groups with unions and networking with Bryn Mawr and Brookwood students, but these efforts were largely unsuccessful. Ransdell's letters to Coit regarding these matters also expressed increasing frustration and suggested a bit of resentment toward this new public relations role as part of her work with the ASW. Two brief samples: "The Union is dead as a door-nail and quite hopeless. Elizabeth Nord [a prominent leader in the northeastern textile unions during this time and Bryn Mawr SSW alumna] is discouraged and disgusted with the officials, and rightly so," and "So far, I have spent my time entirely with the girls, and have seen none of the members of the committee."[134] Ransdell struggled to reconcile her increasingly radical interests with ASW initiatives.

Although the extension programs no longer fell under the SSS's leadership, Ransdell still maintained autonomy over her summer programs, but they would change as well. In 1934, the Federal Emergency Relief Act (FERA) fundamentally altered the SSS's core programming. In order to secure additional funds to keep the program afloat, Leonard applied for monies via FERA in exchange for supporting a "unit of unemployed workers" in teacher education training. These twenty-four new students combined with the unprecedentedly small class of seventeen workers recruited "through regular channels."[135] This small class resulted from several factors explained in the 1934 Director's Report:

> Four hosiery workers . . . dropped out because they feared if they got off they would not be taken on again; two hosiery workers could not leave economic responsibilities for their families; 1 garment worker's . . . company refused her time off; 1 garment worker . . . decided to get married; 1 Amalgamated garment worker . . . was laid off and obliged to get another job; 1 shoe worker . . . apparently lost interest; 1 waitress . . . who had been unemployed for a long time dropped out because she got a job; and 1 waitress . . . had to drop out because of illness.[136]

The majority of students left because they either feared losing their jobs or found a new job, a positive side effect of the long-awaited economic upturn in the South. In addition to the small group of typical students, other concerns arose from the new group of teacher trainees. The SSS received approval for FERA money very late in the planning season, and leadership scrambled to recruit new students and plan their curriculum. Reports indicate that the unemployed unit "had not known what to expect," had "very little industrial background," and did "not have a very clear idea of what they were coming to" before they arrived on campus. Faculty needed to rapidly shift curricula away from workers' education to a more practical program in teacher training, whatever that entailed.[137] This reorientation produced strain for teachers like Ransdell who had grown accustomed to a particular flow in summer programs. Additionally, the poorly conceived solution to this odd set of circumstances only made matters worse. Reports suggest that much instruction during the 1934 season involved the twenty-four teacher trainees sitting on the sidelines of classes observing the methods of faculty as they taught the seventeen "regular" students.[138] Naturally, this was a significant departure from the intimate, discussion-based models of instruction the faculty had previously incorporated in their teaching and presented "difficulties in teaching a 'crowd'" that the instructors struggled to overcome.[139]

Another set of complicating issues arose from the SSS's new affiliation with the ASW. While the SSS had maintained connections to this organization, it had resisted a formal association for almost a decade in order to protect its autonomy. However, the Depression-era financial strain made joining the ASW necessary, much to the SSS leadership's annoyance.[140] Most documentation about this period addresses growing pains associated with these new developments. Little commentary about dramatics programs, other than a brief mention of another outreach project by Ransdell in "the anthracite region of Pennsylvania," exists.[141] The only other reference to SSS labor drama was a mention in Commonwealth College's school paper in March 1934, which stated, "Ransdell will have charge of labor drama projects for a series of workers education projects under the ASW. Pennsylvania Department of Public Instruction will supply unemployed teachers for a number of groups in the anthracite section of the state."[142] As this reference to unemployed teachers implies, Ransdell continued her new job as a teacher of teachers with the ASW in the off-season as well, likely an economic necessity.

By 1935, teacher-training programs had essentially taken over the SSS. Ransdell, while simultaneously continuing as dramatics instructor, also "acted as chairman of the teaching staff of the Teachers' Training Center" carrying "major responsibility for this course."[143] A few dramatics presentations appeared, but they were mostly "comic pictures of the life of the school," some simple student-generated skits, and few scenes from Clifford Odets's *Waiting for Lefty*.[144] In a report on dramatics classes that Ransdell somehow found time to put together while organizing and leading the Teachers' Training Center, she also commented on another competing development that threatened her dramatics program: the motion picture.[145] A great deal of conversation in the dramatics classes now centered around the movies, a form Ransdell worked to integrate into her curriculum but clearly struggled to contextualize within her approach. Mostly, Ransdell directed students to the idea that motion pictures "so seldom" took up "the problems and lives . . . of the working class" and offered labor drama as an alternative.[146] However, the plays she offered as fodder for this idea that drama more effectively took up working-class issues than movies in no way addressed the lives of southern workers. Titles included Paul Peters's *Stevedore*, *Waiting for Lefty*, a translation of Ernst Toller's *Masse Mensch*, and Friedrich Wolf's *Floridsdorf*. The U.S.-centered titles represented narratives from the northeastern industrial centers and dealt with dockworkers (*Stevedore*) and cab drivers (*Lefty*). The German plays by Toller and Wolf were even more obscure. *Masse Mensch* was based on the German workers' movement, and *Floridsdorf* chronicled the February uprising of Viennese workers in 1934. While these titles might have been engaging for Ransdell, a highly educated journalist with roots in radical Left politics and experiences with European workers' movements, they were an undoubted misstep for hooking in her southern students who had little background on U.S. cab drivers, let alone Viennese socialists. Even though popular movies failed to address workers' lives, at least they provided an escape from workers' day-to-day drudgery and generally contained accessible content.[147]

Although classes continued in 1936, the stage was clearly being set for a transition to a coeducational program that radically altered the SSS's pedagogical function. Sensing this inevitable change, Ransdell dug in her heels regarding her desire to introduce students to "some of the outstanding modern plays" and use them to criticize the "intent and value" of "other types of plays with which students are more familiar."[148] The tone of her dramatics reports during this period shows an increasing desperation for maintaining the integrity of her program, an endeavor she had diligently nurtured for eight years. For example, she tersely insisted that her course "aims to develop confidence and self-expression in *all* the members of the group. A few of the students of course have more natural ability at acting than the others. If the aim of the course were to present as perfect a performance as possible, these few would be selected and trained intensively to the neglect of the others."[149] This quote suggests increasing pressure to produce polished performances as part of the summer program, an idea reinforced by the evaluation she wrote in 1936:

> Dramatics at a workers' school has a very different function than that of the usual dramatics course in schools and colleges, or in the typical little theatre movement. The emphasis in a workers' dramatics group or in labor drama as it is sometimes called, should be not so much upon technique, as such, as upon ideas, and how to present those ideas simple [*sic*] and tersely in dramatic form, and in a way that students with a working class background can understand and respond to emotionally.[150]

Clearly, the shifting pedagogical objectives of the SSS, the changing landscape of popular entertainment, and the pressure to generate a product over process weighed heavily on Ransdell. She ended her affiliation with both the SSS and workers' education after the 1936 summer session.

"A Long Time Ago": Beyond the Southern Summer School

Ransdell never worked in dramatics again. Instead, she returned to her activist-journalist roots by joining the staff of the *CIO News*, the official publication of the newly formed CIO.[151] A few months earlier in 1936, the AFL ousted CIO-affiliated unions from the federation, and this historic fracture resulted in, as Robert Zieger notes in his history of the CIO, a "politicization of organized labor," "recasting of racial and ethnic dynamics," and a hinting toward a reawakened "openness to anticapitalist movements."[152] Ostensibly, Ransdell also saw promise in the CIO, especially regarding her work with women in the South, since the organization appeared open to new labor activism initiatives, particularly for women. However, this optimism was for naught. The CIO's founders, given their primary focus on industrial trades, maintained "traditionalist views of the economic, social, and political roles for women" and thus women were once again relegated to the organization's periphery.[153] Ransdell published a few articles during her twenty years as assistant editor of the *CIO News*,[154] but based on titles alone, none of them seem as compelling as her plays or the earlier essays she wrote in conjunction with International Labor Defense.[155] In a particularly poignant and sad turn of events, Ransdell was discharged from her job under the guise of early retirement for participating in unapproved organizing in 1958. Accounts suggest that she "refused her gift" of a wristwatch "with much indignation" during the retirement ceremony.[156] She did not publish again.

To close this chapter, I return to the exchange between Mary Frederickson and Miriam Bonner Camp, one of the few sources that offers insight regarding Ransdell's personality or her students' opinion of her:

> MARY FREDERICKSON: I was interested in Hollace Ransdell's work with labor drama [Laughter]. How did the students react to her, to the plays?
> MIRIAM BONNER CAMP: They enjoyed them; they were very enthusiastic.
> MARY FREDERICKSON: Was she easy to work with?
> MIRIAM BONNER CAMP: Well, I think she had certain standards, and was rather demanding, but I think they appreciated that because they got good results. She was a very able person.
> MARY FREDERICKSON: What was Hollace Ransdell like?
> MIRIAM BONNER CAMP: Oh, she was a charming person, very bright—very bright. That was a long time ago.[157]

This exchange about Ransdell's charm, brightness, demanding nature, and ability coupled with the anecdote about her standing up at her retirement ceremony and indignantly rejecting her well-earned wristwatch helps make sense of Ransdell's decade-long detour into labor drama. Both moments suggest that Ransdell was a radical at her core. When she signed up to lead the SSS labor drama programs, the hopes—the untold possibilities—for radical innovation through education and art were still very real possibilities, and Ransdell wanted a part of the action. Even though she resisted these radical tendencies in the SSS's early years, producing safe pageants and pedagogical vignettes of practical activism, over time she returned to her radical roots in organizations like the ILD and the ACLU. In the face of reawakened red fear and the Great Depression's lingering influence on the southern labor movement, however, by the end of her foray into labor drama Ransdell was back where she started. Instead of radical art that agitated on behalf of, as Mary Frederickson states, "a major social change," she was producing simple dramas with women most interested in producing pleasing plays that showcased their virtuosity as performers. And ASW director Eleanor Coit's watchful eye now monitored her work. The experience had to be demoralizing.

Perhaps these developments in Ransdell's life help explain why, just as she appeared poised to lead the field, her commitment to labor drama so quickly waned in 1936. Her few articles about the topic, "Amateur Dramatics" published in the 1936 ASW *Labor Drama Scrapbook* and "The Soapbox Theatre" published in an April 1935 edition of the National Association for the Advancement of Colored People publication *The Crisis*, offer additional insight. In her ASW article, Ransdell outlines the "confusion in many workers' minds" about why labor drama should be part of the workers' education: "They do not see why it is necessary for them [labor plays] to be different from ordinary plays, and to be put in a class to themselves as though they were strange and outlandish things. . . . They resent the idea that the theme or subject should deal with problems of their working lives. 'We are fed up on it. Give us something different,' they say, 'something romantic with love and excitement and thrills in it such as we see in the movies.'"[158] Here, Ransdell clearly articulates the frustrations with which she wrestled during her final year at SSS. The tide of what theatre historian Thomas Postlewait calls the hieroglyphic stage "whereby a democratic or mass culture enters into a new kind of spectatorship, an optical culture defined by the reign of the eye and the seduction of images," overwhelmed Ransdell's commitment to intellectual engagement with real problems in order to change the world.[159] As Ransdell demanded engagement, her students begged for escape. With those around her no longer interested in the activist dimensions of labor drama, she had little reason to stick with her experiments. The practice of self-reflection she cultivated as SSS labor dramatics instructor ultimately led her to leave the profession. She chose to abandon her efforts in labor drama in the hopes of making a difference elsewhere.

Despite her decision to leave the field, she acknowledged new avenues for this kind of work, particularly in the civil rights movement. In "The Soap Box Theatre," she discussed the use of activist drama in southern black communities. She also identified the next frontiers in the fight for labor drama's legitimacy: "The battle that goes on among the intellectuals as to whether or not propaganda can also be art, passes over the heads of most members of the labor drama classes. They are far too modest to dream of claiming that their simple, spontaneous, and impromptu performances come anywhere near the august realm of art."[160] Perhaps the struggle to place these workers' dramas into the category of art, education, or something new and undefined also vexed Ransdell, and she ultimately moved to a discipline, labor journalism, that made clear the delineation between what counted as art and what did not. For whatever reason, Ransdell's infatuation with labor drama ended quietly, and she slowly drifted into obscurity even as she continued to seek out opportunities for activism at the *CIO News*. Other artists, discussed in Chapters 5 and 6, would take up the mantle of labor drama in the South and advance arts-based activism leading up to, during, and after World War II.

CHAPTER 5

Something Very Different

Southern Labor Drama at Highlander Folk School, 1934–40

We don't mean "boy meets girl" and a happy ending like the Hollywood movies. This is Labor Dramatics—something very different.
Zilphia Horton

In microcosm, the Highlander Folk School, a Tennessee labor college founded in the early 1930s, reflected the growing pains of the newly emboldened labor movement as it pushed into the southeastern United States. In the vanguard of the southern labor movement, Highlander was one of the most influential labor colleges in articulating a unique approach to organizing workers in southern industries. The school was also an evolving institution that fully embraced the nascent civil rights movement, supporting early attempts to undo Jim Crow laws and later supporting efforts of organizations like the Student Nonviolent Coordinating Committee and the National Association for the Advancement of Colored People. In the 1960s, Highlander Folk School hosted civil rights activists, including young Martin Luther King Jr. and Rosa Parks, as part of its commitment to racial integration. Highlander is also a compelling labor institution because, unlike all other schools discussed in this book, it has survived. Currently in New Market, Tennessee, a small rural community roughly half an hour's drive from Knoxville, Highlander, now known as the Highlander Research and Education Center, is committed to "grassroots organizing and movement building in Appalachia and the South" through popular education, participatory research, and cultural work.[1] Those affiliated with the center have worked diligently for eighty-five years to advance social justice issues in rural Appalachia. These efforts include activism around the southern labor movement in the 1930s and 1940s, as well as more successful civil rights activism in the 1950s and 1960s. Currently, Highlander social justice work centers on supporting and organizing Latinx immigrants in the South and engaging southern young people in progressive causes.[2] Throughout this notable history, the school has been subject to scrutiny, violent attacks, protests, and both formal and informal censuring from a host of local, state, and federal agencies. Notably, the Federal Bureau of Investigation maintained an open case file on the school from 1936 until 1963, the contents of which include over a thousand pages of documentation that serves as a rich archival repository in and of itself. Despite the school's trials, or perhaps thanks to them, its history is well known. This rich record persists due to several additional factors, including cofounder Myles Horton's long tenure at the school and his commitment to documenting the goings-on at Highlander since the institution's founding in 1932. Highlander also benefited from hindsight by watching as other left-leaning political institutions, particularly those in the South, were quite literally erased from history.

In regards to labor drama, Highlander maintained a longstanding commitment to cultural life as part of the school's mission. The prominence and longevity of arts-related pedagogy at Highlander is largely thanks to the influence of Zilphia Horton, Myles Horton's first wife. Zilphia and Myles Horton met at Highlander and worked together to advance Highlander causes for more than twenty years. These efforts were only halted due to Zilphia's sudden and untimely death in 1956. Zilphia and Myles's relationship and Zilphia's connection to drama catalyzed labor drama on campus and more broadly for arts-based activism in the South as part of the civil rights movement. Accordingly, this chapter examines the early years of Highlander as a labor institution in the vanguard of several intertwined social justice movements in the South and considers how dramatics, as part of a longstanding commitment to arts-based activism, shaped these efforts.

Reawakening Southern Labor: Roosevelt, Racism, and the New Deal

As discussed in the previous chapter, the southern labor movement was a complicated, fractured, and tense affair. In addition to challenges associated with the Great Depression's impact in the South and the southern

Democrats' longstanding anti-union influence, a new series of trials arose from the movement's development within the political environment of the New Deal. The grip of economic decline between 1929 and 1932, felt acutely throughout the nation, decimated many already impoverished southern agrarian communities. As these dire economic conditions ground on, Republican President Herbert Hoover, previously lauded around the world as "the great humanitarian" who brought aid to ailing European countries after the Great War, could not manage to bring relief to his citizens. New York governor and Democrat Franklin Delano Roosevelt recognized these dire circumstances, particularly within virtually unshakeable Democratic strongholds in the South, and appealed directly to the downtrodden yellow-dog Democrats in Tennessee, Alabama, and Louisiana with his promise of a New Deal for all Americans. This political rhetoric resonated across geographic boundaries, and FDR soundly defeated Hoover in 1932, sweeping the Electoral College with 472 electoral votes. The election also ushered in Democratic supermajorities in both houses of the seventy-third Congress, the first interruption of the Republican stranglehold since Woodrow Wilson's presidency. Thanks to this broad coalition of voters, the 1932 election season was a boon to workers' causes as part of the leftward shift of the Democratic Party. The long-ignored "Solid South" finally seemed to matter to those in power. However, while the South was indeed solid, the coalition built by President Roosevelt was on shakier ground, particularly regarding the issue of race. In appealing to southern Democrats, FDR made an uncomfortable alliance with professed segregationists. The period from 1932 until the lead-up to World War II thus serves as a testament to both the possibilities brought about by New Deal optimism and the challenges associated with a rapidly transforming country with deeply held beliefs about regionalism, economics, and, above all, race in the face of escalating geopolitical instability.

In addition to these troubling realities, discussed in greater detail in both the Introduction and Chapter 4, the Great Depression also threatened to destroy any possibility of improving race relations or undoing the most egregious manifestations of southern Jim Crow laws. The racism brought about by national neglect in the wake of failed Reconstruction efforts once again erupted in the face of widespread economic decline, pitting poor white people against poorer black people. This situation was only made worse as the Republican and Democratic platforms completed a full realignment on issues of race, particularly as the new progressive coalition coalesced with the segregationist yellow-dog southern Democrats as core constituents. As economic desperation accelerated the deterioration of race relations in the South, horrifying laws, including widespread passage of mandated segregation and miscegenation laws and the repeated failure of Congress to pass antilynching bills, intensified the regressive Jim Crow laws and deeply entrenched racism in place since the failure of Reconstruction. The uptick in racial violence as the Great Depression reached its nadir further reflected the South's declining stability. These tensions played out in the young southern labor movement as well. By 1932, more than half of black people were unemployed nationwide, but in the South, reasonable work in any industry, including agriculture, for black workers was essentially nonexistent. Those black southerners able to find work were paid less than their white counterparts, were forced to work in the most dangerous conditions when hired, had no guarantee for sustained employment and tended to be fired before whites, and received no promise they would benefit from government relief offered to similarly impoverished white workers. Thus, the young southern labor movement would be deeply intertwined with the fledgling civil rights movement as activists worked on both issues simultaneously.

As a result of the tenuous New Deal coalition, post–New Deal labor activism in the South did not produce many of its desired outcomes. Efforts to expand industrial unionization from the North and Midwest to the Southeast were, in many ways, failures. Most southern states maintain anti-union right-to-work legislation to this day, barring workers from collective bargaining.[3] The causes of these failures are manifold. Seemingly impregnable institutionalized racism and religious conservatism, lingering economic depression due to failed Reconstruction efforts, and the imperfect transfer of organizing tactics for urban manufacturing workers with a fundamentally different economic system based on agriculture, coal, and textile industries all presented challenges in the southern labor movement. While these tensions played out throughout the South and in all the labor education institutions discussed in this book, Highlander Folk School was the epicenter for many of these struggles. Highlander's ever-changing role in activism demonstrates the evolution of the southern workers' movement and illustrates how education and artistic experimentation were transformed in response to a shifting political landscape in the late 1930s.

Contextualizing the Highlander Labor Drama Experiment

Myles Horton founded Highlander in partnership with colleague Don West as an experimental educational institution in rural east Tennessee in 1932. A remarkable series of learning opportunities and life experiences uniquely positioned Horton to contribute to workers' education and labor advocacy in the South. The son of Tennessee sharecroppers, Horton combined his poor white southern roots with a socially engaged Christian Protestant faith largely grounded in Methodism and Presbyterianism to nurture an abiding interest in social justice for southern communities. These interests led Horton to work with and study at a variety of institutions, including the Tennessee YMCA, the small Cumberland University in Lebanon, Tennessee, New York's Union Theological Seminary, and University of Chicago's sociology department. He was a student of theologian and ethicist Reinhold Niebuhr and sociologist Robert Park. He learned directly from Jane Addams and witnessed firsthand her work with the immigrant settlement houses in Chicago; he read Dewey's *Education and Democracy* when it was first released; and he traveled to Denmark to study the folk school and people's college movements, all before his twenty-eighth birthday. This pedigree positioned Horton in the vanguard of radical and experimental education in the United States during the first half of the twentieth century, and he pursued this mission with fervor. He returned to his home in the politically volatile and economically depressed foothills of Appalachia, otherwise known as the Southern Highlands of eastern Tennessee, to put these ideas about experimental education and social activism into practice. Highlander was born soon after, and drama as a mode of pedagogy was at the core of this long-standing educational experiment.

Highlander, which officially opened in late 1932, was housed on the property of southern education pioneer, historian, suffragist, and former president of Western State College Lillian Johnson in the Summerfield community near Monteagle, Tennessee. This new school continued a long tradition of experimental education and community engagement in this economically depressed region. In fact, Highlander was an extension and expansion of Johnson's decades-long KinCo cooperative project. In 1916, Johnson left her position at Western State College (now Memphis University) and relocated to Summerfield in order to form a new cooperative institution, inspired by the settlement house experiments, that would support the deeply impoverished local community. The center, known as KinCo, supported area farmers through education, provided elementary schooling for local children, and served as a center for cultural life in the area. By 1932, Johnson was preparing for retirement and agreed to lease her property to Myles Horton and his partner Don West for one probationary year for testing out their new school. Unlike Johnson's KinCo community—a Progressive Era institution committed to social uplift without a core guiding political philosophy—Horton and West articulated an explicit and radical commitment to "us[ing] education as one of the instruments for bringing about a new social order" for a "socialistic society" in their new school.[4] They also aimed for Highlander to have an integrated faculty and student body, an illegal proposition given Tennessee's Jim Crow laws. Indeed, Horton and West, emboldened by their study of leftist political theory and immersion in the Southern Social Gospel movement, brought a radical brand of socialism to the South.

The two founders opened Highlander later that year, no doubt inspired by the zeitgeist of optimism for leftist causes during the early Roosevelt administration. Horton's preparations for his southern labor school included a visit to Brookwood, but he found its focus on northern industry philosophically and practically irrelevant for the southern workers whom he hoped to educate.[5] Instead, Horton and West synthesized their experiences with Danish Folk Schools, Jane Addams's settlement houses, and their own seminary training in order to develop a new philosophical and pedagogical approach that was specifically tailored to the Tennessee mountain community. In Horton and West's initial appeal for funds and support, Horton wrote about his desire to "train *radical* labor leaders" in a communal agrarian school where small groups of students and teachers would work and learn together in order to "enable those who would have no educational advantages whatsoever to learn enough about themselves and society."[6] However, Horton and West, given their unique blend of radical politics and organizational pragmatism, realized that the local community would greet this new institution with skepticism, if not hostility, unless they prioritized a strong investment in the local people. Furthermore, teaching socialism to the religiously conservative and staunchly independent mountain community would doom the school. Therefore, Horton and West initially hybridized Johnson's KinCo approach with their new educational experiment, focusing first on engaging the community without promoting political goals. As both a continuation of Johnson's long-standing commitment to cultural endeavors and a reflection of the founders' belief that Highlander would only be successful if it "deal[t] with people in relation to specific problems at specific times and place," the new school included many community engagement opportunities centered on the unique cultural heritage of Appalachia, including amateur dramatics, from its inception.[7]

These community engagement programs paved the way for additional pedagogical initiatives. Only after establishing strong community programming did Horton and West add limited formal classes. These early classes in psychology, cultural geography, and social and economic problems developed organically, born out of conversations among community members otherwise gathering for square dances, music performances, and amateur dramatics productions.[8] In truth, much of the early Highlander curricula developed haphazardly as Horton and West worked through how to best organize their collectivist, democratically governed school. Horton and West also had to work through the challenging disconnect between their academic training and tendency toward intellectualism and the largely uneducated community members who neither had attended school for very long nor had any use for courses in political theory or other seemingly esoteric topics. This struggle, a common refrain throughout the institutions discussed in this book, led Horton to prioritize cultural programs, including labor dramatics, to help bridge the divide and build mutual trust and respect for the local community. Slowly, the school developed a stronger sense of organization around two initiatives: a residential program to prepare leaders in the southern industrial unionization efforts and a community-oriented education extension program designed to support economic uplift in the area.[9] Even with these two foci, there was little delineation between programs as almost everyone attended classes together, community members transitioned to residential students, faculty arrived and departed, and new initiatives were enacted, then ended shortly thereafter. The path forward at Highlander was circuitous at best.

Even though the early Highlander experience was ever-changing, education programs largely focused on the nascent southern workers' movement, and later, the civil rights movement. The school started deliberately small, with fewer than eight residential students and a hundred community members participating in programs during the first year. No one received a salary, and the school relied on student tuition and donations to shore up its finances. Everyone contributed to maintaining Highlander by working the farm and helping with building and grounds maintenance. Ten years later, extension programs reached over a thousand southern workers, but the residential program remained a close-knit affair with fewer than one hundred students in total ever attending the school sessions. These residential sessions took on a variety of forms, from three-month intensives held three times a year in the early years to six-week and two-week sessions on various themes for various constituencies.[10] For example, in its first decade, Highlander hosted work-camp sessions for students to help build new structures on campus as they learned about the labor movement, a series of writers' workshops for students to study literature in relation to social problems, and open-study sessions whereby students and instructors collectively devised the curriculum.[11] Tuition was not insubstantial at roughly five dollars a week in the first years, but it included room and board and was far less than other colleges, which ran in the hundreds of dollars before room and board. In addition to tuition and donations from education and religious leaders, the school also relied on union support and limited sales of farm and forest products, including mistletoe foraged from the area during the holiday season.[12] The school was truly experimental, if not radical, in its structure.

Horton and his team also worked diligently to racially integrate his school, to limited but noteworthy success in the early years. While few, if any, black students attended in the first decade given the risk, the school often hosted black speakers. These lectures were often met with threats of violence from the community, helping solidify Highlander's position as a potentially dangerous institution in the eyes of both local and state law enforcement and many Tennessee politicians. This commitment to integrationist principles also supported the school's later work in the civil rights movement, a complex and well-documented phase in the school's history.[13] By the late sixties, the school, already the subject of decades-long

FBI investigations, endured legal harassment by practically every law enforcement entity in the state of Tennessee, and was the object of a relentless slander campaign in a variety of news media, eventually succumbing to political attacks. The Tennessee legislature successfully revoked the school's charter, the Tennessee Supreme Court upheld the revocation, and the property was auctioned off. Anticipating this legal shuttering, Horton and the leadership had already secured a second charter for the Highlander Research and Education Center, protecting some of the school's rich legacy and history. It remains today, just outside of Knoxville, continuing the fight for social justice.

Early Highlander Labor Drama

Although Myles's first wife, Zilphia, was a sustaining force for labor dramatics starting in 1934, Highlander supported amateur dramatics programs in various forms from its inception. This inclusion of drama reflected the rising prominence of workers' education, political theatre, and amateur dramatics programs by 1930. While this growing popularity is documented in this book's previous chapters, the activities of the Workers' Laboratory Theatre (founded in 1929), the Arbeter Teater Farband (or Artef), the Prolet Buehne (particularly the agitprop turn in 1927–29), and the organizations affiliated with the Little Theatre and nascent community theatre movements also highlight the growing and diversifying theatre scene through the late 1920s.[14] Given these developments, drama would have been an expected addition to any educational program that intended to connect with communities. In 1932, the year of Highlander's somewhat haphazard founding, Don West invited his sister, Jonnye West,[15] to campus to lead a dramatics club with local community members.[16] Although Jonnye West was an amateur with little dramatics expertise, she led the creation of a "young people's group" that produced an "original play built around a local labor situation," along with a production of Tom Tippett's *What Price Coal?* and several other informal pieces.[17] While little documentation of this early work exists, Highlander presumably would have produced plays circulating via labor publications produced by organizations like Brookwood, the Workers' Education Bureau (WEB), the YWCA's Industrial Department, and the Affiliated Schools for Workers (ASW). These productions would have been performed each Saturday on campus for the community night, which included public lectures, singalongs, and other events.

While extant scripts were likely at the core of early Highlander dramatics, local situations, as mentioned in the 1932 first-year reports, also provided source material for study both in dramatics and beyond. At this time, labor organizing among area coal miners and textile workers developed momentum and attracted attention from a host of concerned groups, including the Highlander community. Of particular note was the Wilder strike. In 1932, United Mine Workers Local 4467, one of the few southern union chapters operating at that time, supported a strike against the Fentress Coal and Coke Company in Wilder, Tennessee. In response, the mine owners effectively starved out the striking workers, evicting them from their rented homes and hiring scabs to replace the unionized employees. The striking miners responded by destroying equipment and bombing the railroad bridge used to transport coal from the mine. After these events, the strike turned more violent, necessitating National Guard assistance to keep the peace. In responding to this crisis, Myles Horton, and, by proxy, the young Highlander community, found itself in the middle of the fight, supplying relief to the starving mineworkers and helping raise visibility for the organizing efforts.[18] Horton was arrested by local Tennessee authorities during one strike for collecting information and providing relief. The strike effectively ended after two company guards brutally murdered union president Barney Graham and were quickly acquitted.[19] Through violence, the union was busted. The Wilder strike would haunt the southern labor movement for years to come, reminding organizers of the violent lengths to which anti-labor forces would go to prevent labor organization in the South. More importantly, the outrage produced by the Wilder strike provided initiative for study to determine how to prevent similar incidents among the Highlander community, including those involved in the dramatics programs.

As the nascent southern labor movement encountered disconcerting challenges, the new Highlander school likewise struggled to find its footing. First, the institution faced an uncertain future since Lillian Johnson, still wary of young Horton and West's rather haphazard educational experiment, had not offered to deed her land and property to them.[20] Thus, the two leaders ran the school on limited funds and spent a great deal of time publicizing programs in the hopes of receiving financial support and finding a permanent home.[21] These tensions came with a cost. By mid-1933, West and Horton split over philosophical differences and institutional priorities, concerns only magnified by the ongoing financial strain. West moved to Georgia to organize workers and later started the Southern Folk School.[22] His sister, Jonnye, the de facto dramatics instructor, departed as well, and dramatics programs continued under new leadership. Malcolm Chisholm, a "wrought iron worker, an artist, a maker of marionettes, and writer of plays," joined the Highlander faculty to take over dramatics.[23] Chisholm, a Little Theatre veteran from Chattanooga, served multiple roles on campus, including construction foreman. These skills were necessary, since leaders had secured land in nearby Allardt, Tennessee, and Chisholm would help to build school buildings on their new property in addition to his work with dramatics. Under Mac, as he was known, the community drama program became more closely aligned with the Highlander curriculum regarding specificity to local communities.[24] In doing so, he supervised building a new outdoor performance space in Monteagle, facilitated writing plays about area labor struggles, and supported community engagement with a new marionette program that attracted area children and their families.

Chisholm's work developing original plays about area strikes was particularly significant in the evolution of drama programs on campus. These scripts documented both the aforementioned Wilder strike and the Harriman strike as well. The Harriman strike, one of the first tests of the new federal National Industrial Recovery Act passed in 1933, pitted newly organized hosiery workers against their bosses. The strike, which also required intervention from federal mediators due to the Harriman Hosiery Mills owners' refusal to negotiate, resulted the busting of the new union.[25] Much like the Wilder strike, the Harriman strike was a notable loss in the fight for organizing southern textile workers. It was also a clear failure on the part of the federal government to make good on New Deal promises in the South. Instead, federal inaction served as a salve to southern Democrats who threatened to fracture the New Deal coalition over pro-labor national policy. Highlander faculty and students closely followed the Harriman strike, visiting the site, meeting with workers, and documenting the goings-on. As a result of these efforts, several Harriman and Wilder strikers attended Highlander during the 1934 summer session. In addition to studying labor history and tactics, psychology, and journalism, these worker-students produced and starred in a one-act play about the Harriman strike written by Chisholm. Additionally, the dramatics program continued to gather more information about the ongoing Wilder strike and began drafting a script. Chisholm tasked a student with completing it for the next term.[26] The student newspaper, *The Fighting Eaglet*, described the Harriman play as a "night scene by a railroad culvert" that featured "a railroad watchman," "a bum," and "one of the unemployed hunting work."[27] For the culmination of the summer session, three actual Harriman strikers performed the new play for the local community on the new outdoor stage, which had been completed by Chisholm and his construction team.[28] This first performance paved the way for dramatics as a mode of pedagogy and as a performance conduit connecting resident students with the area community.

These new initiatives in drama spurred other innovative projects, including plans for a labor Chautauqua styled after the now well-regarded Brookwood Labor Players' jitney tours.[29] Highlander was also moving into a more stable period as well. After West's departure, Horton recruited friends Elizabeth "Zilla" Hawes, an organizer for the Amalgamated Clothing Workers of America, and James Dombrowski, a Methodist minister and social justice crusader, to join the Highlander faculty. These friends held philosophies more closely aligned with Horton's views, and by the fall of 1934 the school had formally applied for and received a charter of incorporation from the state of Tennessee.[30] The arrival of Hawes and Dombrowski was also a boon for drama programs, as Hawes had attended Brookwood Labor College and participated in dramatics programs while a student.[31] She introduced the idea for a labor Chautauqua. By this time, Brookwood's programming was so well-established they had published guidelines for producing labor Chautauquas in addition to touring their own versions, training groups in their techniques, and selling numerous source materials including scripts, songbooks, and chants that circulated among workers' dramatics programs.[32] Highlander utilized the Brookwood guide, coupled with Chisholm and Hawes's expertise, to plan and present their first Chautauqua in 1935 to support organizing efforts of the American Federation of Hosiery Workers and the International Ladies' Garment Workers' Union (ILGWU) in the surrounding areas.[33] However, Chisholm departed in the winter of 1934–35 to pursue work as a writer, and plans for dramatics moved into a brief period of haphazard organization. After Chisholm's departure, Rupert Hampton, the public speaking and music teacher, supervised dramatics, helping organize the labor Chautauqua preparations. Hawes also supported the effort by writing *Mopping It Up*, a short propagandistic one-act play that advocated for the passage of the Wagner Act, the legislation that would formally establish the National Labor Relations Board and the right for workers to collectively bargain.[34] The play, adapted from Hawes's organizing experiences in the southern textile mills, reinvented the familiar labor drama plot whereby a group of young hosiery workers plans a strike against their greedy boss. In this case, the moustache-twisting Mr. Grab-It-All is put on notice in a rousing final monologue, delivered to the audience by the lead Girl, who speaks out against the boss's slave wages and unsafe working conditions.[35] The play concludes with a rousing call to action and a song: "We got our rights as human beings and as citizens and as workers. . . . Come on, everybody that thinks I'm right stand up, and sing the song that'll help us win."[36] Stage directions encourage "shouts and cries of 'strike'" from plants in the audience, and the play concludes with "We Shall Not Be Moved."[37] The six-page play, the first extant original work from the Highlander dramatics program, would become an important entry into the school's performance repertoire. During this period, Highlander also recruited a new eight-person cohort of resident students for the winter 1934–35 residential term. Zilphia Mae Johnson, a young Arkansan with strong pedigree in music, dramatics, and Social Gospel Christianity, was among them. She arrived on campus in January 1935 and immediately immersed herself in the Highlander programming while also starting a whirlwind romance with Myles Horton that would culminate in their marriage two months later. Zilphia was poised to lead these programs into a new phase of exciting artistic work.

Zilphia Horton at Highlander

Zilphia Horton was pivotal in shaping drama's significance on the Highlander campus. As a multidisciplinary artist most noted for her work as a pioneering folk musician who wrote "We Shall Overcome" and other protest songs of the civil rights movement, Zilphia galvanized a fledgling labor drama program at the young Highlander.[38] She also oversaw arts-based activism and arts education initiatives on campus. Despite her short career, her contributions to labor dramatics and her work as a bridging figure in southern activist art position her as a key figure in the histories of both radical education and arts-based activism in the United States. Nonetheless, many studies of Highlander have contextualized Zilphia's work as peripheral to the overall accomplishments of the school, particularly given her sudden death just as the civil rights movement gathered steam in the 1950s. As scholar Vicki Carter writes, "At no time . . . was Zilphia taken from the margins and put at the center where her work could be explored as standing on its own. In many ways in fact, the literature of music history acclaimed her work more than the studies of Highlander did."[39] This examination of her contributions to dramatics reframes Zilphia's efforts, helping to both complete the picture of the activist efforts at Highlander and to connect Highlander's experiments in arts-based pedagogy to the lineage of labor drama.

Between 1932 and 1935, the seeds were planted for a more diverse, pedagogically focused workers' dramatics program at the school under Zilphia's leadership. Zilphia Mae Johnson found herself in Tennessee devising arts-based pedagogy by way of a radical Left Presbyterian minister, an angry Arkansan father, and a whirlwind love affair with her instructor, Myles Horton. In 1934, twenty-four-year-old Zilphia Johnson was enmeshed in the nascent southern labor movement and troublingly at odds with her family. The daughter of a coal mine operator, Zilphia had grown up relatively privileged and well educated.[40] She graduated high school in Arkansas and attended College of the Ozarks, receiving a degree in music. Afterward, she taught high school in Oklahoma for a short time before moving back to Arkansas to be near family. At home, she started attending services at Claude Williams's Cumberland Presbyterian Church, which folk musician Lee Hays, subject of Chapter 6, also attended, in Paris, Arkansas. There, she encountered Williams's radical teachings on Christian Socialism. As part of her participation in the church, which also conducted covert and illegal mixed-race church services, she developed an interest in social justice that included the labor movement. Unsurprisingly, Zilphia's father, a prominent coal man, railed against his eldest daughter's involvement in leftist movements, labor organizing, and any association with the radical Williams. Despite her father's vehement objections, Zilphia was undeterred.

The test of wills between Zilphia and her father came to a head when she started working with organizers affiliated with the new Progressive Miners Union at her father's own mine. Outraged, her father threatened to involve local politicians and law enforcement to prevent his daughter from continuing her organizing efforts and to arrest other organizers. When she still refused to stop her work, he disowned her. As a result, Williams, always a mentor-preacher-father hybrid when dealing with his flock of young congregationalist activists, encouraged Horton to flee Arkansas and attend the new Highlander Folk School in Tennessee. She took Williams's suggestion, choosing to distance herself from her father and strengthen her skill set for activism in the southern labor movement via study at Highlander. During her first weeks attending class in January 1935, she and Myles Horton fell in love. They married two months later.

Zilphia's marriage to Myles cemented her role on campus and positioned her to make a long-term contribution to the Highlander educational experiment. Zilphia was a natural fit for leading Highlander's cultural and arts programs since she was a trained musician with an interest in dramatic arts who had studied both subjects prior to her arrival. She was also a prolific artist during her entire tenure at the school and pioneered pedagogical approaches for dramatics, music, and recreation programs at Highlander. This innovative pedagogy was an evolution of the labor arts programs popularized at institutions like Brookwood and in publications from organizations like the ASW and WEB in the late 1920s and early 1930s, but Zilphia Horton's approach to southern workers was pathbreaking. By carefully attending to and representing the experiences of southern workers, she paved the way for arts as a form of activism within both the southern workers' movement of the 1930s and 1940s and the civil rights movement of the early 1950s. She also inspired the work of similar instructors at schools like Arkansas's Commonwealth College and, later, in the folk music scene of the 1940s and 1950s.

While the rapidity of Zilphia and Myles's romance was notable, her growing interest in dramatics and labor activism eclipsed these personal life developments. In truth, their marriage was a fairly minor event in the goings-on in the Highlander community and beyond during early 1935. In Tennessee, the Richmond Hosiery Mills strike at several sites near Chattanooga absorbed the Highlander community. Although Highlander staff and students supported a host of southern labor strikes in Tennessee and Georgia during this period, their participation in the Richmond strike was particularly prominent given the movement's larger goal of attaining a national profile. The strike was indeed high profile due to the death of a striking worker at the hands of an anti-union coworker and drew national attention.[41] The southern labor coalition hoped they would attract support from the federal government and other national labor organizations, including potential backing from the AFL. These hopes were not unreasonable. FDR's New Deal agenda was picking up pace by early 1935, galvanized by the 1934 midterms, which served as a national referendum on FDR's New Deal. The election ushered in an additional nine congressional seats for FDR's Democrats, a rare example of a president's party gaining ground in a midterm election. While the Democratic wins were a boon to progressive causes, the entire labor movement was largely unprepared for its reawakened relevance as part of the New Deal agenda. The subsequent passage of sweeping legislation, including the National Labor Relations Act (NLRA, also known as the Wagner Act) replacing NIRA in mid-1935, repositioned the labor movement front and center in reform efforts and broadened workers' rights to collective bargaining. While these legislative victories should have paved a clear path for an invigorated labor movement in places like the South, the results were worrisome. As different allied workers' groups and labor organizations clamored to set the movement's new agenda for expansion, vicious in-fighting began. The now-infamous formation of the CIO and its subsequent expulsion from the AFL during this time (discussed in the Introduction), highlights these growing pains. Moreover, global uncertainty once again magnified concerns over the socialist and communist influences in the labor movement, a key point of internal disagreement. In 1935 alone, Hitler led German rearmament, a blatant and egregious violation of the Versailles treaty; Mussolini invaded Ethiopia; and deeply concerning reports began to surface out of Stalin's Soviet Union that would be later identified as the beginnings of the Great Purge. These developments further strained efforts to advance the labor agenda, setting the labor movement, with its professed communist and socialist factions that still considered Soviet Russia an ally in the global movement toward industrial unionism efforts, further on edge.

In the midst of these goings-on, Highlander set out to agitate on behalf of the striking hosiery workers in Tennessee. As made evident by the number of such events in which Highlander participated, the art of the strike was evolving into a particularly important pedagogical activity. During this time, students studied labor organizing and strike tactics and put them directly into practice at area Richmond Hosiery plants.[42] Early prototypes of the labor Chautauqua performances featured heavily in the activist strategy, particularly at the satellite Richmond plant in nearby Daisy, Tennessee.[43] Students performed songs and led chants while faculty conducted lectures on labor history for the striking workers. For Washington's Birthday, the school even organized a labor parade through the center of town.[44] While the use of skits and dramatizations are not well documented in these early arts-based activism efforts, the other performance-oriented efforts clearly demonstrate the early stages of this work. These efforts were cut short after a particularly violent incident in which the strikers were fired upon from inside the mill, ostensibly by hired guards, despite police presence at the strike. The Highlander librarian, Hilda Hulbert, and three striking workers were shot. All made a full recovery, but violence once again busted the strike and rightly concerned the Highlanders. The workers returned to their jobs in March 1935 without support from any national labor organizations, and the Highlander community returned to their school grounds to regroup.

With their librarian recovering from her gunshot wound, Highlander students and staff continued pushing forward their commitment to workers' education and labor organization. The labor Chautauqua continued to be central to these efforts. In summer 1935, Highlander produced its first full Chautauqua. The arts program, now led by Hawes and Hampton, integrated their earlier contributions of Hawes's *Mopping It Up*; a new play entitled *We Ain't a-Goin' Back*, a dramatization of an Ohio onion-weeder strike by Hazel Cunard published by the Socialist Party of Ohio; a series of square dances to tunes like "Pop Goes the Weasel"; a slideshow of photographs from the Richmond Hosiery strike; and several "labor ballads and mountain songs."[45] The cast of nine was made up of both Highlander students and young performers from the local high school.[46] While the labor Chautauqua program was modeled after Brookwood, Highlander's version directly related to southern industries, embraced southern culture and popular mountain folk art forms, and documented the actual work of ongoing southern labor struggles. The Chautauqua was a hit, and the High-lander community performed it again in Atlanta as part of the ILGWU convention and in Huntsville, Alabama, as part of organizing efforts with the United Textile Workers.[47]

This work galvanized Zilphia Horton's commitment to labor dramatics. By fall of 1935, she had departed Highlander to begin graduate training in music at College of the Ozarks, but withdrew from classes shortly thereafter, opting instead to attend the recently opened New Theatre School in New York City. By November, she had made arrangements to attend a four-month training session in "the innovative developments in the use of dramatics, both in the 'legitimate' theater and the left-wing or Agitprop Theatre."[48] Perhaps Zilphia responded to a call issued by a *New Theatre* magazine editorial in September 1934, just a few months before she departed for New York City, calling for the professionalization of "the revolutionary theatre arts" through more formal training.[49] This editorial reflected the booming workers' theatre movement, particularly in the Northeast, and, more important, the move toward formal workers' theatre training schools, which labor colleges saw as a possible way to expand their reach.

In the case of the New Theatre School, members from Group Theatre, the Theatre Union, and the Theatre Collective were instrumental in its founding. An outgrowth of informal classes held in the *New Theatre* magazine offices, the school was formally established in 1935, the same year Zilphia Horton attended. John E. Bonn, a prominent director who would later supervise the German theatre group as part of the Federal Theatre Project, served as director, and faculty included artists like J. Edward Bromberg, Elia Kazan, and Lee Strasberg.[50] Classes consisted of acting, play analysis, history of the theatre as a social factor, stage makeup, playwriting, directing, and theatre management. Through this curriculum, actor-students were taught skills in improvisation and Stanislavskian techniques in psychological realism, the day's cutting-edge acting techniques.[51] As historian Douglas McDermott observes about the pedagogies employed at the early New Theatre School, "the improvisations were of situations and problems which affected the working man, since these were the problems of the characters in the Theatre Union plays."[52] The grounding in theory and practice Horton received from her studies with the New Theatre School directly influenced her work at Highlander.[53]

Horton immersed herself in the New Theatre School pedagogy and took advantage of her first visit to New York City by seeing as many shows as possible and attending additional courses in other theatre education programs. New York City in late 1935 was an exciting place for workers' theatre. August 1935, only two months before Zilphia arrived in the city, marked the official rollout of the Federal Theatre Project (FTP), and pilot projects had begun in the city the prior year. As a result, New York City served as an epicenter for this unprecedented federal investment in theatre and hosted some of the FTP's most substantial and diverse productions. During Horton's time in New York, both Elmer Rice and Phillip W. Barber served as regional directors of the city's FTP projects, and a number of subprojects, including the famous Living Newspaper and "Negro" units, including Orson Welles's *Macbeth*, rehearsed new works in preparation for national tours. In addition to FTP programming, non-FTP left-leaning and workers' theatre productions were also plentiful. Clifford Odets's *Waiting for Lefty* and *Awake and Sing!* had premiered earlier that year. Horton may even have seen the Theatre Union's English-language premiere of a controversial new work, *The Mother*, by a young and mostly unknown German playwright named Bertolt Brecht, who was visiting the United States for the first time to collaborate on the production in late 1935.[54] Finally, many workers' education programs were pioneering dramatics as pedagogy in their curricula. For example, the ILGWU's education department, under the leadership of Mark Starr, Louis Schaffer, and Fannia Cohn, had founded the ILGWU Players and supported the founding of Labor Stage Incorporated, which leased and renovated the Princess Theatre for producing workers' theatre productions.[55] Cohn was also publishing essays about the pedagogical role of "social drama" in workers education.[56] Clearly, the timing of Horton's visit to New York City was fortuitous.

Despite the palpable energy in the New York City workers' theatre scene during her visit, Horton was not fond of the city. As a lifetime resident of the rural South, she disliked the crowded, fast-paced environment.[57] She also struggled to make ends meet given the high cost of city living, and much of the time she could have spent taking advantage of additional training or otherwise enjoying theatre was consumed with making enough money to pay her bills. She took a job as a maid at one of the Girls' Service League clubs, a philanthropic organization that provided temporary housing to homeless young women. The position provided room and board, but the dormlike conditions were largely undesirable and required Horton to work during the day.[58] In addition to her classes in the afternoons and evenings and her daily work as a maid, she also took on a second job in a church choir, requiring her to stay in the city over weekends and holidays; she missed her first Christmas married to Myles due to her obligations to the church choir. Her letters to Myles during this period suggest Zilphia's time in the Big Apple was profoundly influential on her art practice, but also exhausting. She completed her classes in March 1936 and returned to Highlander shortly thereafter, happily moving into a one-room log cabin with Myles.

While Zilphia was in New York, Hampton and Hawes kept the dramatics program afloat, remounting *Mopping It Up* it for a local junior high school, producing puppet plays created by Myles's sister Elsie Pearl, and presenting mock debates as part of the public speaking program.[59] However, Hampton departed in February for a one-year leave of absence but did not return. By spring 1936, Zilphia had taken charge of arts and culture programming, including Highlander labor dramatics. The skills acquired during her New Theatre School training coupled with her previous experiences and expertise in music and amateur theatre provided Horton the contextual knowledge she needed to guide students in the creation of activist-oriented theatre and music for decades. This work began immediately with the formation of the Highlander Players, a touring group that wrote new plays, improvised using workers' issues germane to the South, and toured productions throughout the area. By summer, Horton was listed as the primary instructor for a "a very inspiring" course in labor dramatics that focused on "being able to present labor problems in the form of entertainment."[60] The school's informational recruitment pamphlet echoed this sentiment, stating that the dramatics class would be focused on "experience in presenting workers' problems in plays."[61] This articulation of educational philosophy marked an important shift in the rhetoric regarding labor dramatics. Until this moment, the motivation behind dramatics programs was haphazard at best and confused at worst. For example, Mac Chisholm's work had focused on workers documenting their own stories, as in the case of the Wilder strikers. In contrast, plays like Hawes's *Mopping It Up* were entirely fictional, drawing influence from striking textile workers and other extant plays. All plays were presented in a variety of contexts for a host of different reasons and for widely divergent audiences. Several plays premiered at the community theatrical nights for local residents who were not necessarily interested in labor organization or even affiliated with the industries or topics central to the dramatic works. The Highlander dramatics students utilized other productions, as in the case of the Chautauqua performances, as on-site propaganda pieces to provoke workers to action. Other productions served as entertainment at labor organization meetings while still other pieces celebrated the close of the Highlander school sessions. Overall, the pre–Zilphia Horton dramatics program lacked a clear purpose and mission.

Dramatics programming came into focus under Horton's leadership, with a new emphasis on drama as a method to teach workers about labor problems through entertainment. This focus also reflected changes in the school as well. By summer 1936, Highlander's overall institutional focus had shifted toward organizing efforts with tenant farmers and sharecroppers. These efforts directly connected with the Southern Tenant Farmers' Union's (STFU) founding in 1934. As one of the first integrated southern labor unions, the STFU was formed by both black and white members of the southern outposts of the Socialist Party to aid in more equitable distribution of New Deal farm subsidies provided by the Agricultural Adjustment Administration to actual farmers over the financially stable landowners who employed the impoverished itinerant workers and sharecroppers. This focus on New Deal policies and independent farmers and sharecroppers—who, unlike southern textile workers, were not dependent on business leader compromise at the bargaining table—meant the STFU leaders were more successful in their organizing efforts. By late 1936, the union had expanded to five southern states and had membership in the tens of thousands.[62] As the STFU grew, it also found national backing by affiliating with the newly formed CIO, who had recently been ousted from the AFL due to the Congress's commitment to inclusive industrial unionism and antiracist values. However, the perceived radical orientation of the STFU, which included its commitment to racial integration and its affiliation with the Socialist Party, caused concern. While Highlander had already attracted negative media attention given its presence in southern labor strikes, its work with the STFU, particularly around race, positioned it as a serious menace in the views of many conservative Tennesseans. It is no coincidence that the FBI formally opened its decades-long investigation of Highlander in 1936, just as their work with the STFU ramped up.

Even though Highlander's work with agricultural communities situated it in rough political waters, this new focus provided a labor audience for productions generated in Horton's dramatics programs. By the end of 1936, Highlander had presented plays or dramatic sketches for the United Textile Workers in Chattanooga; at a workers' education conference in Roanoke, Virginia; for the ILGWU, the Auto Workers Union, a forerunner of the United Auto Workers, and the International Union of United Brewery, Flour, Cereal and Soft Drink Workers of America in Atlanta; at a meeting of the Knoxville Central Labor Union; and to Tennessee Valley Authority workers building the Norris Dam near Clinton, Tennessee.[63] They also presented various works at institutes held on the Highlander campus during the year.[64] While details about the actual titles are somewhat unclear, notes suggest these 1936 performances retained the variety nature of the earlier Chautauqua and included improvisational skits, songs, a marionette play with music called *Company Union Boy*, and several staged readings.[65] One of the few extant skits from this period, "The Men Behind the Man Behind the Guns," was clearly tailored to a specific audience and detailed the efforts to organize a "labor-management production committee" between two plants producing barbed wire.[66] A separate untitled comedic piece critiques company union policies that undermine national organizations like the CIO. It follows a quack doctor as he dispenses "company union" medicine to workers with grievances about the company union policies. The medicine causes each of the workers to "get happy, then pass out," dropping dead, one by one.[67] The critique of tainted company union efforts undermining the larger labor movement and harming workers is clear. These short skits served as prototypes for longer, more developed works that the dramatics students generated in subsequent years.

Gumbo *and* Labor Spies: *Highlander Drama 1937–39*

By winter 1937, the dramatics program tailored all their new plays specifically to agricultural concerns. In addition, the winter 1937 session also ushered in another new and noteworthy student: Lee Hays. Hays, most famous

FIGURE 4. Production photograph of *Gumbo* featuring Lee Hays (left), 1937. Photographer unknown. Courtesy of Highlander Center Archives.

for his folk music career with the Weavers and the main subject of Chapter 6, attended Highlander on the recommendation of Claude Williams, the same preacher who had encouraged Zilphia Horton to flee her overbearing father. In fact, Hays and Horton had attended church together in Arkansas, both developing their interest in social justice causes by way of Williams. Hays immediately immersed himself in Horton's dramatics classes during his time at the school. Given their familiarity with one another, Hays and Horton appeared to work together closely, supporting and challenging one another. Together they produced their first play, *Gumbo*, the first published text and one of the best-known works from the Highlander dramatics program. *Gumbo* (see Figure 4 for a production photo) marked an important shift toward more serious fare in dramatics programming for the school. Titled after the sobriquet used for the thick black delta mud found in southern Arkansas, Mississippi, and Louisiana, the drama chronicles the murder of a black farmer, Frank Newell, after he tries to organize on behalf of the STFU in southern Arkansas.[68] When comparing the work to the rather simple and explicitly propagandistic pieces that preceded it, *Gumbo* is quite sophisticated and emotionally wrenching.

The narrative details the real and present threat of death for labor organizing and participation in the South, especially for black workers. In the play's first scene, Frank learns that local white landowners have murdered his friend Jessie for union organizing. Friends let Frank know that he is next on the list and urge him to flee, but as he's running away, the white Landowner and the "Riding Boss," Big Boy, played by Lee Hays in the student production, catch him. The two men berate and threaten Frank, promising to both "build a bridge across the Arkansas river" with the bones of black union organizers and "to learn some of you . . . how to respect white men!"[69] The exchange ends when the two men shove Frank into the trunk of a car, his fate clearly sealed.[70] The next scene cuts to Frank's home, where his wife, Sister Newell, anxiously waits for Frank's arrival home, soothing their baby as Frank's friends unconvincingly attempt to reassure her that Frank is safe. Slowly, the chorus begins to sing "Gumbo," an original spiritual developed for the production that crescendos with Sister Newell's screams as men carry in Frank's body. In the final scene, Frank's funeral, a fellow sharecropper impassionedly delivers the pro-labor eulogy that concludes with the cast and audience joining in to sing "We Shall Not Be Moved."[71]

In this unflinching look at the dangers associated with organizing in the southern labor movement, *Gumbo* was innovative in both content and form. Regarding content, *Gumbo* avoids caricatures of cartoonish villainous bosses and hyperbolic worker-heroes who easily triumph, unlike many plays produced by workers' groups during this period. Instead, the work reflects lived experiences, chronicled in the various instances of violence members of Highlander experienced and in several documented accounts well known to southern activists at this time. As the school newspaper notes, two STFU students attending the session "supplied the historical material," reminding readers that this narrative was more truth than fiction.[72] *Gumbo* also demonstrated refinement of the Chautauqua variety form that had dominated Highlander productions up until this period. Although the play still contained music, songs were embedded within the narrative and designed to support the plot. Additionally, the nine-page play was the most polished example of an original work from the school up to this time and included stage directions and suggestions for production.[73]

Records suggest the play had reasonably high production values, and it toured once again to the ILGWU and the Automobile Workers Union in Atlanta and to surrounding union organizations in Tennessee.

While the play was a significant step toward a more relevant form of theatre for southern workers, it was not immune to the influence of institutionalized racism that pervaded the South, particularly in regards to its representation of black characters. Specifically, Highlander students' representation of this narrative reinforced racist performance paradigms even as it intervened in the politics of racial violence and discrimination inherent to labor activism. First and foremost, producing *Gumbo* was an ideologically complicated affair since mixed-race casting would have been impossible given Jim Crow laws at the time. Instead of risking arrest, the all-white Highlander Players produced the play with white actors portraying several roles in blackface (see the center actor playing Frank in Figure 4). If the use of blackface performance and its associations with minstrelsy stereotypes were not concerning enough, *Gumbo* was performed almost entirely for white audiences. Since almost all labor unions and workplaces were still segregated at this time in Georgia and Tennessee, the two states where the play toured, the audience would have been distanced from the lived experiences of the characters represented on stage. Moreover, the play was performed for textile and automobile workers, not sharecroppers. Last, *Gumbo* borrowed heavily from southern playwright Paul Green's 1927 Pulitzer Prize–winning play, *In Abraham's Bosom*, in which a mixed-race farmworker murders his half-brother, a white man, in a fit of rage, then is murdered by a white mob in retaliation.[74] It turned out *Gumbo* was more minstrel plantation drama with a labor bent than theatre for social justice.

Tensions about these concerns appear in substantive exchanges via letters between Lee Hays and Zilphia Horton. In a letter evaluating the production, Hays directly took up the issue of blackface with Horton, describing it as "the most important thing about the play that requires discussion."[75] He was deeply critical of the decision to use blackface, questioning its legitimacy in relation to Highlander's larger views on racial equality.[76] Moreover, he suggested that blackface performance in a play about black labor organizers is "seldom convincing" and not "authentic" in its representation of dialect and characterization.[77] Hays placed the blame for this stereotyping on the lack of engagement on the part of dramatics students with actual black workers and labor organizers. Instead of speaking with individuals, the dramatics students instead drew on "academic" accounts from white workers distanced from these lived experiences. Although Horton's response to this particular letter has not survived in the archives, she likely received the feedback with open-mindedness and steered dramatics away from these stereotypes. After this foray into the lives of southern sharecroppers, the dramatics programs turned back toward white textile workers. Even though *Gumbo* was an important step forward, the dramatics program still had much to learn about making timely and relevant theatre for all southern workers.

Summer 1937 brought about additional changes for Highlander regarding its commitment to southern textile workers beyond dramatics. First and foremost, the school did not hold a residential summer session, opting instead to conduct a variety of satellite programs in support of the newly formed Textile Worker Organizing Committee (TWOC).[78] This CIO-backed committee called for large-scale organizing efforts for textile workers, and Highlander staff, some of the most experienced southern labor organizers, committed themselves to the effort. Faculty scattered to textile mills in LaFollette, Tennessee; Greenville, South Carolina; and Lumberton, North Carolina.[79] No documentation of dramatics in these programs exists, even if performances may have been included haphazardly and informally utilized as community-building pedagogy.

By fall, the experimental satellite programs had concluded, and everyone reconvened back in Monteagle to prepare for another residential session for winter 1938, with most students in attendance coming from ILGWU or TWOC in areas where the satellite programs had occurred.[80] Dramatics were back on as well. However, the lingering impact of the wide-scale organizing efforts continued to shape the Highlander community. For dramatics, Horton was called on to teach about art and music in Clarksville, Arkansas. Thus, two instructors shared the responsibility of leading dramatics with Horton during this time: Ruby Norris and Gwyn Roe. The school paper announced that Roe, an artist from New York City, would lead dramatics, but unforeseen circumstances delayed her arrival. Norris, an economics professor at Vassar, had joined the staff to lead labor history classes, but she was also a playwright and took up supervision of dramatics until Roe arrived.[81]

Norris's main contribution included adapting and directing a new play entitled *Labor Spy*. The work was based on socialist journalist Leo Huberman's 1937 exposé *The Labor Spy Racket*, which documented testimony given to the United States Senate's Civil Liberties Committee chaired by Wisconsin Republican Robert M. La Follette Jr. regarding the use of spies hired by businesses and industries to monitor and undermine labor organizing efforts.[82] Reports from Highlander's winter 1938 session chronicled this new three-act's development. First, the students read Huberman's book together, with the account noting that "several had actually participated in the same situations described in the book."[83] The situations referenced here and also taken up as the central plot point of the play included the recruitment of long-time employees and high-profile labor organizers as spies for management. These informers would receive substantial under-the-table compensation from the security firms to report on labor organizing even as they served in positions of leadership within their unions. Students familiar with these labor espionage efforts worked closely with Norris to develop a "realistic" and "truthful" play that "illustrates very vividly the point of Mr. Huberman's book."[84] The development process for *Labor Spy* demonstrates a clear commitment to working with real-life situations familiar to the dramatics students, in contrast to the flaws present in *Gumbo*. As a result, the work is one of the more sophisticated and nuanced plays developed by the students during this period.

The play follows the story of Tom Chattuck, a weaver employed by the fictional Southern Textile Corporation. An underpaid and overworked churchgoing employee described as "intelligent," "responsible," and "mature," Tom jumps at the chance to provide Mr. Pinkman, a new and mysterious representative of company stockholders, efficiency reports on the textile mill where he works.[85] In reality, Pinkman works for William J. Burns International Detective Agency, a real agency implicated in numerous nefarious acts, including several labor espionage incidents during the 1930s.[86] Sufficiently duped by Pinkman, Tom submits a series of generic reports that comment broadly on the physical needs impacting worker efficiency.[87] He receives substantial compensation for doing so, making it possible to put a down payment on a car, buy his wife new glasses, and have his daughter's tonsils removed, all unaffordable luxuries prior to securing his new side job.[88] Just as Tom's family settles into their more comfortable lifestyle, Pinkman arrives at the family's door, demanding more detailed reports that reveal labor activism on the part of employees. Tom initially refuses, but Pinkman threatens to leak receipts of Tom's additional income to his coworkers, thus revealing him to be a spy. Pinkman also promises him additional money if he ramps up the reports. Although deeply torn, Tom acquiesces. In the play's final scene, Tom's colleagues expose him. During a poorly run and poorly attended union meeting, clearly sabotaged by Tom, who still spies even as he has been elected union secretary-treasurer, leadership announces that five union leaders have been simultaneously dismissed from their jobs due to supposed "inefficiency."[89] Tom attempts to dissuade the union leaders from calling a strike, but Freddie, a fellow coworker and union member, cries foul and accuses Tom of spying. Tom protests, but Freddie details how Burns company representatives had also tried unsuccessfully to recruit him. Following this damning accusation, Tom is "kicked out" as the union members shout him down. The play concludes with everyone in the union meeting "breaking out into song."[90] With *Labor Spy*, Highlander dramatics participants had successfully created an exciting melodrama with direct relevance to the southern labor movement. Highlander leadership published both *Gumbo* and *Labor Spy*, selling each for twenty-five cents. As a result, both were included in the 1938 Affiliated Schools for Workers publication *Annotated List of Labor Plays*.[91] *Gumbo* and *Labor Spy*, original works that shifted conversations about representing the New Deal–era labor movement, were the first two Highlander plays to find a broader audience in the national workers' theatre movement.

The dramatics team toured a selection from the play to a Chattanooga meeting of the TWOC on January 28, 1938, and then performed it in full for the Highlander community two days later. Even with the play's melodramatic qualities, its specificity and relevance in 1938 renders it a time capsule. In addition to documenting shocking testimony included in the Huberman book, the play also comments on more granular disputes in the labor movement as it entered a moment of crisis that would irreparably fracture it and damage its influence. These crises also arrived despite, or perhaps directly as a result of, FDR's 1936 reelection, the most lopsided win in U.S. history in which he carried forty-six states, received more than 60 percent of the popular vote, and secured 523 electoral votes. This overwhelming victory extended to the legislative branch and many state governments as well. It was a galling defeat to Republicans that called into question the party's viability, mordantly summed up by Arthur Vandenberg, one of the sixteen remaining Republican senators, in a *Saturday Evening Post* piece entitled "How Dead Is the G.O.P.?"[92] Not dead at all, as it would turn out. The humiliating 1936 election galvanized the party remnants, a group with plenty of time on their hands to strategize a comeback. They capitalized on a 1937 recession that produced anxiety regarding the New Deal's effectiveness, stoking fears that another round of severe economic decline was on the way.[93]

Additionally, as the Democratic reign continued, factionalism divided a once-unified left alliance as internecine conflicts broke out like wildfires. First, Roosevelt's executive influence was increasingly seen as too concentrated and overreaching, exemplified by the outcry against the Judicial Procedures Reform Bill in 1937. The legislation, negatively nicknamed "the court-packing plan," proposed to give Roosevelt the opportunity to appoint up to six new Supreme Court justices by allowing a sitting president to nominate replacements as soon as justices turned seventy years old. Republicans seized the opportunity to critique this proposed expansion of executive power, equating it with a move toward dictatorship. Regarding labor, the acrimonious AFL-CIO split had by 1938 exposed an exploitable divide regarding business and industrial unionism and the influence of socialism and communism within workers' groups. Mushrooming geopolitical instability helped make the Republican platform relevant as well. The year 1938 ushered in Hitler's announcement of the Anschluss in Austria, Japan's invasion of China, an escalating Spanish Civil War in which a number of U.S. leftists including Highlander's own Mac Chisholm had fought and died, the conclusion of the Moscow show trials, and the Yezhovshchina phase in Stalin's Great Purge. These developments would challenge the Democrats' continued commitment to neutrality and present an opportunity for Republicans to distinguish themselves against whichever controversial position the Democrats would take regarding the impending war in Europe. Highlander's *Labor Spy* picked up on practically all of these tensions in addition to concerns more central to the southern labor movement. By including discussion about the potential concerns over the communistic influences in the CIO and the ongoing tensions with the AFL, the play also tackled the exploitative nature of company unions and the concrete struggles of organizing workers.

FIGURE 5. Student-illustrated cover of *Lolly Pop Poppa*. In *Five Plays About Labor*, Highlander Folk School. Box 2, Folder 9, Eveline M. Burns Collection. Courtesy of Highlander Center Archives and Kheel Center, Cornell University.

FIGURE 6. Production photograph of *Lolly Pop Poppa* produced at Highlander Folk School, 1938. Photographer unknown. Courtesy of Highlander Center Archives.

Labor Drama's Maturation at Highlander

By summer of 1938, Zilphia Horton had returned to Highlander and taken over all recreation programs from Ralph Tefferteller, the departing recreation instructor who had run nondramatics programming since 1935. By this point, Lee Hays was leading his own dramatics programs at nearby Commonwealth College, putting into practice the training he received with Horton. Now that she was in charge of all cultural programs, Horton's prior experimentation and training coalesced into a rigorous and focused dramatics program. In the summer of 1938 dramatics participants wrote and produced several new works, including *Lolly Pop Poppa*, a musical farce of the familiar narrative about a group of young workers who force out the boss, this time set in the southern context of a textile factory (Figures 5 and 6), and a musical western melodrama, *Wild Nell, Pet of the Plain, or the Supreme Sacrifice*. By the summer of 1939, dramatics students had written four additional plays, presented them at a variety of union-sponsored events, and published them in a new volume entitled *Five Plays About Labor*.[94] The collection of plays produced during 1938 and 1939 showcases the diversity of theatrical styles with which Highlander experimented during this period as well. One drama, *North-South*, originated from a speech given by a union president and engages with the "sectional antagonism" between the northern and southern labor movements. *Look Ahead Dixie* focuses on the cotton industry and features a thrilling courtroom drama. Another, quasi-Meyerholdian pageantry-inspired piece, *Stretch-Out* is a pantomime about overwork.[95] The short score includes drumbeat-signaled action and actors, representing symbols of labor, moving in a syncopated dance, and was described as "skeptically rehearsed but well received."[96] Overall, this period of dramatics class allowed for increased experimentation, from the nonlabor Wild West melodrama of *Wild Nell* to the avant-garde *Stretch-Out*.

During this flurry of activity, Horton and her new assistant, Ethel Chouteau Dyer Chapin, an actor who had worked extensively in labor dramatics in the United States, England, Germany, and the USSR and who later studied with Erwin Piscator at the New School, also generated several essays and reports documenting their pedagogical practices.[97] These substantive accounts provide some of the only glimpses into the day-to-day pedagogical practices in the Highlander dramatics classroom in 1938 and 1939. The introduction included in *Five Plays About Labor* provides insight into the process of writing the plays:

> Each one was made up in about eight hours for an audience before it was written down. The actors, therefore, didn't have exact lines to memorize. They simply knew the situation and what sort of person they were playing and talked accordingly. So the lines of the script should not be taken word-for-word. No busy worker could be expected to learn some of the long speeches by heart. But if he understood what they contained he should be able to say them in his own words.[98]

This description captures the improvisational foundation on which Horton built her later methods. Horton's devising process, a short intensive session in which worker-students produced a narrative in skeletal outline then improvised dialogue during performance, was quite simple. These ideas were echoed in similar reports from 1939, wherein Horton asserted, "I'm inclined to question the value of script form. . . . Improvised plays always look pretty poor written down."[99] In this conception of labor drama pedagogy, Horton suggested that text should play a secondary role to the improvisational work of collaborating on an original drama based on participants' lived experiences. These conversations about pedagogical practice and philosophy also allowed Horton and Dyer the chance to articulate the unique nature of labor drama: "If any of [the students] looked on the course as frivolous or feared it as designed for artists . . . these notions were dissolved in the first class session. . . . When we speak of dramatics, we don't mean plays as some of you know them. We don't mean 'boy meets girl' and a happy ending like the Hollywood movies. This is Labor Dramatics—something very different."[100] Horton and Dyer upheld the notion that anyone could participate in making a theatrical production, but that labor drama was not simply for fun. Instead, they emphasized a commitment to drama's capacity to have tangible social impact both for participants and for the groups and audiences who engaged with these performances and texts, a far cry from figures like Doris Smith and Hazel MacKaye in the early labor dramatics experiments. Last, these essays also stressed the accessibility of these techniques: "You don't have to have a stage to put on these plays. They can be done in a room, or out-of-doors. If you don't have a curtain the actors simply walk on and offstage at the beginning and end of each scene, carrying their properties with them."[101]

Horton's writings about drama-based pedagogy serve as some of the first guidelines for producing plays with workers in the South.

Martin Dies and the War: The End of Highlander Labor Drama

By early 1937, Highlander attracted local and national attention, both for good and for ill. On a positive note, in 1937 a team of documentary film-makers that included Elia Kazan shot a short film, *People of the Cumberland*, narrated by novelist Erskine Caldwell, at Highlander. In 1938, the film premiered at the Cameo in New York City and received a mention, albeit brief and sharply critical, in the *New York Times*.[102] It played several more times in New York and even at the World's Fair in 1940.[103] The school was attracting attention from less sympathetic parties as well. A local reporter from the *Nashville Tennessean* named John McDougal Burns posed as a student and published a red-fear exposé in his paper in 1939. The series included a stand-alone article on drama with the headline, "Highlander School Uses Drama with Students to Spread Communism Doctrine in Tennessee."[104] In it, Burns notes that the newly formed Dies Committee, later known as the House Un-American Activities Committee, had "heard of the school's flare in the dramatic field," and conservative politician Walter Steele, in historic testimony, had stated that Highlander's plays were "among the other separate communistic and radical theatrical branches in the United States."[105] Highlander was marked in what would become a notorious chapter in the censoring of American artists. Horton's improvisation-based dramatics classes continued much the same, but the Burns articles foreshadowed drama's decline at the school. First, Horton increasingly turned attention to music, her first love, over dramatics. The school also shifted aims, moving toward a focus on CIO officer training, then curtailing programming by 1942 owing to the war effort. After the war, Highlander would live on, turning its focus to the civil rights movement, where Horton would make her most well-documented contributions to folk music and protest songs. The school would also face increased scrutiny for these efforts, particularly from the state of Tennessee. These legal attacks culminated in the Tennessee legislature revoking the school's charter and seizing its buildings and land in 1961.

While external forces would ultimately shutter both workers' education and labor dramatics at Highlander after World War II, Horton's contributions to southern labor drama are significant in their support of a network for politically engaged artists in the South. As will be shown in the next chapter, she directly influenced the dramatics programs at Commonwealth College under the directorship of Lee Hays and others who would try to carve out a space for a uniquely southern theatre movement after the war. While these efforts would prove largely unsuccessful, the arts-based activism of the civil rights movement, primarily oriented around music and visual art, would continue for many years to come. Horton's unexpected death from acute uremic poisoning in 1956,[106] only three days before her forty-sixth birthday, also stopped her work just at the moment where she was poised to lead new efforts in the civil rights movement. Like many others described in this study, Zilphia's contributions to labor dramatics in the earliest phases of her lifelong devotion to activism helps complete her biography, bringing attention to her contributions to the southern labor movement and demonstrating how her long-standing commitment to arts and politics in the South supported her later, more prominent work in the civil rights movement.

CHAPTER 6

Lee Hays, a Preaching Hillbilly, and the FBI

The Last Gasps of Labor Drama
at Commonwealth Labor College, 1932–39

> *Occupational therapy is not our function.*
> Lee Hays

> *This institution for a number of years has been brought to the attention of this Office and of the Bureau from time to time as being a Communistic institution.*
> Fred Halford, Special Agent in Charge (Arkansas), Federal Bureau of Investigation

Evangelical preachers, real-deal communists, and crimes of anarchy define this final case study of labor drama's evolution during the interwar period. The story of labor drama at Commonwealth Labor College in rural Mena, Arkansas, reveals both the increasing radicalization of pedagogical drama in residential labor colleges as the movement metamorphosed in the late 1930s and an expanding landscape for arts-based activism in the face of new social justice initiatives after World War II. This growing radicalization introduced new challenges that demanded revolutionary change from dominant structures, even as those structures turned against the labor movement's most left-leaning arms. Commonwealth's labor drama endeavors between 1937 and 1939 serve as an example of the last gasps of such programs.

Commonwealth, an institution that focused on educating students about the needs of agricultural workers in the racially divided and socially conservative southern United States, formed in 1923 and closed in 1940. Tracing the year-to-year history of Commonwealth is challenging since, as discussed later, Polk County police destroyed all of the school's records in the 1940s. However, a few extant sources remain, and historians and former students have attempted to keep Commonwealth's legacy alive. The school was the longest running residential labor college, and when it closed, it was the last of its kind. The founders, Kate O'Hare and William Zeuch, former students of Ruskin College, set out to create a secular labor college comfortably grounded in the Democratic Socialist Party's political views that also left open a space for a diversity of approaches for studying the labor movement.[1] The pair started their program, a residential agriculture-based commune-style school with a four-year curriculum in labor studies, in the Ouachita Mountains of northern Louisiana. After a tumultuous beginning, the college relocated several times and settled in Mena, Arkansas, in December 1924.[2]

The school had a working farm designed to be self-sufficient, and all students and staff, including faculty, were expected to earn their keep through manual labor in the fields or domestic duties on campus. Commonwealth covered around 70 percent of expenses through the college's agriculture programs.[3] Students were charged a reasonable but significant tuition of around fifty dollars a semester, most of which was covered by sponsorship and scholarships from donors and labor organizations. Faculty received no compensation. Most students and staff were young—the youngest of any group considered in this study—with almost everyone under forty. The school was coeducational, and student cohorts averaged between forty and fifty students. Most students came from the Northeast or Midwest, and while the campus would have welcomed black students, the hostile environment and legal climate of segregation prevented even black speakers from visiting campus.[4] Students' schedules generally included class in the morning, farm work in the middle of the day, and informal study and recreation in the evening.

Commonwealth was one of the most fascinating labor education institutions for a single important reason: the school tolerated the missions of radical leftist political groups despite its location in rural, racially divided, and religiously conservative Polk County, Arkansas. Commonwealth was and continues to be a radical anomaly within Arkansas's history. In regards to its support of leftist political groups, even though the school endorsed no official doctrine, calling itself, like many other programs, a "non-sectarian, non-propaganda institution" that "sponsors no particular religion, political or economic dogma," the opposite was true. The small institution maintained a philosophy of total academic, religious, and political freedom for the worker-students who attended, but this supposed freedom made room only for left-leaning, politically minded worker-students. Religious and political conservatives, students seeking a more traditional college experience, and even a few "sex experimenters" who happened upon the campus after hearing of its tolerant values were summarily denied admission or quickly booted from the school.[5] As expected, the presence of self-proclaimed socialists, communists, independents, and trade unionists inspired outrage from the staunchly Democratic and fervently anti-union residents who lived near the school. Commonwealth proved an ever-present red thorn in the conservative side of many a rural Arkansan between 1922 and 1940.

Of course, many of the allegations lobbed against Commonwealth from the locals were true. The school taught Marxism, harbored communists, organized agricultural unions, fought for racial integration of labor organizations, and generally displayed a shockingly honest approach to living one's radical left beliefs. Given this commitment to leftist politics, Commonwealth fared poorly at mitigating attacks on its reputation, particularly toward the end of its tenure in Polk County. For example, how could Commoners, a catch-all term for students, staff, and faculty of Commonwealth College, convince their religiously conservative neighbors that the school did not endorse atheistic communism when the school's director, in sworn testimony to the Arkansas legislature, self-identified as an anticapitalist atheist who supported communist ideology? The school was simply in direct ideological and political opposition to the community that surrounded it, and it paid a hefty price for its commitment to its ideological and pedagogical beliefs. Moreover, unlike Highlander, the school did little to help its case with locals by failing to form lasting, meaningful ties to the surrounding community. While the college attracted a diversely leftist student body mostly from the North and West, it infrequently admitted southern students who could provide a connection to local Arkansans. As a result, the school regularly defended itself against charges by its neighbors of being a free-love atheistic commune harboring Bolshevist terrorists. The red threat of tiny Commonwealth College attracted so much attention that local, state, and government agencies like the Arkansas State Assembly and the FBI monitored and later successfully shut down the school.

Unfortunately, Commonwealth's relationship to the surrounding community was only one factor threatening the school's existence. When the Commoners were not alienating themselves from the surrounding community, they spent a large amount of time responding to internal fractures among the student body and school leadership. Many of these problems arose from the students drawn to Commonwealth's school doctrine, which, in theory, positioned the school as a utopic space of educational freedom. As is the unfortunate truth with most aspirational utopias, Commonwealth's operated effectively only in the abstract. In reality, the Commoner experience was, by and large, defined by internal revolts. Part of the problem lay with the student body. Young labor activists, mostly between ages eighteen and twenty-five, arrived on campus with remarkable passion for study of the labor movement. The school's bucolic setting in rural Arkansas combined with its promise of doctrine-free education and opportunities for work and study of the southern labor movement attracted these energetic, outspoken young people. Unfortunately, these passionate students perpetually attempted to radicalize and re-radicalize the school, much to the consternation of faculty and school leadership. One exasperated teacher spoke to this concern in an anonymously written 1933 article designed to recruit new teachers: "Many Commonwealth students consider themselves more mature politically than the liberal and would think of themselves as having something to teach him rather than something to learn from him."[6] These "politically mature" students regularly attempted to redefine and reshape the school via Commonwealth's admirable but largely ineffective and time-consuming governing structure, by which the whims of all students and staff received attention, no matter how extreme the idea.

With this open-door policy in regards to school governance, the school's leadership was perpetually engaged in either a lead up to, fallout from, or immediate crisis in response to student uprisings. Students called for more (or less) political activism on the part of the college, more (or less) authoritative leadership, more (or less) representation by students on the governing board, and more formal (or less formal) affiliations with different labor organizations and political groups, in addition to myriad other concerns. In fact, these uprisings were so common they might be seen as the only constant experience shared by Commoners during the school's seventeen-year existence. These internal conflicts, discussed with greater specificity in regards to labor dramatics later in the chapter, created tensions so great that students struck against the college, faculty abandoned teaching in support of students, labor organizations severed ties with the school, and leadership was repeatedly forced out. In defending the school's egalitarian no-official-doctrine values, Commonwealth leadership constantly negotiated the complicated task of governance in the face of their constituents' radical ideologies about education, politics, and activism.

In addition to external attacks from the Mena community and internal attacks from politically mobilized students, Commonwealth also cautiously navigated geopolitical instability in the period leading up to World War II. By 1936, the unfinished business of World War I shifted popular opinion of leftist politics and labor activism from skepticism toward hysteria. While the United States had never fully integrated leftist or radical political groups, with the Palmer raids, the first Red Scare, and the government crackdown on the IWW's communist contingency still very vivid memories from the prior decade, New Deal legislation opened space for more tolerant attitudes toward communist and socialist ideologies in government. Nevertheless, fear of the Soviet republic never drifted far from view. By 1936, the United States once again looked toward the Soviet Union with increasing suspicion, especially given the signing of the Stalin constitution that same year. This nervous distrust toward the Soviet regime, and, by proxy, the communist ideologies found in Marxist-Leninist philosophies, only increased with Stalin's purge of Red Army military leaders in 1937 and the Great Purge in 1938. The situation grew even more worrisome with the signing of the Nazi-Soviet Nonaggression Pact in August 1939, only weeks before the British declared war on Germany. With the Soviets aligning themselves with the Nazi regime, U.S. citizens and leadership easily conflated the oft-suspect tenets of communism, once in direct opposition to the Axis powers, with fascist rule. As a result, the United States zeroed in on the Soviet regime and its supposed goal of integrating Marxist/Leninist philosophies into U.S. politics as a clear and present danger.

Given this newly reawakened fear, interest in or association with communism in the United States during the late 1930s was an increasingly dangerous affair, particularly for members of the increasingly politicized and radicalized labor movement. Predictably, opponents of labor, namely conservatives and anti–New Deal Republicans still reeling from labor's influence on their devastating loss during the 1936 presidential campaign, picked up on the sublimated red fear that once again bubbled to the surface. They began an aggressive campaign to reignite anticommunist fervor.[7] In this campaign, conservative antilabor leaders correctly, albeit nefariously, directed attention to communism's influence within labor's leadership. As a result, politically influential labor organizations like the newly formed CIO, the Labor Non-Partisan League, the American Labor Party, the United Automobile Workers, and other groups fell under intense scrutiny for their inclusion of Communist Party members within their organizations.[8] The adversarial relationship and resulting factionalism between the AFL and CIO, discussed in greater detail in the opening and previous chapters, further complicated the role of labor organizations and radicalism between 1936 and 1939.

Back in Arkansas . . .

Somehow, in the midst of this chaos, Commonwealth College, a tiny institution with a student body never exceeding sixty students and a faculty made up entirely of volunteers, set out to navigate these forces and continue its mission of developing future leaders of the labor movement in the deep South. Clearly, Commonwealth faced uphill battles of Sisyphean proportions throughout its existence, but internal and external factors converged in a moment of unprecedented crisis for the school in the latter half of the 1930s. Reverend Luther D. Summers, pastor of Mena's First Baptist Church, launched a full-scale attack on the school in September 1936 by preaching weekly sermons about the evils of Commonwealth.[9] Commonwealth's paper, the *Fortnightly*, documented Summers's attack in articles entitled "Bearing False Witness from the Pulpit," "The One Man Circus," and "Preaches Violent Sermons."[10] The shifting tone of these articles, from humorous, sarcastic descriptions of Summers as "a magician at a carnival" pulling "another Red Herring" from his hat, to "Reverend Summers repeatedly accuses the school of being atheistic, godless, communistic, socialistic, believing in free love, Negro equality. . . . Virtually every Sunday sermon delivered by Reverend Summers within the past four months has sought to build up hatred against the college," demonstrates the growing intensity of Summers's campaign against the school.[11] The Summers threat grew so worrisome that Commoners issued a request for readers of the school paper to write the Mena Chamber of Commerce "urging action to stop Summers' violent attacks."[12] By January 1937, the student body and school leadership, once bemusedly annoyed by Summers's antics, now considered the fallout from his attack a serious threat to the school's survival.

Commoners were right to fear Summers. In September 1937, he published a free fifteen-page pamphlet entitled "Communism and Commonwealth College Unmasked," a compendium of his sermons. In it, the fiery preacher asserted:

> When this institution was first established in Polk County, Arkansas, the citizens were led to believe that it was a school in which poor boys and girls could obtain an education with little expense; that is, if they were willing to work part of their time. The citizens of Polk County welcomed such an institution, feeling that it would be a blessig [sic] to their people. It finally dawned on the citizens of Mena and Polk County that this was an institution *in which radicals were being trained to further the cause of Communism in this state and other states.*[13]

The tract continues, describing the prior year's investigation of the school by Arkansas's General Assembly, at which Lucien Koch, the school's vibrant twenty-three-year-old director, testified that the school was supposedly, "atheistic . . . that Communism was being taught and that revolutionary movements were being organized among the student body and morals were at a very low ebb."[14] Summers was correct in his assertions about much of Koch's testimony; Koch *had* asserted his personal atheism, denied belief in capitalism "as it now operated," admitted to both socialist and communist factions on the campus, and even acknowledged seeing "indecent activities" and "illegal co-habitation" at the school.[15] However, Summers's twist of Koch's testimony toward an image of Commonwealth as a radical anarchist training ground that immediately threatened the Mena community was a gross exaggeration. In reality, Commoners kept to themselves and even set out to demystify the Commoner experience for locals by holding campus open houses, but the ideological chasm between the residents of Mena and the Commonwealth school community was simply too vast. The fallout from Koch's provocative testimony accompanied by Summers's pulpit attack on the school resulted in the Arkansas State Assembly announcing a new sedition bill that directly targeted the school in 1937.

The bill, coupled with a newly formed Summers-led "Citizens' Committee" focused on closing the school, caused the *Fortnightly* to announce, "The college is again under fire from its enemies."[16]

Reverend Summers's campaign against Commonwealth was just the tip of the iceberg. From within the school, a group of militant communist students had grown so powerful that they forced out the already quite radical director, Lucien Koch, in September 1935.[17] The departure of the charismatic and popular Koch created an immediate power vacuum, unfortunately, just as Commonwealth garnered increased national attention as a southern communist enclave, much to the chagrin of school supporters and allied labor organizations like the Southern Tenant Farmers' Union (STFU). Given the burgeoning national fear of communism, these southern labor organizations viewed any association with it as a threat to their work, and thus, they warned the school administration to deal with the radical faction of students on campus or lose union support. Several new directors stepped up, starting with Richard Babb Whitten, a moderate socialist handpicked by the recently departed Koch. Whitten was charged with the task of ridding the campus of its communist faction, but this task was much too difficult, and he remained for less than a year, passing off his duties to Charlotte Moskowitz, the school's administrator and an undoubted sympathizer with the Commoner communists.[18] After Whitten's departure, a tumultuous director's search commenced, ending with the controversial appointment of Arkansas's own "Preaching Hillbilly," Reverend Claude Williams, in August 1937. In an unexpected twist, Williams acted as a surprising catalyst for revolutionizing drama at Commonwealth.

Williams, the same preacher who had nudged Zilphia Horton and Lee Hays to attend Highlander, was a forty-two-year-old Presbyterian minister from Tennessee with a notable track record of political activism. The Arkansas presbytery had booted Williams from his church for preaching to mixed-race congregations; he served jail time for organizing on behalf of unemployed agricultural workers; and he collaborated with STFU and the American Federation of Teachers on organizing workers' education for sharecroppers of all races.[19] In 1936, the year prior to his appointment as director, Williams had famously endured a beating from Tennessee law enforcement on his way to give the eulogy at a murdered black sharecropper's funeral in Memphis. Williams's social justice pedigree combined with his deep commitment to his Christian faith positioned the Preaching Hillbilly as solid choice for the school's new leader.

However, Reverend Williams faced a pitched battle. The goal of reorganizing Commonwealth to eliminate communist influences meant boisterous, outspoken Williams would be introduced as a deradicalizing force, an odd role for an outspoken personality with clear ties to practically all radical left political movements in the South—including the Communist Party.[20] Even Moskowitz, the aforementioned secretary and communist sympathizer, and her husband, Raymond Koch, director Lucien Koch's brother, asserted in their memoir, "It was Claude's dubious luck to be available at that particular time."[21] Given the increasingly tense factionalism among the different personalities working in southeastern labor politics, the diminished funds available as the school reorganized and sought new financial donors with less radical political ties, and the labor college's shifting role in response to the CIO's founding and programs like the Works Progress Administration brought about by New Deal legislation, Williams seemed doomed to fail.

Early Commoner Drama

Even though Williams failed to save Commonwealth, the new leader was instrumental in developing labor drama programs at the school. Drama had existed at Commonwealth in a variety of forms since the program settled in Polk County; however, by 1936, the school's drama program, much like the school itself, struggled to find its footing given the discontinuity of leadership. Between 1932 and 1936, the school hosted at least eight different volunteer dramatics instructors of various backgrounds, from students studying theatre at four-year universities to directors working regularly in workers' theatre on Broadway. Despite this haphazard leadership, Commonwealth's labor drama program was an integral component of the school's cultural life. In the early days, participation in full-length productions was a popular extracurricular activity for students. For example, in 1926, the first year Commonwealth published the *Fortnightly*, students and staff produced at least two full-length productions under the direction of Alice Hanson, the public speaking teacher: Kichizo Nakamura's *The Razor*, with "clear traces of the influence of Ibsen and Strindberg," and Nicholas Evreinov's *The*

Merry Death.[22] The next year, Helen Bellman, wife of the school's sociology instructor, supervised drama as part of her music program at the school. She directed Lady Gregory's *The Rising of the Moon,* which included a backdrop of "tan blankets" and a resourceful cast of four that "surmounted the property difficulties."[23] By 1929, the "monthly theatrical in the Commons" appeared as a regularly scheduled component of campus life.[24] In addition to formal productions, early Commoners regularly incorporated collaborative, informal works into school celebrations like May Day, holiday celebrations, or school-closing festivities. Mass recitations, dramatic readings, original farces, minstrel performances, satirical skits about campus life, and other variety acts featured regularly in the monthly theatrical sharing as well. Some examples include a Thanksgiving "farce in which students aped the foibles of their campus elders," two original dramas based on "The Charge of the Light Brigade" presented at the December student program, and a lecture on Greek drama's role in the labor movement.[25] Overall, drama was an integral component in early Commoners' lives.

Among these diverse dramatic offerings, a series of "stunt" plays were the most interesting early performances in regard to drama for pedagogical purposes. These stunts, practical jokes executed through performance, incorporated playful uses of the agit-prop fourth-wall-busting techniques celebrated in many well-known workers' theatre productions like *Waiting for Lefty.* In these events, dramatics students identified moments of oppression specific to campus life and employed theatre to open a dialogue among the school community. In the following example, William Zeuch, the school's first director, helps students explore tensions between the open-minded student body and his stodgy reputation as a social conservative:

A kimonoed woman, yawning, opens the door of her apartment. A young man enters, embraces her. Pantomimes that he would like to remain for the night. The woman gives him a pair of pajamas. He goes into another room, returns decently pajamaed. They embrace again, are about to walk off stage when the door smashes open. A man rushes toward the couple. . . "Here, here!" Father Zeuch protests from the audience. "This sort of thing won't do!" The audience is thrown into an articulate confusion. The indignant actors, Irving Weissman, Fannie Schlefstein and Herman Erickson remonstrate and demand a hearing of their pantomime. The audience shouts, "Go ahead!" The actors now speak their parts and unfold the prosaic story of a young brother who "runs in" on his married sister unexpectedly, asks to be put up for the night, is loaned his brother-in-law's pajamas, and meets the brother-in-law himself just as he is about to go off to bed. The spectators laughed, ignorant of the fact that Father Zeuch was "planted" in the audience and that the point of the skit depended upon his conscientious objection.[26]

In this example, Father Zeuch (as he was known on campus) plays himself from the audience, interrupting the supposedly salacious skit and attempting to censor it. The students plead their case, causing Zeuch to concede and allow the performance to continue. As it turns out, nothing scandalous occurs. The stunt serves as a performative pedagogical tool. Students engage in the process of overturning the dominant power structure even though the power structure, stodgy Father Zeuch, is in on the joke and gives up power only to be proved wrong by the students. After the performance ends the students realize they have been pranked, via the school newspaper and likely campus rumors about Zeuch's involvement. Although no record exists documenting any conversations about this particular stunt, the performance created a space for students to engage with the ethical, aesthetic, or pedagogical implications of the acts being performed. Given the school's dialectical model of instruction, it is highly likely that students discussed the stunt in these terms. This example, one of many, demonstrates how pedagogic drama techniques worked in tandem with early dramatics at the school.

Commonwealth's early efforts in drama demonstrate how performance techniques supported the school's overarching objectives of open education via experimentation. These programs nurtured community development on campus, with students and staff sharing responsibilities of devising, producing, acting, and technical production with limited resources. The content focused on political themes relevant to Commoners' studies in regard to labor issues or on the day-to-day life of Commonwealth. Aesthetic quality was secondary to community-building and pedagogical objectives. This early paradigm for labor dramatics as an inclusive, proudly amateur extracurricular activity endured throughout the school's existence, proving a challenge for later dramatics instructors who hoped to improve the quality of dramatic offerings.

The thriving extracurricular drama program prompted school leadership to incorporate a formal drama course into the curriculum. The study of drama appeared in several formats in the school's early years and evolved along with the larger workers' theatre movement. Commonwealth's early curricula included a course in modern drama, a literature-based course oscillating between an official requirement and an elective in the first few years of the school.[27] The literary, text-focused drama that dominated in the school's earliest full-length productions, like the productions from Lady Gregory and Evreinov, reflect the modern drama class's influence. The school even requested dramatic literature from "Strindberg, Porto-Riche, Widekind [sic], Pinski, Benavente, Pirandello, Molnar, and Andreyev" in a school newspaper notice asking for new dramatic materials.[28] However, modern drama courses were no longer offered by 1931, the same year the *Fortnightly* first employed the term "labor dramatics" in connection with the school's theatrical goings-on.[29] In this reference to labor dramatics, the authors describe an "extracurricular" program offered alongside reading groups, writing clubs, and a "modern poetry circle."[30] This shift away from a literature course to a program in practice-oriented labor dramatics coincided with the school's founding director, Father Zeuch, departing Commonwealth. The new guard, led by Lucien Koch, redirected the school's pedagogical focus to labor activism whereby "education now presumed action."[31] With the new emphasis on more experimental and politically minded pedagogy, labor drama, with its potential to inspire activism, also gained prominence as an integral part of the school curriculum.

During the Koch era, labor dramatics reverted to an extracurricular program for a short time, but retained a clear connection to student coursework. For example, a 1933 course description offers the following note: "If there is sufficient demand, courses of study will be worked out for those interested in labor drama."[32] Course listings for the 1934 summer term included labor drama as the only extracurricular activity alongside classes in Marxism, "Labor Journalism," and "Farm Problems," suggesting drama would serve as the primary bridge between learning and leisure on campus.[33] By fall 1934, teachers at Commonwealth listed labor drama as a uniquely categorized course "in that they are carried on by the entire group under the direction of a faculty member."[34] These subtle shifts in program descriptions showcase the school's attempt to best place labor drama into the Commoner experience as it slowly shifted from a socially oriented extracurricular to an integral component of the school curriculum.

Despite labor drama's undeniable prominence on campus by 1934, the dramatics instructor position did not appear to be a priority among school leadership. When not tacked on to other instructors' responsibilities, the position most often fell to the wives of male instructors. For instance, modern drama was taught by both "Mrs. John Kirkpatrick," the modern history teacher's wife,[35] and Helen Bellman, wife of the sociology professor.[36] Both taught the modern drama course as an ancillary interest to their work in music at the school. Later, Beatrice Carlson, wife of the school's Marxism teacher, Oliver Carlson, oversaw drama at various intervals between 1932 and 1934.[37] Like previous instructors, Carlson lacked expertise in drama and primarily taught English. As a result, the school promoted her as "active in directing amateur dramatics" in school catalogs, a clear acknowledgment of her lack of advanced-level drama training.[38] Other instructors included wives of students, like Alice Ettinger, wife of Manfred Ettinger; students with other interests, like Agnes "Sis" Cunningham, who specialized in music; and occasionally former students who dabbled in drama, as in the case of instructor Vaughn Albertson, an English professor at the University of Texas who directed the dramatics program during the 1932 summer quarter.[39] The few exceptions to the slew of amateur instructors included Ben Low, a working theatre professional interested in the leftist theatre movement who drifted to Commonwealth after spending time at the New Llano Cooperative Community, a socialist commune in Louisiana.[40] Overall, most dramatics instructors came to Commonwealth with labor drama as a secondary interest in their larger careers or areas of study. Consequently, the program's development was, at best, haphazard.

Peter Frye's appointment as labor drama instructor in 1935 changed this trend. Frye's arrival on campus signaled a more significant investment in labor drama. A Canadian who moved to New York City in his late teens, Frye worked extensively in leftist theatre movements during the first half of the twentieth century. He studied with Michael Chekhov and taught drama at both the American Theatre Wing and Erwin Piscator's Dramatic Workshop in the New School for Social Research in New York after his time at Commonwealth. Also, like so many others discussed in this study, he fell under suspicion for communist sympathies during the McCarthy era and, as a result of blacklisting, he emigrated to Israel in 1954. There, he led Tel Aviv University's drama department until his death in 1991. Despite this resume, when twenty-year-old Frye arrived at Commonwealth, he was a young artist just starting his exploration of leftist theatre practices. Commonwealth was an ideal location to experiment with aesthetic frameworks and artistic philosophies shaping the northeastern labor movement. Frye also had unprecedented experience in theatre and a complex understanding of the ideological and pedagogical complexities of labor dramatics, particularly when compared to preceding instructors. His credentials, as published in the *Fortnightly*, reinforce this idea: "A background of seven years of varied theatrical experience (four of them spent in teaching), [he] comes to direct Commonwealth dramatics 'keenly interested in experimentation along the line of finding new American theatre-forms in the light of the political need for more articulate dramatic expression.'"[41] The rest of this description, a detailed and theoretically sophisticated narrative about Frye's specific interest in labor drama, reveals a shift in thinking about the program. Instead of a community-building extracurricular, as it had been previously, Frye suggested dramatics could also be a pedagogically valuable course that supported the labor movement's needs and the school's mission related to education as activism.

During Frye's tenure, labor drama secured legitimacy on campus by earning a place in the course offerings. In Fall 1935, the paper announced, "Labor Drama under Peter Frye is now a full-time part of the curriculum, with regular class periods, an advance from its former status as an evening and spare-time activity."[42] This announcement was accompanied by a lengthy course description, the thesis presented with concise clarity: "A formal course in labor drama at Commonwealth must in this sense at least be largely experimental."[43] Frye articulated four guiding principles for his course:

A. The students are essentially non-actors.
B. None of them has the signal intention of leaving the college to engage solely in the work of building the workers' theaters.
C. Most students seek only an elementary knowledge of theater-practice as an aid in some other task.
D. The aim of the course will therefore be to adapt the theory and practice of revolutionary theater to the particular requirements of Commonwealth students without, however, telescoping our artistic principles.[44]

Along with these principles, Frye also outlined an admirably ambitious plan to produce a great number of plays during his first year.

While Frye's ideas were inspiring and innovative, they failed to materialize in any significant form during his brief tenure on campus. In total, Frye directed two productions, only one of which included original or experimental material, and he departed the school by the spring quarter of 1936. For his productions, Frye played it safe, producing Odets's *Waiting for Lefty* in November 1935, ten months after the Group Theatre's January premiere in New York City. While ten months might seem a short time to consider a play a safe bet, particularly in regard to labor drama scripts, *Waiting for Lefty*'s popularity in 1935 was spectacular, securing its place as the iconic text, if one could ever exist, of the labor drama movement. The *New York Times* review had asserted that the show "is clearly one of the most thorough, trenchant jobs in the school of revolutionary drama," and it had been published in *New Theatre* magazine earlier in 1935 after winning the magazine's play contest.[45] By this time in 1935, just about everyone in labor drama circles knew *Waiting for Lefty*. Given *Lefty*'s popularity by the latter half of 1935, it was a solid choice for program-building around a dramatics course committed to synthesizing theory and practice in revolutionary theatre, but it was not particularly experimental. Nonetheless, the Commoner community seemed excited that their New York City–based dramatics teacher brought big-city hits to rural Arkansas. In a review of Frye's production, Clay Fulks, longtime faculty member and strident drama supporter, lauded the Commoner take on *Lefty*, enthusiastically asserting that it "embraces a new 'verve and realism' causing the audience to rise en masse and shout STRIKE! *Waiting for Lefty* certainly deserves its fame."[46] However, Fulks's review reads as more of an endorsement of Frye's decision to bring the white-hot *Waiting for Lefty* to rural Arkansas than an evaluation of Commonwealth's production of the play. Fulks's vague commentary on Commonwealth's *Lefty* makes more sense when read alongside his review of the second performance accompanying the Odets pieces.

Frye also directed a new adaptation of Erskine Caldwell's short story *Daughter*. The dark story chronicles the imprisonment of a black sharecropper who has murdered his eight-year-old daughter. After hearing her wail for months due to chronic starvation, the father treats the murder as a desperate act of mercy. Following his arrest, a mob of white men gathers outside the man's cell, threatens him, and eventually breaks into the jail. The story ends with the Sheriff, who has been protecting the man, walking away, ostensibly letting the mob murder him. In response to Frye's new adaptation of this work, Fulks offered a much less celebratory review of this new work, describing it as "far inferior."[47] In fact, Fulks's limited positive feedback focused on one of the student performers who "handled the crow-bar at the jail door with the resolution of a bold and intrepid proletarian."[48] The rest of the review is a rather inflammatory critique of Frye's new work, a text that Fulks described as "too obviously the work of over-ambitious adolescents."[49] The core of Fulks's critique:

> The main character is "a simp almost too weak to win any respectful sympathy"; it is not necessary to make the sharecropper out a stark simpleton in any effort to win sympathy for him. In the first place the typical southern sharecropper is not a simpleton and, in the second place, readers and audiences, taken by and large, don't waste good sympathy on congenital simps—there are too many deserving Democrats. It is the actual condition of millions of sharecroppers of something like normal human intelligence and of at least a modicum of strength of character—a condition apparently hopeless under capitalism—that calls for the highest efforts of the literary workers.[50]

Fulks's harsh assessment of Frye's new work as an oversimplified and insulting depiction of black southern workers, likely in blackface and reliant on minstrel stereotypes, echoes other critiques mentioned throughout this book, including many of texts generated by Zilphia Horton at Highlander and Hollace Ransdell at the Southern Summer School. Again, the new drama teacher, in an attempt to create entertaining theatre, reduced the complexities of workers' struggles to polemic didacticism, and the actors depicted laborers as hyperbolized and racist stereotypes while simultaneously oversimplifying their struggles in regards to the labor movement. This critique recalls a similar idea brought up at the 1936 doom-and-gloom workers' theatre conference discussed in the opening chapter regarding how theatre-makers had gone wrong in not representing real workers on their stages. Fulks's critique highlighted these serious concerns, particularly as artists and activists attempted to translate the northern labor movement's cultural forms and political tactics to the South. Frye, a northerner, created his southern sharecroppers as bumbling racist clichés, demonstrating little connection or appreciation of the actual lived struggles of sharecroppers or the complex power dynamics at play in southern race relations, particularly among the poorest workers. Fulks, a lifetime Arkansan, was offended.

The offense overshadowed any political commentary on the southern labor movement possible through Frye's new work, and, while fair, Fulks's critique was a low blow for a new instructor clearly interested in experimental initiatives. Although Frye made a miscalculation in crafting *Daughter*, this error was a likely consequence of the fact that he was, in fact, an "overambitious adolescent" at the start of his career. Perhaps this critique by Fulks discouraged the young teacher, since Frye left quietly by the end of the summer quarter to join the Workers' Theatre in Chicago and did not offer much comment on his work at Commonwealth later in life.[51]

Despite missing the mark with *Daughter*, Frye had an impact on campus dramatics programs that boosted labor drama's popularity. By the start of Claude Williams's official tenure as director in fall 1937, the program had grown quite popular not only on campus, but in the surrounding communities and within other labor education circles as well. Frye expanded Saturday night performances to include productions off-campus and began to invite the local Arkansans living near the school. Unlike most of the problems related to the school's geography, in this instance, location worked in Commonwealth's favor. In rural Arkansas, quality entertainment, particularly of the theatrical variety, was in short supply, and local community members positively received the Saturday night theatricals to which they were now invited on a regular basis. Although he had not managed to overcome common traps in crafting his scripts, Frye had managed to reach out to the Polk County community and produced both *Waiting for Lefty* and *Daughter* for local residents.[52] Frye's precedent of sharing the school's productions with the community served as one of the most important outreach tools as Commonwealth transitioned to the Williams era and navigated political turmoil between 1936 and 1939.

In the summer of 1937, after Frye's departure, Commonwealth student Mara Alexander Gilbert took the helm of theatrical production, extending Frye's work. Gilbert had extensive theatrical experience; she had acted on Broadway, organized on behalf of the Theatre Union, and directed her own troupe called the Contemporary Players.[53] Gilbert's biography marks a shift of the kinds of students attracted to Commonwealth in regard to theatre. For the first time, Commonwealth was serving as an outpost for workers' dramatics in the South. Instead of taking over drama as an ancillary interest, Gilbert arrived at Commonwealth as a student with a strong background in theatre, and she wanted to adapt these methods for a uniquely southern labor drama movement. With this respectable resume in actor training and professional theatre, Gilbert moved beyond acting and directing and explored her interest in teaching while at the school. Even though her work appears haphazard, perhaps the result of her taking over the summer theatre programs as a student volunteer during a period when no instructor was on staff and, more important, the school had no director, she managed to keep the program afloat for several months until new director Williams arrived. One of the Preaching Hillbilly's first tasks was to call twenty-two-year-old Lee Hays to take over dramatics courses.

The Preaching Hillbilly and the Lonesome Traveler

Lee Hays, the self-styled Lonesome Traveler best known for his later involvement with Pete Seeger in the folk group the Weavers in the 1950s and 1960s, found himself teaching drama to a group of young radicals in rural Arkansas at age twenty-two. He was one of the most unlikely candidates for the position of dramatics instructor in the school's history, even among the plethora of wives and students who defaulted into drama at Commonwealth, but he was also the most famous and the most uniformly beloved instructor associated with Commonwealth College. Hays's biography follows a similar path as other drama instructors discussed in this book. As a young man, Hays committed himself to social justice issues. This commitment contributed to his work in the Weavers, a musical group who inspired a generation of young people toward activism via folk music with iconic songs like "If I Had a Hammer" and "Kisses Sweeter Than Wine." As part of his work fighting society's injustices, he also sympathized with leftist and radical political movements. Consequently, he fell victim to the systemic blacklisting of politically engaged artists during the 1950s and was forced into relative obscurity until McCarthyism subsided. Afterward, Hays drifted away from society, summing up the experience with sarcastic wit: "Having a listed number with no fear of Trotskyite crank calls is a huge relief."[54] He lived simply in a New York City suburb until his death in 1981 from complications related to his lifelong battle with diabetes, a condition complicated by alcoholism and smoking. However, Hays's time at Commonwealth preceded this turmoil. The Lonesome Traveler arrived at Commonwealth a young idealist, long before blacklisting destroyed his career and left him disempowered and disillusioned.

The seeds of social justice were planted early in Hays's life. He grew up in Arkansas during the peak of racial unrest in the South. His father, an itinerant Methodist minister, was on the front lines of social unrest in the South, and Hays saw firsthand the volatile mix of entrenched racism and extreme poverty among the agricultural workers of all races to whom his father preached. When Hays was thirteen, his father died in a car accident. This cataclysmic life event upended young Hays's world since at the time of his father's death, Hays, the youngest of four children, was the only child still living at home. While Reverend Hays had provided for his three older children's high school and college educations through his work with the Methodist church, no provision had been set in place for Lee. The reverend's untimely death coupled with the emotional devastation experienced by the remaining Hays clan at the loss of the family patriarch left young Lee virtually forgotten. Consequently, the thirteen-year-old was left to "make my own 'educational advantages.'"[55] With his mother experiencing a complete mental breakdown requiring institutionalization, and his siblings attempting to figure out their own lives in the thick of the Great Depression, Hays was, at best, an afterthought for his family. After completing his high school diploma at Emory Junior College Academy, a Methodist boarding school, sixteen-year-old Hays was unexpectedly uprooted by his brother and forced to move with him to Ohio. Plucked from his home state, with little hope for the future in light of the Depression, Hays started working at the public library and cultivated a voracious appetite for banned books. Devouring any literature stamped with the black "Unfit for Children" label, Hays developed his nascent radical leftist sensibilities: "Somewhere along in there, I became some kind of Socialist."[56] By 1934, Hays, now twenty, was ready for something new. He left Cleveland and returned to Arkansas. Although he initially planned to pursue his bachelor's degree at Hendrix College in Conway, Arkansas, his father and siblings' alma mater, he changed his mind, and instead, took to wandering with no particular goal in mind. During this period, Hays met the Preaching Hillbilly, Claude Williams. Williams changed Hays's life.

Hays's relationship with Williams directly shaped Hays's approach to and interest in activism, especially in regards to labor drama. As Doris

Willens, Hays's biographer, asserts, "Indeed, from 1934 to 1949, Claude was the dominant figure in Lee's life—a surrogate father—a man of the cloth but with a radical difference."[57] Williams's unique blend of intellectual, passion-driven, and undeniably Southern Christian Marxism appealed to Hays, a young man who still held tightly to his father's religious conviction and piety despite his turn toward radical politics. The two formed a fast bond, and their relationship supported Hays's development of a social group and a place to belong. Through his associations with Williams, Hays encountered a group of young southerners, much like him, who were committed to the study and enactment of labor activism through the leftist interpretations of Christianity found in Christian Marxism, Christian Socialism, and the Social Gospel movements. As discussed in the previous chapter, in this group, Hays met young Zilphia Johnson, who would lead him to the Highlander Folk School in Tennessee. There, he explored theatre as a vehicle for social activism as one of Zilphia Horton's students. Hays was an active participant Horton's drama program, and he borrowed directly from her program and its values when he took over the position of Commonwealth labor dramatics instructor in 1937.

As previously mentioned, Hays joined the teaching staff at Commonwealth amidst a time of crisis. Accordingly, Williams's appointment of Hays can be read as an endorsement of Hays as an ally in Williams's deradicalization efforts. Hays's theatrical expertise was of secondary importance. In truth, Hays had no formal training in theatre and only a passing preexisting interest. In a 1982 interview, Hays stated about his time at Commonwealth, "I was teaching dramatics, as little as I knew about it."[58] Unlike his mentor, Horton, and the most recent string of dramatics instructor predecessors, Hays had not studied at New York theatre institutions. He had little practical experience in theatre, even in amateur settings. Most came from his work with Horton at Highlander during the spring and summer 1937 quarters, a total of ten weeks learning techniques for labor drama. During this time, he largely contributed through playwriting, only collaborating on one piece of theatre, the aforementioned *Gumbo* about a murdered black sharecropper, under the close guidance of Horton.[59] Still, upon twenty-two-year-old Hays's arrival at Commonwealth, the school paper announced, "He has been assistant to the drama director at Highlander Folk School. . . . Lee brings with him to Commonwealth valuable experience and ability."[60]

This assertion was partially correct. A few years earlier, Hays had drifted to New York for a brief period of study as a resident of Judson Memorial Church. There, he made one short documentary film, *America's Disinherited*, about southern sharecroppers and the STFU. Few people viewed *America's Disinherited* outside of New York City's leftist elite because of the film technology Hays used; labor organizations had no access the projectors capable of playing the eight-millimeter film on which Hays had recorded the project. This brief filmmaking experience was the "valuable experience and ability" that Hays supposedly brought with him to campus. It seemed that a few weeks of dramatics training and short film were enough of a pedigree for Commonwealth.

Whatever Hays lacked in experience, he made up for with his theoretical knowledge, general intellectual inquisitiveness about the subject, and commitment to the program. On the same day the *Fortnightly* announced his appointment, the paper also published an essay written by Hays about his plans for the dramatics program. In it, he states, "Emphasis will be placed upon the drama as a weapon for union organization."[61] He follows this assertion with an outline of the course, "a survey of professional plays of social content and of special interest to labor" with an ancillary study of professional theatre and motion picture institutions "as influencing and molding opinion."[62] First, Hays conceptualizes labor drama as weapon, a far cry from Brookwood's A. J. Muste and his milquetoast assertions about a quasi-militaristic labor drama genre that marched, sang, and waved flags. Second, Hays fully integrated the influence of film into his course from the beginning, acknowledging the increasingly influential presence of the growing movie industry. Together, these two developments reveal Hays's connection with popular and mass cultural forms and his commitment to and knowledge of an increasingly radical labor movement. In addition to the study of dramatic texts and films, he also describes the course's practical components: "Most important, students will write and produce their own plays out of their common experiences and ideas. They will learn how to use dramatics in attacking their own social, economic, and organizational problems. These plays will be produced on the college stage and before workers' audiences in the Southwest."[63] He includes "labor songs, mass chants, and other theatricals" as part of the coursework, a nod to the comprehensive role he viewed labor drama would serve on campus.

However, the creation and production of plays that attacked southern labor injustices, as determined by Commonwealth labor drama students, was Hays's primary pedagogical objective.

Hays's strongly worded course description foreshadowed his spirited and focused commitment to teaching labor drama. He also encountered many challenges. First, developing an actual curriculum proved particularly challenging for the young artist since he had no formal dramatic or pedagogical training and was expected to maintain the wildly popular extracurricular Saturday night theatrical program. Each Saturday, the group performed a new work that Hays had to "think up" for the school's neighbors.[64] Somehow, Hays managed it all. Unlike Frye, who seemed to bog down in the practicalities of both Commonwealth life and the challenge of mounting productions, Hays was prolific in his theatrical production. In October of the same year, a month after he arrived, he published a request for "copies of labor or social-protest plays or skits" in order to meet his objectives of studying "as many plays as possible."[65] By January, the school collected over two hundred new drama texts.[66] In November, he sent Max Cohen, the school's industrial manager, on a side trip to New York City to procure even more resources for the labor drama program, including forging contacts with the New Theatre League and the American Writers Union.[67] By mid-November, Hays produced his first skit, an adaptation of Florence Lasser's International Ladies' Garment Workers' Union pamphlet, "Who Is Getting Excited?," the ever-popular narrative about female garment shop workers who take on their mean, brutish bosses. Even though the performance derived from an extant text, Hays made clear that this first production served as a resource for learning "the qualities most productive of dramatic effect" for new works. He also announced the next production's performance date as less than a month away.[68]

From Ninety-Seven Cents to Hushpuppy: Lee Hays's Experiments in Labor Drama

True to his word, on December 4, 1937, Hays led students in *Ninety-Seven Cents*, a courtroom drama about a young worker named Helen accused of attacking her boss after receiving a paycheck for ninety-seven cents. The one-act play showcases the creative experimentation upon which Hays based his program. The dramatic narrative opens with darkness. A disembodied "pompous" voice of a factory owner describes the Southern Dress Company's arrival in a fictional southern town called Jefferson.[69] Through a series of eight blackouts within the three-page work, the voice promises "increased prosperity" for the town, describes free medical care as part of the company's compensation packages, outlines a workers' education program, and promises to be a "conscientious employer."[70] Over the course of the drama, these promises turn out to be thinly veiled lip service paid to community leaders designed to hide the northern company's plan for exploitation of its new southern workers. Between the copious blackouts, a courtroom drama unfolds. A series of witnesses, from Helen's fiancé to her corrupt coworker Lucy, testify on behalf of Helen or on behalf of the boss, George Butler. Through this dialectical testimony regarding Helen's guilt or innocence, the audience learns that Helen has violently attacked her cheapskate supervisor and now, the court must decide if she acted in self-defense or with premeditated malice. The play ends without resolution. The defense attorney finishes his closing argument by turning from the imagined jury to the actual audience: "The bench is not here—the bench is there—with the citizens who view this trial. They review this case, and they shall pass judgment. When will their voices be heard?"[71] The play ends with yet another blackout.

Most of the play's structure, from the mean-boss-versus-female-worker narrative to the final moment of the play when a character asks the audience to react to the drama, follows paradigms found in many labor drama texts.[72] In addition to its predictable plot, the text rests heavily on narrative description instead of dramatized action, and it struggles to find flow given the disjointed back-and-forth between the dark stage, the pompous disembodied voice providing exposition, and Helen's trial. The play also takes itself very seriously, with stilted, overly dramatic dialogue: "Helen Bryant is not on trial here! The Southern Dress Company is on trial!"[73] However, despite the play's obvious faults, it also serves as an important example of how and why the pedagogy of labor dramatics worked in practical terms.

Within its clunky structure, Ninety-Seven Cents showcases students' attempts to incorporate compelling theatrical techniques in creating new and relevant plays for southern audiences. For instance, the play explores strategies for breaking down separation between audience and performer. The stage directions included actors planted in the audience who yell out responses to the testimony and enliven the production from outside the drama. Even though the technique is the same as employed in the earlier "stunt" skits with Father Zeuch, as well as countless other workers' theatre productions like *Lefty*, these audience-performer interactions are the most exciting part of *Ninety-Seven Cents*. When Lucy, Helen's coworker, testifies against her, a "girl in the audience" shouts, "You're a liar, Lucy Andrews! I saw the big yellowbelly pushing Helen around that day! And what's more every word she said was true! How much are you paid to make this speech, Lucy?"[74] "Much banging of the gavel" ensues, and a bailiff exits the stage, enters the audience, and drags the girl out. As she's being dragged, she screams, "You can't keep me from talking!"[75] Later, when Tom, Helen's fiancé, takes the stand, the audience erupts with shouts of affirmation after Tom alludes to plans for a strike percolating amongst Southern Dress Company's workers: "That's why the company don't want us to talk—afraid we'll start something they can't stop!" Voices respond with, "You tell em, Tom! We're talkin' now!"[76] By manufacturing audience involvement through the performance of spectator outrage, the dramatics students gave their audiences permission to rise up within the dramatic moment and pursue their goal of utilizing drama as a weapon for change. The reality of the production's overall failure, a fact that Hays asserts in a later evaluation of the play, does not diminish the pedagogical significance of dramatics students' experimentation with strategies designed to reach their unique southern audiences.

Similarly, the predictable plot structure of *Ninety-Seven Cents* overshadows the pedagogical significance and social relevance of the play's major theme: the exploitation of southern workers by northern industry. The process by which the group selected this theme is clearly outlined in an article published a week before the premiere: "The theme was selected because of its pressing interest all over the South, and its direct relation to the labor movement nationally."[77] The plot, while simple, reveals a nuanced understanding of the problem of carpetbagging during the 1930s. Carpetbagging, in which northern business owners moved South to exploit southern workers, was one of the most prominent and uniquely southern labor issues during this time. As northern corporations looked south for cheap land and labor, particularly after organizing successes in the North raised pay and improved working conditions, thus cutting into business profits, the need for both education and organizing around this practice was increasingly critical for the nascent southern labor movement. The play captures many challenges associated with carpetbagging. For example, the play addresses the good sense found in promises of community uplift via welfare capitalism that had become a de rigueur strategy employed by corporations to gut unions. This concern was increasingly evident in the South, as corporations looked for rural communities ravaged by the Great Depression that would welcome jobs while sacrificing rights guaranteed to northern workers in similar industries. By giving voice to issues that directly affected southern workers, Ninety-Seven Cents spoke to new audiences, albeit in an imperfect fashion.

Although no review of Ninety-Seven Cents appeared in the Fortnightly, increased enrollment in labor dramatics under Hays's leadership suggests that his program resonated with the Commoner community. By the start of the winter term, "Workers' Dramatics," as the course had been retitled, was "enlarged to include virtually the entire student body."[78] Hays divided the students into three groups, with each researching and devising a new play. One group, directly supervised by Hays, focused on the lives of sharecroppers. A second group, directed by student Rosalie Stinson, centered their work on the struggles of the "independent farmer." The third group, guided by the school's secretary-treasurer and mimeograph/printing teacher, Don Kobler, would write an industrial play. The paper announced that these three new plays would be performed for the "appropriate audience" during the quarter, with the productions traveling off-campus and into surrounding communities for performances before local workers, an unprecedented program expansion.

In this flurry of activity, Hays also found time to develop his curriculum and further explicate his increasingly complex understanding of labor drama's function within the Commonwealth community and, by proxy, the southern labor movement. In a lengthy essay entitled "Dramatics at Commonwealth Must Serve the Needs and Aspirations of Labor Audience," a rhetorically sophisticated and inspiring work that reflected the author's preacherlike passion deriving from his father and Claude Williams, Hays opens with three questions:

► What is labor drama?
► What part should it play in workers' education in the southern labor movement?
► How can Commonwealth produce plays worthy of the worker audiences and get them before those audiences?[79]

While these questions might first appear rudimentary, in reality they reflect the first instance in which a Commonwealth dramatics instructor carefully considered both theoretical and practical motivations behind labor drama specific to the Commonwealth community. In pursuit of clarifying these complex ideas, Hays wrestles with the larger theoretical foundations undergirding labor drama while also narrowing his focus to Commonwealth as a unique microcosm where these larger principles might be enacted. By thinking locally in regard to his Workers' Dramatics classes, he engaged with the techniques and narratives that would support the school's unique contribution to the larger field instead of simply re-creating or replicating other groups' work. To return to Hazel MacKaye's earlier "variegated shoots" metaphor regarding the importance of the earth in which the "generic seed" of labor drama was planted, Hays thought carefully about his uniquely fecund south Arkansan soil.

In the remainder of the essay Hays described his Workers' Dramatics program as exclusively engaging with southern labor issues. In establishing a foundation for his unique approach, Hays assessed the state of southern labor drama as "casual and immature affair. We find very little writing about dramatics and know of no group which tries systematically and consistently to develop drama for southern workers, in any form."[80] He continues, evaluating the pedagogic goals of the few workers' education programs in the South that incorporated drama, appearing to take particular aim at his friend Zilphia Horton's Highlander program. In this evaluation, he critiques the Highlander program's focus on process over product, the "chief benefit of preparing and producing plays is to the players themselves . . . the experience of preparing the play is paramount."[81] Hays states, matter-of-factly, "*Occupational therapy is not our function. We are amateurs . . . but our job is to make plays of consuming interest to the workers who view them.*"[82] In this assertion against "occupational therapy," Hays implicitly critiques goals associated with almost all other labor drama programs, including Horton's. By rejecting the privileged state of process-oriented work designed specifically for the participants' development or pleasure, Hays's critique serves as an indictment of the status quo in pedagogic labor drama and, more importantly, advances theoretical conversations about the function of drama in education more broadly.

Though he critiques labor drama's focus on process, Hays does not privilege the product, as is the case with many external assessments of labor drama. Instead, he suggests that the performance, the live event in which performers and audience come together and share in a moment of collective meaning-making, should be valued as much as the act of workers generating theatre. Essentially, workers' theatre should neither be process-over-product nor product-over-process. Instead, labor drama should be thought of as process *and* product. By addressing the importance of what happens live, in both the presentation and creation of labor drama, Hays offers an important analysis about students' experiences with labor drama, how they learn, and why that learning is important. Accordingly, he castigates amateur groups for resting too comfortably within their amateur status and for accepting the process of creation as the apex of labor drama's pedagogic function. Most crucially, he calls for a theatre that "cannot wait for the arrival of fully developed professional playwrights," one that is "recognizable in speech, action, and principle to the workers who view the plays," no matter who creates it.[83] Hays also refuses the idea that amateur labor drama meets its pedagogic objectives even if it is politically insignificant, poorly constructed, or culturally irrelevant for the audiences who see it. Instead, he demands that amateurs use their intimate knowledge of issues they hope to change and craft an authentic theatre that simultaneously makes meaning for both the creators and their audiences.

By valuing process and product equally, Hays opened new possibilities for workers' drama programs. Through this dual focus, labor drama might transcend the bourgeois nature of professional theatre, an art form dominated by money attached to the product of performance. It might also break free from the strictures placed on performance that chiefly valued the worker's participation, not the audience's experiences, in assessing value. Even as Hays concedes that the creation of theatre that intimately connects to the lives of both workers who watch and workers who create is a "a large order," he holds up the recent production of *Ninety-Seven Cents*, however imperfect, as a prototype for his program. He closes his essay with the following: "To Sum Up: Our stage is 'any spot which can become a target for witnessing eyes.' . . . We are forging techniques which will help bring workers' education closer to the daily struggles of southern workers."[84] With this essay, Commonwealth began an intense phase of theatrical experimentation focused on these principles.

As a result of Hays's sophisticated experimental approach to theatrical production, Commonwealth dramatics courses stood at the vanguard of southern labor drama and perhaps even theatre practice as a whole. Between the fall of 1937 and Hays's departure in the fall of 1939, Commoner dramatics students produced over twelve original full-length plays and countless skits, short dramas, and scene sketches. Hays outlines this remarkably prolific time in a 1939 report entitled "From 97¢ to Hushpuppy," which he presented at the second annual meeting of the Commonwealth College Association in February 1939.[85] The address demonstrates the evolving aesthetic and thematic styles of Commoner labor drama. The list is impressive:

- ► *97¢*: Our first play, about "southern carpetbaggers of industry." Produce for the first annual meeting of the association. Published. Produced elsewhere.
- ► *One Bread, One Body*: Our best play. Written and produced several times for local audiences, and for the annual convention of the STFU. Published. Produced elsewhere.
- ► *Get Going, George*: A play written and produced for several farmer's union locals in east Arkansas. Published. Produced elsewhere.
- ► *Backbone of the Nations*: Another play for the farmer's union, produced for Calhoun County locals in south Arkansas.
- ► *The People's Right*: A play about the poll tax. Produced for local audiences.
- ► *Sow the Seed Deep*: A play about farm relief, produced for local people.
- ► *Risen from the Ranks*: A play with hand puppets.
- ► *Haymarket*: A play about May Day.
- ► *We Are Not Alone*: About the Blytheville boys, falsely accused of rape. Published, used by the NAACP as a reading. Sent to a large number of Arkansans, urging them to free the boys by protesting. Apparently they did, for Governor Bailey's secretary wrote me asking me to "tell my friends" to stop writing the governor, an indication that popular protest was having its effect.
- ► *Hushpuppy*: The Oklahoma show, consisting of:
    - ■ *The People' Press*, a play about the Midwest Record.
    - ■ *The Pecan King*, a play about the new wage and hours bill.
    - ■ *Hushpuppy and the Admiral*, a marionette play.
    - ■ Numerous Toby skits and songs.

- ▶ *Ci-Cio*: An unproduced marionette play.
- ▶ *Jack and the Beanstalk*: An unproduced play for hand puppets.
- ▶ Numerous skits and sketches.[86]

He closes this list with the following emphatic assertion: "We took our plays to 3000 people. 2000 saw them produced by other groups. All our published plays have been sold out. The market for worker' plays—easy to produce, well planned to meet the money limitations of workers' groups, and with specific appeals—is wide open."[87] These descriptions demonstrate Commonwealth's increasing focus on the southern labor movement and commitment to generating original works. Commonwealth's new plays also met the needs of diverse groups, from the NAACP to the STFU. Furthermore, they served as tools for tangible political change, as indicated by Hays's note on *We Are Not Alone*.

Most important, this collection of new works directly engaged with the changing landscape for southern labor and the challenges of activism of any stripe in the expansive and economically depressed South. Hays's dramatics report includes invaluable reflection about both of these issues as well. In the introduction, he asserts, "Every group works within certain cultural limitations. Its program must be fitted to the needs of its members, or of those whom it addresses. *To ascertain its limitations is the first big job of any group, and it is the point at which most groups fail.*"[88] This statement alludes to the challenges weathered by the drama students during Hays's tenure. In a continuation of his analysis, Hays faults other labor drama organizations' use of "an Odets production or some similar ambitious play which may have won fame on Broadway" for their lack of suitability for specific labor groups and geographic regions, again drawing attention to the flawed methodology of reproducing labor drama hits for audiences who do not connect with the content.[89] Hays returned to this notion later in his life, describing tensions between his students' desires to create theatre and the needs of the southern audiences they hoped to address: "A lot of the kids were from New York and the East, and naturally they inclined toward plays like *Waiting for Lefty* and *Private Hicks*—exactly the wrong kind of stuff for west Arkansas hill farmers who didn't know about New York taxi drivers, didn't care about them, and thought plays about them to be in the worst possible taste."[90] This tension inspired Hays to develop a specifically southern approach to labor drama.

Hays and his students created Toby skits as an accessible, popular form for southern workers. The beloved "golden hearted son of toil," Toby was a white hillbilly stock character who wove together vaudeville traditions and evolutions of minstrelsy in southern popular performance. At his core, Toby spoke the language of the poor white southerner. Toby became a "dumb but inevitably triumphant" hero for Hays's unique brand of southern workers' dramatics.[91] The dramatics program discovered that workers more clearly understood labor issues through the comic musings of Toby since "he is usually a native of the South. . . . Nothing slick. Nothing foreign in their accents. They twang in Arkansas, drawl in Mississippi, and close up both nostrils in North Carolina. Just like the man on the street."[92] By reconceptualizing the Toby character, Commoner dramatics generated a vehicle that could speak to "millions" of unorganized southerner workers: "Toby is our own discovery, though he has been under our noses for generations. He's a difficult character, but we have made great progress in using him, and 900 Oklahomans who saw him approved of him completely."[93] Hays felt so strongly about the importance of Toby that he mentioned him in several discussions of labor drama, including the aforementioned dramatics report in which he states, "We must develop this medium. It is the only way we know to reach unorganized workers—and if we can do this, we shall be doing what workers' theatres ought to be doing but are not."[94] Toby demonstrated Hays's commitment to finding new forms that spoke directly to area communities. He insisted that Commoner dramatics was "sold on no theatre dogma, no school of method" and asserted that his program would "not produce Broadway plays for Arkansas audiences."[95] In yet another evolution of his pedagogic approach, Hays's experimentation and innovation suggested a southern workers' theatre might be housed at Commonwealth.

Hays spoke frankly about challenges he and his students encountered in pursuit of a uniquely southern workers' theatre. He did not sugarcoat his descriptions, willingly and openly addressing the difficulties of leading a course without pedagogic precedent as an instructor forced to learn alongside his students. Many of the challenges and failures of Commonwealth's dramatics program derived from the group's negotiation of a collaborative pedagogy within the reality of severely limited resources. The Commoner dramatics students and faculty "had to write our own plays, build our own equipment, and finally, build our audiences."⁹⁶ No easy task. In a section of the essay entitled "We Have Worked Collectively," Hays discusses his strategy for tackling these challenges: "The 'approach' is no one man's idea. It has been developed by teachers and students, exerting collective effort. *We have many things to learn about working together*, but our approach is right, our purposes are clear and with adequate organization most of these problems will be solved."⁹⁷ The assertion that dramatics participants have "many things to learn about working together" is refreshingly honest.

Hays also describes the practical challenges involved in making a new theatre for workers in the rural South with students new to drama. These difficulties include finding labor audiences, building equipment out of tin cans, and performing in unorthodox spaces such as a country school where "hogs had taken over the building and released a brigade of fleas."⁹⁸ Hays also reminds Commonwealth leadership about the challenges of engaging with dramatic learning at a school that relied on egalitarian and collective labor: "The director has been switched from kitchen to office, from mimeographing to dishwashing, from bread baking to office work and back again."⁹⁹ Likewise, he expresses concern over the school's open approach to learning that allowed students to pursue their academic interests with extreme flexibility, meaning drama students would regularly drop in and out of the course as their interests waxed and waned. Indeed, the challenges faced by Commoner drama students would vex the most seasoned theatre professional.

Even in the face of undeniable challenges, Hays's southern labor drama program elicited attention from a variety of labor and theatre outposts. The school toured several original productions throughout the South, presenting performances at the STFU convention, The Farmer's Educational and Cooperative Union, the Indiana Farmers' Union, the Dallas Civic Federation, and the local community in 1938 and 1939. A variety of labor organizations, including the Arkansas Farmers' Union, the Farmers' Union Institute, the Religion and Labor Foundation, and the *Midwest Daily Record* purchased, published, or produced Commonwealth's dramas. Hays started a new course in Union Recreation as an extension of Workers' Dramatics to help students develop cultural entertainments and activities for the campus as "a practical exercise in arranging such programs for union meetings," and he published *Commonwealth Labor Songs*, a compendium of thirty original songs developed through the arts programs on campus.[100] Dramatics activities on campus continued to grow and gain increasing national attention.

As a result of these exciting goings-on, Commonwealth attracted several recent graduates from the New Theatre School. By the end of 1938, the school had developed a reputation as an innovator in southern labor drama techniques.[101] New students developed workers' puppet theatre, drafting an unpublished pamphlet entitled "Marionettes for Unions" that included guidelines and blueprints for constructing puppet stages.[102] Claude Williams's 1938 Director's Report cites dramatics as one of "Commonwealth's best drawing cards for students and support," and describes the dramatics program's evolution into "postgraduate work for students who have already attended professional theatre schools."[103] Both Hays and Williams called for increased support of the labor drama program and a continued commitment to developing "The Commonwealth Approach."[104] Even Charlotte Moskowitz and Raymond Koch, members of the group replaced in Williams's 1936–37 reorganization, acknowledged Lee Hays's leadership. They identified drama as the sole exception in an otherwise grim time during which Commonwealth "continued to lose old ground while failing to gain in new directions," asserting, "these dramatic expeditions . . . were the high points of educational achievement during this period."[105] In the history of labor drama, Hays was among the most successful in carving out a future for his programs.

The Traveler Wanders On: Concluding Commoner Labor Drama

The newly invigorated dramatics programs and Hays's tireless commitment to his students were not enough to save the school. By the summer of 1939, Reverend Summers's attacks, political infighting among various southern labor groups, the lead-up to World War II, and the threat of communism brought Commonwealth's problems to a head. Williams ran afoul of the STFU after being accused of allowing communist-sympathizing students to remain on campus. With this public rejection from one of the most prominent southern labor unions that was also one of Commonwealth's strident supporters, Williams was forced to resign. Shortly after, he announced a medical leave of absence that would require him to leave the post of Commonwealth director.[106] Hays departed soon after, stalling exciting possibilities for Commonwealth's labor drama program. The New Theatre League, inspired by the work of the Federal Theatre Project and the Coffee-Pepper bill, had looked to the school as a potential outpost for a new Southern Theatre School. Unfortunately, these efforts were for naught. The school closed in the summer of 1940 after a "quasi-legal lynching" from the local government, which included a formal investigation by the FBI and a lien against the school for failure to pay fines for the crime of "anarchy."[107] As an indication of how deeply ill will toward the school was felt, when Commonwealth's equipment was auctioned off, Reverend Summers bought the library, destroying practically all of the labor drama materials along with most of the school's resources. Later, a majority of school documents and records mysteriously disappeared from the Polk County Courthouse during the 1940s. They have never resurfaced.

After his departure from Commonwealth, Lee Hays wandered once again to New York City. There, he continued to make art, but mostly in the form of music. In one of the few discussions Hays engaged in about his time directing drama at Commonwealth, an essay published in *People's Songs Bulletin* in 1948, he assessed his time in Mena, Arkansas: "Perhaps we borrowed considerably from 'Waiting for Lefty,' for the burden of his lectures was usually, 'Don't wait for the organizer to come and tell you what to do. Fight your own fights. Make your union strong the way you want it to be, then you can make it strong by your own efforts.'"[108] It seems the need to strengthen his activism led Hays, like Ransdell, MacKaye, and so many others, away from drama. After his time at Commonwealth, he wrote only a few musical dramas that continue to sit, unpublished, in his archive at the Smithsonian. One of the dramatic texts, an outline for a work entitled "Space Cantata," is a musical production for children. The other, entitled "Corey," is a new adaptation of his beloved Toby shows.[109] A musical career reshaped this labor drama instructor into the voice of leftist political folk music in the 1940s, and blacklisting in the early 1950s quieted his activism for many years thereafter. However, his involvement with Commonwealth dramatics as an energetic, inexperienced young artist undoubtedly ignited his passion for arts-based activism. While it might be easy to attribute that success to his artistic talent, especially given his professional accomplishments later in life, it is more accurate to suggest that he benefited from the collective wisdom and labor of women like Smith, MacKaye, Ransdell, Horton, and others artists mentioned in the prior chapters.

Unlike other programs discussed in this study, Commonwealth was a truly radical school with a radical curriculum and radical students. This affiliation with extremism exacted a high price, and the literal destruction of Commonwealth's enduring records marks an important moment of erasure. For conservative Arkansans it was not enough to shut down Commonwealth; they wanted to obliterate its memory. The literal destruction of this school's archive is one of the most prominent examples of a widespread obfuscation of the historical record of leftist theatre initiatives in this period. Nonetheless, Commonwealth labor drama programs provided a vital space for artists and activists to think through a uniquely southern approach to arts-based activism and points to the challenges and attacks that destroyed many legacies for activist performance in the United States.

CONCLUSION

Labor Drama's Legacies

Labor audiences should not be expected to fight for something they do not want to see.
Herbert Kline, editor of *New Theatre*, at Brookwood Theatre
Conference, 1936

Returning to the End

To conclude this study of amateur dramatics, labor activism, and experimental education, I return to the Brookwood Labor College and the ill-fated 1936 workers' theatre conference. In sharp contrast to the vibrancy of Brookwood's programs during Hazel MacKaye's tenure during the 1920s, by the late 1930s, the school was in dire straits. Chairman A. J. Muste, the once-moderate Christian Socialist interested in toeing the AFL party line, had become radicalized in his views, further distancing himself and his school from mainstream organizations. He departed in 1933 over a faculty dispute regarding the teaching of Marxism on campus and took with him a core of loyal donors and supporters. More important, he left behind a reputation for Brookwood as a radical establishment no longer in step with the needs of labor education or the labor movement. A financial crisis at the school closely followed Muste's departure, and by summer 1936, only months after leaders lamented the supposedly failing workers' theatre movement, Brookwood closed. By this time, Portland Labor College was also long shuttered, with Doris Smith working at the new Portland Civic Theatre and producing massive Oregon Trail pageants to celebrate and, in many ways, rewrite the state's history. Hazel MacKaye was no longer working in theatre. Hollace Ransdell would resign from the Southern Summer School later in 1936 just as both Zilphia Horton and Lee Hays entered trying times at their institutions as the FBI closely followed their actions. Bryn Mawr's summer program would close in controversy in 1938, and Commonwealth College would be shuttered for good in 1940. Leadership at Highlander, the only institution that remains of those discussed here, probably watched these closures and, both in an act of self-preservation and in a necessary shift to pressing issues, refocused their efforts on the civil rights movement. Still, they faced scrutiny by the FBI and harassment from the Tennessee government until the 1970s, and the massive Highlander FBI file was only declassified in 1984. As these examples demonstrate, the 1936 workers' drama conference was indeed a harbinger for the contraction of labor drama, workers' theatre, and workers' education.

But what had gone wrong? Could help for the labor drama experiments chronicled through these pages be found in the workers' theatre conference minutes? Were labor drama leaders, as noted by *New Theatre* magazine editor Herbert Kline, asking their students to "fight for something they do not want to see"?[1] Would dramatic narratives with "mass heroes" have helped, as Kline recommended? Would funding playwrights to write better plays or returning to mass-spectacle labor pageants help invigorate labor drama programs in workers' education institutions? It may be simpler to look at the various institutions chronicled in this book, with their volunteer teachers, underfunded programs, and experimental curricula, and assert that they were simply unable to weather hostile government sentiment at both the local and national levels. Indeed, a fracturing leftist coalition, and perhaps most devastatingly, a second world war based on nationalistic and fascistic perversions of the core beliefs of many of these artists, educators, and institutions certainly damaged these programs. Additionally, McCarthyism decimated many left-leaning artist communities, particularly between 1939 and 1955 with House Un-American Activities Committee–sponsored investigations and sworn testimony leading to the arrest and imprisonment, silencing, deportation, and blacklisting of numerous artists. While some theatrical organizations fought back against some of these policies, the real danger of anti-left sentiment during the second Red Scare nonetheless curtailed a great deal of theatrical work, especially in communities discussed in this book. The lingering effects of these efforts to systematically silence left-leaning artists allied with the labor movement reverberate through the committee's hearings records; through the voluminous FBI files about many of these institutions; through the precipitous decline in union participation since the 1950s; and last, through the anti-labor right-to-work laws in twenty-seven U.S. states in 2018.

However, instead of dwelling on labor drama's decline and obscurity, I close this study by examining other lineages of labor drama in an effort to start longer conversations about how and why drama with workers, particularly as a form of pedagogy, was transformed into new and often unrecognizable forms. In doing so, I position labor drama as a space for vital and productive experimentation that provided numerous constituencies, all of whom cared deeply about the intersections among activism, education, and performance, opportunities to nurture new ideas, take risks, and ultimately wrestle with the challenges of being politically engaged artists and citizens. Furthermore, these spaces of experimentation, which include not only workers' colleges but also many other types of classrooms, recreation halls, basements, and living rooms where a few people make a go at new theatre, house the remnants of performance experiments otherwise lost in broader historical accounts of U.S. theatre. More often, artists in these spaces came from marginalized groups, amateur circles, and underdocumented communities, yet they shaped the evolution of performance in the United States. While the variegated shoots of these labor drama programs may not have blossomed into a robust pedagogical and artistic tradition, their influence ripples through multiple politically oriented performance and pedagogical forms.

Political Theatre and Political Art

Given the erasure of materials and silencing of many labor drama artists who also participated in workers' education, histories of political performance provide avenues to explore the legacies of labor drama. Given the HUAC's assault on left-leaning artists in the 1940s and 1950s, tracing the evolution of political theatre oriented toward the labor movement in the United States has been a difficult endeavor. While the movement most certainly contracted, recent scholarship has demonstrated that certain forms of workers' theatre and protest performance continued, as in the case of theatre scholar Ann Folino White's 2015 study, *Plowed Under: Food Policy Protests and Performance in New Deal America,* and Chrystyna Dail's 2016 study of Stage for Action. Furthermore, the wholly experimental nature of most labor drama initiatives resulted in many programs becoming artistic incubators for students who later developed more prominent and well-documented theatre of the political left in the United States. For example, the dramatic, political, and pedagogical experimentation that occurred in labor college classrooms often connected to more well-known performance initiatives and political endeavors, including the International Ladies' Garment Workers' Union's *Pins and Needles*, the founding of the Hedgerow Theatre, and the left-leaning productions of the Federal Theatre Project. These forms also paved a way for other forms of arts-based activism of the 1950s and 1960s, as demonstrated by the legacies of Lee Hays and Zilphia Horton, who both moved away from theatrical performance and toward music. Horton also contributed to the arts-based activism in the civil rights movement as Highlander Folk School evolved into an outpost for this new wave of activism.

Theatre for Youth and Applied Theatre

When conceived of as a pedagogical intervention, labor drama also offers a productive area of inquiry in theatre and drama for youth. Historians of theatre for youth in the United States have only begun to explore the historiographical complexities associated with documenting the genealogies of theatre with, by, and for young people. The history of labor drama complements extant histories of creative drama pioneers like Alice Minnie Hertz, Constance D'Arcy Mackay, and Winifred Ward in the early twentieth century. These pioneers, almost all upper-class white women working during the Progressive Era, employed pedagogical drama in their work with young children in a variety of organizations, including the Junior League and various settlement houses. Many of these figures collaborated with early labor drama instructors as well. For instance, Hazel MacKaye worked directly with Constance D'Arcy Mackay, and Doris Smith's most significant theatrical contribution was in her work with children in the Portland Junior Civic Theatre School. Many children's theatre and theatre for youth companies still operating today started in these Junior League programs and settlement house initiatives.[2] Since few other historical investigations of experimentation in pedagogical drama during this period exist, scholars justifiably, but steadfastly, conceive of the field as shaped and constrained by its focus on young children and its reliance upon appropriate and normative subject matter that reinforces a limited set of values and ideologies grounded in the work of these important but ideologically complicated figures. This focus on the normalizing force of drama in children's lives suggests that the field developed out of a very narrowly defined set of conditions in which few, if any, radical or experimental ideologies influenced work with drama and young people. This history of labor drama helps construct a fuller picture of theatre for youth that includes not only normalizing but also highly radical impulses, providing one avenue to see how radical ideas in young artists in the 1920s and 1930s evolved into Junior League community drama in the 1950s postwar context. Moreover, contextualizing the field's radical dimensions helps shape the histories of educational theatre and drama, including the advent of youth theatre programs in professional theatres, theatre programs in K-12 schools, and the founding practices that would shape the applied drama and applied theatre fields.

Labor Drama's Significance

Although this book tells many tales of woe, these labor drama experiments remind artists and scholars interested in intersections between art, activism, and education to apply a broad lens when engaging with historical records around performance. The students and teachers chronicled in this book utilized drama methods to fuse practical ideas and skills for labor organizing with theoretical knowledge that supported the labor movement's philosophical foundations. These labor drama participants had fun, escaping reality for a short time as they generated and sustained communities based around new art. They wrote original skits and sketches about their lived experiences and integrated popular aesthetic forms into their productions, connecting their art to their lives. They generated these new works with meager resources and still brought together unique and specific audiences, bridging ideological and cultural differences among those within and outside these experimental institutions. Students made personal connections to abstract concepts, not only creating moments for contemplation, but also practicing tangible action for change. They rehearsed revolutions. Smith, MacKaye, Ransdell, Horton, Hays, and the countless other students, teachers, and activists mentioned in these pages offer glimpses of the messy and valuable work inherent to creating new performance. Their stories also demonstrate the undeniable tensions regarding race, class, gender, and geography found in the fraught processes of building coalitions for activist art and social change more broadly. Above all, the work of artists and educators described in these chapters lays bare the unpredictable nature of path-breaking art, highlighting the importance of experimentation, failure, collaboration, capitulation, and risk in the complex endeavor of making new performance.

NOTES

Chapter 1

Epigraphs: Bonchi Friedman, *Miners* in *Staged Action: Six Plays from the American Workers' Theatre*, ed. Lee Papa (Ithaca, NY: ILR Press, 2009), 159–84. Minutes from Workers' Theatre Conference, Theatre Institute, n.d., Box 10, Folder 19, Brookwood Labor College Collection, Archives for Urban and Labor Affairs, Walter Reuther Library, Wayne State University, Detroit, Michigan (hereafter cited as Brookwood Collection).

1. "Students Writes Play—*Miners*," *Brookwood Review*, Feb. 1926, 183–84. Friedman undoubtedly took inspiration from Ernst Toller's *Masse Mensch*.

2. Ibid.

3. Ibid.

4. "New Theatre League Schools," *New Theatre*, April 1935, 22. See also Chapter 6's conclusion regarding the proposed but unrealized role of Commonwealth as a Southern outpost of the New Theatre League.

5. Minutes from Workers' Drama Conference, Theatre Institute, n.d., Box 10, Folder 19, Brookwood Collection.

6. Ibid.

7. Ibid.

8. Ibid.

9. Ibid.

10. James C. Davies, "Toward a Theory of Revolution," *American Sociological Review* 27, no. 1 (1962): 5–19. http://www.jstor.org/stable/2089714.

11. See Michael Denning, *The Cultural Front: The Laboring of American Culture in the Twentieth Century* (Brooklyn, NY: Verso, 1998). The American Labor Party formed in 1936 as a further left alternative to FDR's Democratic Party, and the Communist Party USA was also a viable left alternative at this point, although the Palmer raids in 1919–20 had destabilized it to a degree.

12. See Drew Chappell, "Constructions of *Revolt of the Beavers* and Notions of the Child Audience: Controversy in the Federal Theatre Project," *Youth Theatre Journal* 21, no. 1 (2007): 41–53.

13. While I speak about pedagogical drama programs as part of workers' education in commenting on this decline, the workers' theatre movement, which included plays for, about, and with workers, continued and metamorphosed both during and after World War II. See the Conclusion for additional discussion.

14. The IWW had a robust theatrical arm as well. See Michael Schwartz, *Class*

Divisions on the Broadway Stage: The Staging and Taming of the I.W.W. (New York: Palgrave Macmillan, 2014).

15. Franklin Delano Roosevelt, "Acceptance Speech, Chicago, July 1932," in *Great Speeches* (Mineola, NY: Dover, 1998), 14.

16. This assessment is an oversimplification of the issues that also involved industrial versus craft trades, the issues of race and ethnicity, and the tolerance of anticapitalist influences in the organization. See Robert H. Zieger, *The CIO, 1935–1955* (Chapel Hill: University of North Carolina Press, 1995), for additional discussion about the CIO's history.

17. After twenty years and a series of controversial negotiations, the two federations reunited into the contemporary AFL-CIO in 1955.

18. Quoted in A. J. Muste, "Workers' Education in the United States," *Religious Education* 24, no. 8 (1929): 738, https://doi.org/10.1080/0034408290240808.

19. Egon Bittner, "Radicalism and the Organization of Radical Movements," *American Sociological Review* 28, no. 6 (December 1963): 928–29. In addition to Bittner's work, I also recommend Mark Irving Lichbach's *The Rebel's Dilemma* (Ann Arbor: University of Michigan Press, 1998) and Donald Egbert's work, including *Social Radicalism and the Arts: Western Europe* (New York: Knopf, 1970).

20. "Southern Summer School for Women Workers in Industry," pamphlet (Baltimore: Southern Summer School for Women Workers in Industry, n.d.), Cornelia Barker Papers, Manuscript Archives and Rare Book Library, Robert W. Woodruff Library, Emory University, Atlanta, GA.

21. For further discussion of progressivism, see Leuchtenburg's "Progressivism and Imperialism: The Progressive Movement and American Foreign Policy, 1898–1916"; Cocks, Holloran, and Lessoff's *Historical Dictionary of the Progressive Era* (Lanham, MD: Scarecrow Press, 2009); Hogan's *Rhetoric and Reform in the Progressive Era* (East Lansing: Michigan State University Press, 2003); Kloeppenberg's *Uncertain Victory: Social Democracy and Progressivism in European and American Thought, 1870–1920* (Oxford: Oxford University Press, 1986); Robert H. Wiebe's *The Search for Order, 1877–1920* (New York: Hill and Wang, 1967); and Alan Dawley, *Struggles for Justice: Social Responsibility and the Liberal State* (Cambridge: Harvard University Press, 1991).

22. See Thomas C. Leonard, *Illiberal Reformers: Race, Eugenics, and American Economics in the Progressive Era* (Princeton: Princeton University Press, 2016).

23. John Dewey, *Art as Experience* (New York: Minton, Balch & Company, 1934), 2–3.

24. See *Experience and Nature* (1925); *The Public and Its Problems* (1927); *Individualism Old and New* (1930); *Art as Experience* (1934); *Liberalism and Social Action* (1935); *Experience and Education* (1938).

25. "Labor Expunges Tribute to Dewey," *New York Times*, Nov. 29, 1928.

26. John Dewey, "Labor Politics and Labor Education," *New Republic*, Jan. 9, 1929.

27. Thomas Postlewait, "The Hieroglyphic Stage: American Theatre and Society, Post-Civil War to 1945," in *The Cambridge History of American Theatre Vol. 2*, ed. Don B. Wilmeth and Christopher Bigsby (Cambridge: Cambridge University Press, 1999), 107–8.

28. Herbert Kline, "Writing for Workers Theatre," *New Theatre*, Dec. 1934, 22–23.

Chapter 2

Epigraph: Albert Maurer, "Fifth Session: Sunday Evening, April 15, 1923," *Workers' Education Yearbook*, 142.

1. Brooks Atkinson, "The Play; 'The Revolt of the Beavers,' or Mother Goose Marx, Under WPA Auspices," *New York Times*, May 21, 1937.

2. The Portland Labor Players were referred to by many different names in the press and publicity during this time, including the Labor College Players, the Labor Temple Players, the College Players, and the Portland Labor College Players. I've opted for the Portland Labor Players for clarity and consistency.

3. "Labor College Notes and Comment," *Oregon Labor Press* (Portland, OR), Oct. 20, 1922, 6. Also cited in Jerry Lembcke, "Labor and Education: Portland Labor College, 1921–1929," *Oregon Historical Quarterly* 85, no. 2 (July 1, 1984): 117–34, doi:10.2307/20613967 ("Labor College Notes and Comment" hereafter cited as "LCNC"; *Oregon Labor Press* hereafter cited as *OLP*).

4. Some experiments in this period include the 1915–16 production of *The Weavers* produced by Emanuel Reicher at the Garden Theatre in New York City as part of the American People's Theatre project for "working class audiences" (in "American People's Plays," *New York Times*, Oct. 31, 1915); the early works from little theatres throughout the country; the settlement house programs by figures like Jane Addams; and the pageantry productions from figures like Alice Paul, Glenna Smith Tinnin, and Hazel MacKaye in the suffragist movement, as well as labor pageants from the early 1910s, including the Paterson pageant of 1913, discussed in chapter 3. See Cheryl Black, *The Women of Provincetown, 1915–1922* (Tuscaloosa: University of Alabama Press, 2002); Charlotte Canning, *The Most American Thing in America: Circuit Chautauqua as Performance* (Iowa City: University of Iowa Press, 2005); Dorothy Chansky, *Composing Ourselves: The Little Theatre Movement and the American Audience* (Carbondale: Southern Illinois University Press, 2005); David Glassberg, *American Historical Pageantry: The Uses of Tradition in the Early 20th Century* (Chapel Hill: University of North Carolina Press, 1990).

5. Philip Sheldon Foner, *Women and the American Labor Movement: From the First Trade Unions to the Present* (New York: Free Press–Collier Macmillan, 1982).

6. See A. Mitchell Palmer, "The Case Against the Reds," *Forum* 63 (1920): 173–85; Christopher M. Finan, *From the Palmer Raids to the Patriot Act: A History of the Fight for Free Speech in America* (Boston: Beacon Press, 2007), 2–37.

7. Warren G. Harding, "Address before Home Market Club at Boston, Massachusetts, May 14, 1920," in *Rededicating America: Life and Recent Speeches of Warren G. Harding* (Indianapolis: Bobbs-Merrill, 1920), 223.

8. Lewis Levitzki Lorwin and Jean Atherton Flexner, *The American Federation of Labor: History, Policies, and Prospects* (Washington, DC: Brookings Institution, 1933), 225–28. These numbers would decline substantially during the early twenties, particularly as the economy improved.

9. At this point, comprehensive K-12 education was still a quite new idea, with most states requiring education for children only through the elementary or primary grades (roughly up to between ages ten and twelve). Most children only attended school for five years in total. Just 10 percent of potential students attended high school in 1920, with most young people going to work in their early teens. This number had increased somewhat to approximately 23 percent by 1950. See David Tyack, "Ways of Seeing: An Essay on the History of Compulsory Schooling," *Harvard Educational Review* 46, no. 3 (Sept. 1, 1976): 355–89.

10. Both Charles A. Beard and Walter Vrooman, Ruskin Hall Founders, attempted a U.S. outpost of the Ruskin Hall movement in 1899 and 1900, but the AFL refused to support it. "Ruskin Hall Movement," *New York Times*, Sept. 10, 1900; "A New Educational Movement," *New York Times*, Aug. 12, 1899.

11. David Brody, *Labor Embattled: History, Power, Rights* (Champaign: University of Illinois Press, 2005), 25.

12. Clyde W. Barrow, "Counter-Movement within the Labor Movement: Workers' Education and the American Federation of Labor, 1900–1937," *Social Science Journal* 27, no. 4 (Jan. 1, 1990): 395–417.

13. Ibid., 398.

14. Elizabeth McLagan, *A Peculiar Paradise: A History of Blacks in Oregon, 1778–1940* (Portland: Oregon Black History Project Georgian Press, 1980).

15. Alana Semuels, "The Racist History of Portland, the Whitest City in America," *Atlantic*, July 22, 2016.

16. See the state's exclusion laws in 1846 and 1857 and the antimiscegenation law in 1867. Additionally, when admitted to the union in 1859, it was the first state to do so with an exclusion law in place that protected only the rights of white citizens.

17. "LCNC," *OLP*, Oct. 20, 1922, 6.

18. Roberta Lanouette, "This Is Your Life, Doris Smith!" Unpublished playscript, "Smith" folder, Box 111, Portland Civic Theatre Records: 1915–2000, Oregon Historical Society.

19. "Music Briefs," *Sunday Oregonian*, Oct. 22, 1922: 9.

20. "College for Workers May Be Started," *OLP*, May 21, 1921, 1; see also the unpublished thesis by Gerhard Rangvald Flood, "History and Educational Program of the Portland Labor College," Oregon State University, 1940.

21. "LCNC," *OLP*, Sept. 9, 1921, 1.

22. Ibid.

23. Ibid.; Flood, "History and Educational Program," 30.

24. Lembcke, "Labor and Education," 118.

25. Flood, "History and Educational Program," 34–37.

26. "LCNC," *OLP*, Nov. 10, 1922, 9; Flood, "History and Educational Program," 44.

27. "LCNC," *OLP*, Oct. 20, 1922, 8.

28. "Women's Activities," *Sunday Oregonian*, Oct. 22, 1922, 10.

29. Ibid.

30. Ibid.

31. Ibid.

32. Ibid.

33. Flood, "History and Educational Program," 47; "LCNC," *OLP*, Nov. 17, 1922, 8. Local unions further subsidized the PLCA, paying one cent per member per month.

34. Ibid, 55. "LCNC," *OLP*, Jan. 19, 1923, 5.

35. "LCNC," *OLP*, Nov. 10, 1922, 8.

36. "LCNC," *OLP*, Jan. 19, 1923, 5.

37. "Labor Temple Players Cast," *OLP*, Nov. 17, 1922, 1.

38. Ibid.

39. See Chansky, *Composing Ourselves*.

40. "LCNC," *OLP*, Dec. 1, 1922, 8.

41. "Three One-Act Plays Are to Be Presented," *OLP*, Dec. 1, 1922, 4; Richard Harding Davis, *Miss Civilization* (New York: Charles Scribner's Sons, 1911).

42. Marjorie Benton Cooke, *When Love Is Young* (Alexandria, VA: Alexander Street Press, 2012).

43. Ernest Schwarztrauber, "Educational Value of Dramatic Work in Labor Colleges," *Report of the Annual Conference on Worker's Education in the United States* (New York: Workers' Education Bureau, 1923), 140–42.

44. Harold Haynes, "Workers' College Players," *OLP*, Feb. 9, 1923, 4.

45. Ibid.

46. Ibid.

47. "LCNC," *OLP*, Feb. 23, 1923, 5.

48. Spencer Miller to Ernest Schwarztrauber, Feb. 8, 1923, Letter, "Correspondence 1908 Dec. 2–1929 Feb. 24" Folder, Box 1, Ernest E. Schwarztrauber Papers, 1894–1953, Wisconsin Historical Society. Spencer Miller to Ernest Schwarztrauber, Feb. 13, 1923, Letter, "Correspondence 1908 Dec. 2–1929 Feb. 24" Folder, Box 1, Ernest E. Schwarztrauber Papers, 1894–1953, Wisconsin Historical Society (hereafter cited as Schwarztrauber Papers).

49. Ibid.

50. "LCNC," *OLP*, Jan. 12, 1923, 5; "LCNC," *OLP*, Jan. 19, 1923, 5.

51. "LCNC," *OLP*, March 2, 1923, 5.

52. Ibid.

53. "LCNC," *OLP*, March 9, 1923, 5.

54. Ibid.

55. Ernest Schwarztrauber to R. M. Hughes, Feb. 24, 1923, Letter, "Correspondence 1908 Dec. 2–1929 Feb. 24" Folder, Box 1, Schwarztrauber Papers.

56. Flood, "History and Educational Program," 105–8.

57. "We Herewith Submit," Portland Labor College Budget Report, Aug. 3, 1923, "Correspondence 1908 Dec. 2–1929 Feb. 24" Folder, Box 1, Schwarztrauber Papers.

58. "LCNC," *OLP*, March 9, 1923, 5.

59. "LCNC," *OLP*, March 16, 1923, 5.

60. Spencer Miller to Ernest Schwarztrauber, Feb. 13, 1923, Letter, "Correspondence 1908 Dec. 2–1929 Feb. 24" Folder, Box 1, Schwarztrauber Papers.

61. Schwarztrauber, "Educational Value."

62. Ibid., 141.

63. "Labor College to Demonstrate for A.F.L. Delegates," *OLP*, May 4, 1923, 1.

64. "Labor Players in Final Appearance Repeat Triumphs," *OLP*, May 2, 1923, 1.

65. Ibid.

66. Lord Dunsany, *The Glittering Gate*, in *Five Plays* (Holicong, PA: Wildside Press, 2002).

67. "Labor Players in Final Appearance Repeat Triumphs," *OLP*, May 25, 1923, 1; "College Players to Entertain at the Gresham Fair," *OLP*, July 20, 1923, 1.

68. "LCNC," *OLP*, June 29, 1923, 6.

69. Ibid.; Flood, "History and Educational Program," 61.

70. Ernest Schwarztrauber to Louise Budens, Sept. 17, 1923, "Correspondence 1908, Dec. 2–1929, Feb. 24" Folder, Box 1, Schwarztrauber Papers.

71. "Forty-Third Annual Meeting of American Federation of Labor," *Monthly Labor Review* 17, no. 6 (December 1923): 173.

72. See Jennifer Luff's chapter, "Becoming Commonsense Anti-Communists" in *Commonsense Anticommunism: Labor and Civil Liberties between the World Wars* (Chapel Hill: University of North Carolina Press, 2012), 62–118.

73. Ibid.

74. "Labor College Players" (unpublished program), "Articles and Reports" Folder, Box 2, Schwarztrauber Papers; "LCNC," *OLP*, Jan. 9, 1925, 5; "LCNC," *OLP*, Jan. 23, 1925, 5; "LCNC," *OLP*, Jan. 9, 1925, 5.

75. "Labor College Players: Final Performance of the Season" (unpublished program), "Articles and Reports" Folder, Box 2, Schwarztrauber Papers.

76. Lembcke, "Labor and Education," 127.

77. "History of the Portland Civic Theatre," Box 1, Folder 8, Portland Civic Theatre Records: 1915–2000, Oregon Historical Society.

78. "Obituary–Doris Smith," *Oregonian*, Oct. 7, 1972.

79. Ibid.

Chapter 3

Epigraphs: Hazel MacKaye, "Drama and the Labor Movement," *Brookwood Review*, May 1925, 1. A "Very Dead Corpse" quoted by Helen Norton, "Brookwood in Its First Decade," *Labor Age*, May 1931, 18–19.

1. James W. Robinson, "The Expulsion of Brookwood Labor College from the Workers' Education Bureau," *Labour History*, no. 15 (Nov. 1, 1968): 64–69, doi:10.2307/27507910. Robinson's article also discusses the school's connection to the AFL and Workers' Education Bureau.

2. Ibid., 66.

3. See Richard Altenbaugh's "'The Children and the Instruments of a Militant Labor Progressivism': Brookwood Labor College and the American Labor College Movement of the 1920s and 1930s," *History of Education Society* 23, no. 4 (1983): 395–411, http://www.jstor.org/stable/368076, and *Education for Struggle: The American Labor Colleges of the 1920s and 1930s* (Philadelphia: Temple University Press, 1990) for additional discussions about the formation of Brookwood Labor College.

4. Helen Norton, *A Survey of Brookwood Students, 1921–1931* (Katonah, NY: Brookwood Labor College, n.d. [1932?]), 1; Helen Norton, "Brookwood in Its First Decade," *Labor Age*, May 1931, 18–19.

5. Norton, *A Survey*, 1.

6. See Clyde W. Barrow, "Playing Workers: Proletarian Drama in the Curriculum of American Labor Colleges, 1921–37," *Journal of Arts Management and Law* 20, no. 4 (1991): 5–29, and Richard Altenbaugh, "Proletarian Drama: An Educational Tool of the American Labor College Movement," *Theatre Journal* 34, no. 2 (1982): 197–210, for additional discussions regarding the negotiations of the role of cultural and arts education, specifically dramatics, in workers' colleges.

7. Percy MacKaye, *Epoch: The Life of Steele MacKaye, Genius of the Theatre* (New York: Boni & Liveright, 1927), 357.

8. Karen J. Blair, "Pageantry for Women's Rights: The Career of Hazel MacKaye, 1913–1923," *Theatre Survey* 31, no. 1 (1990), 23–46; Percy MacKaye, *Epoch*.

9. Of Hazel MacKaye's brothers, Percy was a noted pageant director and playwright, Benton was a conservationist who steered the creation of the Appalachian Trail, and James was a pioneering engineer.

10. Blair, "Pageantry," 33.

11. Percy MacKaye, *Caliban by the Yellow Sands: Shakespeare Tercentenary Masque* (Garden City, NY: Doubleday, 1916), 158, 220.

12. Blair, "Pageantry," 33.

13. Percy MacKaye, *Epoch*, lxv.

14. See David Glassberg, *American Historical Pageantry: The Uses of Tradition in the Early Twentieth Century* (Chapel Hill: University of North Carolina Press, 1990) for additional discussion.

15. Ibid., 284.

16. "Miss Hazel MacKaye, A Pageant Director," obituary, *New York Times*, Aug. 12, 1944; Blair, "Pageantry," 24–26.

17. Jean H. Baker, *Sisters: The Lives of America's Suffragists* (New York: Hill and Wang, 2006), 5.

18. Blair, "Pageantry."

19. Ibid., 31.

20. Ibid.

21. Ibid., 33.

22. "Faculty Minutes," April 21, 1925, Box 7, Folder 11, Brookwood Labor College Collection, Archives for Urban and Labor Affairs, Walter Reuther Library, Wayne State University, Detroit, MI (hereafter referred to as Brookwood Collection); Lillian Schachat, "Brookwood Presents *The Weavers*," *Brookwood Review*, Jan. 1925, 3.

23. Schachat, "Brookwood Presents *The Weavers*," 3.

24. "Faculty Minutes," April 30, 1925, Box 7, Folder 11, Brookwood Collection.

25. "Faculty Minutes," May 6, 1925, Box 7, Folder 11, Brookwood Collection.

26. Ibid.

27. "Of Interest," *Brookwood Review*, May 1925, 5.

28. "Faculty Memorandum," n.d., Box 7, Folder 9, Brookwood Collection.

29. Hazel MacKaye to A. J. Muste, July 10, 1925, Box 43, Folder 13, Brookwood Collection.

30. Hazel MacKaye, "The Drama and the Labor Movement: Some Problems Involved," unpublished essay, n.d., Box 43, Folder 13, Brookwood Collection.

31. Ibid., 1.

32. Ibid., 3.

33. Ibid.

34. Ibid., 2.

35. Ibid., 3.

36. Ibid., 1.

37. Ibid., 2.

38. Ibid., 4.

39. Ibid.

40. Dana was ousted from his professorship along with professor James Cattel for associations with the antiwar organization People's Council of America for Democracy and Peace. The resulting outcry solicited "public resent" from Charles Beard and John Dewey, and Charles Beard resigned from Columbia in response. "Quits Columbia; Assails Trustees," *New York Times*, Oct. 9, 1917; Hazel MacKaye to A. J. Muste, Aug. 4, 1925, Box 43, Folder 13, Brookwood Collection.

41. Hazel MacKaye to A. J. Muste, Aug. 10, 1925, Box 43, Folder 13, Brookwood Collection.

42. A. J. Muste to Hazel MacKaye, Aug. 10, 1925, Box 43, Folder 14, Brookwood Collection.

43. Hazel MacKaye to A. J. Muste, Sept. 12, 1925, Box 43, Folder 14, Brookwood Collection.

44. "Brookwood Opening Postponed Until After A. F. of L. Convention," *Brookwood Review,* Oct. 1925, 4.

45. Hazel MacKaye, "Notes on Class," in unpublished Notes and Class Plans, ML-5 (214): 6, Papers of MacKaye Family, 1751–1990, Rauner Special Collections Library, Dartmouth College, Hanover, NH (hereafter referred to as MacKaye Family Papers).

46. "Labor Drama Has Initial Success," *Brookwood Review,* Jan. 1926, 1–2.

47. The play is more commonly titled *The Dollar,* but MacKaye and Brookwood both list it as *A Dollar* in their writings and publications.

48. "Labor Drama Has Initial Success," 1–2.

49. Hazel MacKaye, "To Dramatize Workers' Lives," *Brookwood Review,* Dec. 1925, 1.

50. Ibid.

51. Ibid.

52. "Labor Drama Has Initial Success," 1.

53. A. J. Muste, "Dramatizing the Labor Movement," *Brookwood Review,* Dec. 1925, 2.

54. Henri de Man, "Labor's Challenge to Education," *New Republic,* March 2, 1921, 16–18.

55. A. J. Muste, "Dramatizing the Labor Movement," *Brookwood Review,* Dec. 1925, 2.

56. Dick Pels, "The Dark Side of Socialism: Hendrik de Man and the Fascist Temptation," *History of the Human Sciences* 6, no. 2 (May 1, 1993): 75–95, doi:10 .1177/095269519300600204.; Henri de Man, "Labor's Challenge to Education," *New Republic,* March 2, 1921, 16–18.

57. Pels, "The Dark Side of Socialism," 75–76.

58. Ibid., 75; Zeev Sternhell, *Neither Right nor Left: Fascist Ideology in France* (Princeton: Princeton University Press, 1995), 302.

59. Muste, "Dramatizing," 2.

60. Ibid.

61. Ibid.

62. Ibid.

63. Ibid.

64. "Labor Drama Has Initial Success," 1.

65. "Faculty Minutes–Oct. 28 1925." Box 7, Folder 11, Brookwood Collection.

66. "Labor Drama Has Initial Success," 4.

67. Ibid.

68. Ibid.

69. Ibid.

70. "Dramas of Toil Are Staged at Brookwood Labor College," *New York Times,* March 7, 1926.

71. "Brookwood Players Appear in New York," *Brookwood Review,* March 1926, 2.

72. "N.Y. World Comments," *Brookwood Review,* Jan. 1926, 1.

73. "Dramas of Toil," 12.

74. "Faculty Minutes," Dec. 16, 1925, Box 7, Folder 11, Brookwood Collection.

75. "Faculty Minutes," Dec. 22, 1925, Box 7, Folder 11, Brookwood Collection.

76. "Student Writes Play—*Miners,*" *Brookwood Review,* Feb. 1926, 183–84; Bonchi Friedman, *Miners* in *Staged Action: Six Plays from the American Workers' Theatre,* ed. Lee Papa (Ithaca, NY: ILR Press, 2009), 159–84.

77. "Student Writes," 2.

78. Ibid.

79. Ibid., 1.

80. Friedman, *Miners,* 163; "Faculty Minutes," Jan. 1, 1926, Box 7, Folder 11, Brookwood Collection.

81. "Faculty Minutes," Jan. 1, 1926.

82. Friedman, *Miners,* 163.

83. "Faculty Minutes," May 26, 1926, Box 7, Folder 11, Brookwood Collection.

84. Paul L. Murphy, Kermit Hall, and David Klaassen, *The Passaic Textile Strike of 1926* (Belmont, CA: Wadsworth, 1974); Albert Weisbord, *Passaic: The Story of a Struggle Against Starvation Wages and for the Right to Organize* (Brooklyn, NY: AMS Press, 1976); "Passaic Strikers Like 'Shades of Passaic,'" *Brookwood Review,* May 1926, 2.

85. Hazel MacKaye, "Budget: Shades of Passaic," in unpublished Notes and Class Plans, ML-5 (214): 6, MacKaye Family Papers.

86. "Passaic Strikers Like 'Shades of Passaic,'" 3.

87. Ibid.

88. Hazel MacKaye, "Dates," in unpublished Notes and Class Plans, ML-5 (214): 6, MacKaye Family Papers.

89. Arthur Hopkins, "Moonshine," unpublished playscript, ML-5 (214): 16, MacKaye Family Papers.

90. "The Brookwood Labor Players Present One-Act Plays," Playbill, ML-5 (214): 16, MacKaye Family Papers.

91. Hazel MacKaye, "Notes," in unpublished Notes and Class Plans, ML-5 (214): 6, MacKaye Family Papers.

92. "Listening in on Limbo: A Dialogue in Shade Lane," unpublished manuscript, ML-5 (214): 16, MacKaye Family Papers.

93. Ibid.

94. "Henry Ford Applies for a Job at the Edison Plant," unpublished skit, ML-5 (214): 16, MacKaye Family Papers.

95. Hazel MacKaye, "Expenses," in unpublished Notes and Class Plans, ML-5 (214): 6, MacKaye Family Papers; "Outdoor Theatre Used," *Brookwood Review*, May 1926, 2–3.

96. Hazel MacKaye, "The Tailor Shop, words written and dances devised by students of Brookwood Labor College, under the direction of Miss Hazel MacKaye," unpublished playtext, "1926 Folder," American Labor Education Service Records, 1927–1962, Kheel Center for Labor-Management Documentation and Archives at M. P. Catherwood Library, Cornell University (hereafter referred to as ALES).

97. Ibid., 1.

98. Gus Tyler, *Look for the Union Label: A History of the International Ladies' Garment Workers' Union* (Armonk, NY: M. E. Sharpe, 1995), 159.

99. Ibid., 159–65.

100. MacKaye, "The Tailor Shop," 2.

101. Ibid., 2.

102. Ibid., 3.

103. Ibid., 2.

104. Ibid., 3.

105. Ibid., 4.

106. Ibid., 5.

107. Ibid., 6.

108. Ibid.

109. A. J. Muste, "The Year at Brookwood," *Brookwood Review*, May–June 1926, 2.

110. "Faculty Minutes," May 5, 1926, Box 7, Folder 2, Brookwood Collection.

111. Ibid.

112. Tippett was professor of economics at Brookwood from 1927 until 1933 and would go on to write the labor play *Mill Shadows*.

113. "Coal Miner Actors," *Kokomo Daily Tribune*, Nov. 4, 1926, 13.

114. Ibid.

115. Hazel MacKaye, to A. J. Muste, July 21, 1926, Box 47, Folder 19, Brookwood Collection.

116. Ibid.

117. Hazel MacKaye, "Plays for Workers," *Workers' Education*, May 1926, 11–17; Hazel MacKaye, "A Labor Drama Council," *Workers' Education*, Feb. 1927, 16–32.

118. MacKaye, "Plays for Workers," 17.

119. MacKaye, "A Labor Drama Council," 27.

120. Ibid., 26.

121. Ibid.

122. Ibid., 27–31.

123. "Miss Hazel MacKaye," 11.

124. Ibid.

125. Norton, "Drama," 18.

126. Ibid.

127. Arthur Calhoun, "The Social Significance of Labor Dramatics," *Workers' Education*, May 1926, 18–20.

Chapter 4

Epigraph: Miriam Bonner Camp, interview with Mary Frederickson (#4007), *Southern Oral History Program Collection*, 1976: University of North Carolina–Chapel Hill.

1. Miriam Bonner Camp, interview with Mary Frederickson (#4007), *Southern Oral History Program Collection*, 1976, University of North Carolina–Chapel Hill.

2. See Karyn Hollis, *Liberating Voices: Writing at the Bryn Mawr Summer School for Women Workers* (Carbondale: Southern Illinois University Press, 2004); Joyce Kornbluh and Mary Frederickson, eds., *Sisterhood and Solidarity: Worker's Education for Women, 1914–1984* (Philadelphia: Temple University Press, 1984); Diane Balser, *Sisterhood and Solidarity: Feminism and Labor in Modern Times* (Boston: South End Press, 1987); Rita Heller, "Blue Collars and Bluestockings: The Bryn Mawr Summer School for Women Workers, 1921–1938," in Kornbluh and Frederickson, eds., *Sisterhood and Solidarity*, 107–46; Eileen Boris and Annelise Orleck, "Feminism and the Labor Movement: A Century of Collaboration and Conflict," *New Labor Forum* 20 (2011): 33–41; Michelle Haberland, *Striking Beauties: Women Apparel Workers in the U.S. South, 1930–2000* (Athens: University of Georgia Press, 2005); and Alice Kessler-Harris's work, *Out to Work: A History of Wage-Earning Women in the United States* (Oxford: Oxford University Press, 2003), and *Women Have Always Worked: An Historical Overview*, 2nd ed. (Champaign: University of Illinois Press, 2018), for additional investigations of women in the labor movement, particularly in the South.

3. Marion Crain, "Feminizing Unions: Challenging the Gendered Structure of Wage Labor," *Michigan Law Review* 89, no. 5 (1991): 1155–57.

4. Ibid.

5. See Gale Ahrens's edited collection of Parsons's writings (*Lucy Parsons: Freedom, Equality and Solidarity: Writings and Speeches, 1878–1937* [Chicago: Charles H. Kerr, 2004]); Carolyn Ashbaugh's biography of Parsons (*Lucy Parsons: An American Revolutionary* [Chicago: Haymarket Books, 2013]); and Gregor Gall's *Sex Worker Unionization: Global Developments, Challenges and Possibilities* (New York: Springer, 2016).

6. See Alice Kessler-Harris, *A Woman's Wage: Historical Meanings and Social Consequences* (Lexington: University Press of Kentucky, 1990).

7. See Philip Sheldon Foner's chapter on the Great Depression (*Women and the American Labor Movement*, 298–317), Crain, "Feminizing Unions," and Mary Triece, *On the Picket Line: Strategies of Working-Class Women During the Depression*

(Champaign: University of Illinois Press, 2007), particularly chapters about labor organizing for women before World War II for additional discussion of the developments (177–236).

8. Martha May, "Bread Before Roses: American Workingmen, Labor Unions, and the Family Wage," in *Families in the U.S.: Kinship and Domestic Politics*, ed. Karen V. Hansen and Anita Ilta Garey (Philadelphia: Temple University Press, 1998), 143.

9. Foner, *Women and the American Labor Movement*, 299.

10. See Southern Summer School director Louise Leonard McLaren's essays "The South Begins Workers Education" (1928) and "Workers Education in the South" (1935) for additional discussion of the ASW's approach to workers' education for women in the South.

11. The organization later became the American Labor Education Service (ALES) in 1934 and disbanded in 1964.

12. See Gladys Palmer's Department of Labor Bulletin, *The Industrial Experience of Women Workers at the Summer Schools, 1928 to 1930*, No. 89 (Washington, DC: Women's Bureau, United States Department of Labor, 1930), and the edited collection of essays about workers' education for women edited by Joyce Kornbluh and Mary Frederickson, *Sisterhood and Solidarity*, for additional discussion of these programs.

13. Richard Dwyer, "Workers' Education, Labor Education, Labor Studies: An Historical Delineation," *Review of Educational Research* 47, no. 1 (Jan. 1, 1977): 179–207, doi:10.2307/1169973.

14. Mary Frederickson, "Recognizing Regional Differences: The Southern Summer School for Women Workers," in Kornbluh and Frederickson, eds., *Sisterhood and Solidarity*, 147–82. Mary Frederickson, "Louise Leonard McLaren" in *Notable American Women, The Modern Period*, ed. Barbara Sicherman and Carol Hurd Green (Cambridge: Harvard University Press, 1980), 452–53.

15. Mary Frederickson, "The Southern Summer School for Women Workers," *Southern Exposure*, 4, no. 4 (1976): 70–75.

16. See Ann Firor Scott's essay, "After Suffrage: Southern Women in the Twenties," *The Journal of Southern History* 30, no. 3 (1964): 298–318, https://doi.org/10.2307/2204836, and Glenda Elizabeth Gilmore, *Defying Dixie: The Radical Roots of Civil Rights, 1919–1950* (New York: W. W. Norton, 2008), for additional discussion.

17. Hollis, *Liberating Voices*, 33; Hilda Worthington Smith, *Women Workers at the Bryn Mawr Summer School* (New York: Affiliated Summer Schools for Women Workers in Industry and American Association for Adult Education, 1929), 1.

18. M. Carey Thomas, "Address," in *Women Workers at the Bryn Mawr Summer School* (New York: Affiliated Summer Schools for Women Workers in Industry and American Association for Adult Education, 1929), 255–64.

19. Thomas qtd. in Smith, *Women Workers*, 356–57.

20. Smith, *Women Workers*, 5.

21. "Bryn Mawr Constitution," Article II, Section 1, in Smith, *Women Workers*.

22. Smith, *Women Workers*, 304.

23. In addition to Smith's *Women Workers*, see also the 1986 documentary film *Women of Summer* and Hollis, *Liberating Voices*, as well as extensive archival resources available through Bryn Mawr College, University of Wisconsin–Madison, and Cornell University.

24. Smith, *Women Workers*, 96.

25. Heller, "Blue Collars and Bluestockings," 116–18; and Susan M. Kingsbury, "Original Plan for a Summer School for Women Workers in Industry, Bryn Mawr, Pennsylvania," in Smith, *Women Workers*, 265–70.

26. Hollis, *Liberating Voices*, 100.

27. Ibid., 101.

28. See Carter's publications, including *The Play Book*; her article on labor drama featured in the *Journal of Adult Education*; *Everyman's Drama*; and her numerous anthologies and bibliographies of labor drama plays.

29. "Southern Summer School for Women Workers in Industry," pamphlet (Baltimore: Southern Summer School for Women Workers in Industry, n.d.), Cornelia Barker Papers, Manuscript Archives and Rare Book Library, Robert W. Woodruff Library, Emory University.

30. Louise Leonard, "The South Begins Workers' Education," *American Federationist*, Nov. 1928, Folder "Southern Summer School 1928," Box 111, American Labor Education Service Records, 1927–62, Kheel Center for Labor-Management Documentation and Archives, M. P. Catherwood Library, Cornell University. Ithaca, NY, 3 (hereafter referred to as ALES Records).

31. See Paul Salstrom's study of Appalachia's economic history, *Appalachia's Path to Dependency: Rethinking a Region's Economic History, 1730–1940* (Lexington: University Press of Kentucky, 2015).

32. Louise Leonard, "Workers' Education in the South," *Vassar Quarterly*, 1935, 2–6.

33. Ibid., 4.

34. Ibid., 1–2; Louise Leonard, "Director's Reports" (1929–37), Folders "1929" through "1936," ALES Records.

35. Leonard, "Worker's Education in the South," 4–5.

36. "Southern Summer School" pamphlet, "Southern Summer School 1928" Folder, Box 11, ALES Records.

37. "Director's Reports," 1928–37; "Central Committee Minutes," 1927–37, Box 111, Folders "Southern Summer School 1927" through "Southern Summer School 1937," ALES Records.

38. Leonard, "Director's Report," 1929, 2, ALES Records.

39. "Faculty Minutes, Feb. 5 1924," Folder 11, Box 7, Brookwood Collection. I cannot confirm Ransdell's attendance beyond a reference to "Hollace" being retained as English tutor in faculty minutes in 1924, but several other authors make

reference to her attending Brookwood, including Mary Frederickson, who interviewed Ransdell in 1975.

40. "Sacco and Vanzetti collections," Series 1, Box 32, Mrs. Walter Frank Collection, 1927–1963, Robert D. Farber University Archives & Special Collections Department, Brandeis University, Waltham, MA.

41. Samuel Walker, *In Defense of American Liberties: A History of the ACLU* (Carbondale: Southern Illinois University Press, 1999), 179.

42. See La Rue McCormick and Malca Chall, *Activists in the Radical Movement, 1930–1960: The International Labor Defense, the Communist Party* (Oakland: University of California Press, 1980).

43. Her essays and reports include "Prisoners of the Passaic Strike," Joint Committee for Passaic Defense (American Civil Liberties Union and the International Labor Defense), 1926; "Greasing the Rails for Passaic Strikers," *Labor Defender*, Jan. 1927, 5, 15; "Negro Miners Plead for Union Sympathy," *Labor's News: The News Magazine of the Labor Movement*, 15, Federated Press, 1928; "The State versus Thomas Regan, Textile Worker," *Labor Defender*, April 1927, 54; "Guilty! of What?" *Labor Defender*, May 1927, 69–70; and "Jack Rubenstein and 'Whitey' Adamchesky," *Labor Defender*, June 1927, 85, 95.

44. Elizabeth Dilling Stokes, *The Red Network: A "Who's Who" and Handbook of Radicalism for Patriots* (New York: Arno Press, 1936).

45. "Proposed Plan for Summer School for Industrial Women in the South," unpublished document, "Southern Summer School 1927" Folder, Box 111, ALES Records.

46. "Central Committee Meeting Minutes," Aug. 4, 1929, "Southern Summer School 1920" Folder, Box 111, ALES Records.

47. Leonard, "Director's Report," 1928, 2.

48. Leonard, "Workers' Education in the South," 6.

49. Leonard, "Director's Report," 1929, 7.

50. Hollace Ransdell, *Work and Wealth: A Modern Morality Play*, Southern Summer School for Women Workers in Industry, 1929.

51. Ibid.

52. Ibid., 3.

53. Ibid.

54. Ibid., 5.

55. "Southern School for Women Workers Closing Third Session," *Women's Wear Daily*, Aug. 22, 1929, "Southern Summer School 1929" Folder, Box 111, ALES Records; "High Spots of the Southern Summer School 1929," unpublished news release, "Southern Summer School 1929" Folder, Box 111, ALES Records.

56. "High Spots," 4–5.

57. Joel I. Seidman, "The Yellow Dog Contract," *Quarterly Journal of Economics* 46, no. 2 (1932): 348–61.

58. Hollace Ransdell, *Oh Mr. Yaller Dog Take Him Away: A One-Act Sketch Taken*

from Life in a Mill Village, Southern Summer School for Women Workers in Industry, 1929, 1.

59. Ibid., 1–2.

60. Ibid., 2.

61. Ibid.

62. Ibid., 3.

63. Ibid., 3–4.

64. Ibid., 5.

65. Ibid., 8.

66. Ibid.

67. Ibid.

68. Ibid., 9.

69. "Southern School for Women Workers Closing Third Session."

70. Ibid.

71. Ibid., 3.

72. "Staff Gossip," *News of Southern Summer School for Women Workers in Industry,* 1, no. 1 (Feb. 1930), 3; Camp interview.

73. Louise Leonard, "Worker's Risks and How to Meet Them," unpublished course plan, "1930–Southern Summer School" Folder, Box 111, ALES Records.

74. "Central Committee Meeting Minutes," 1.

75. "Statement Concerning the Fourth Session of the Southern Summer School for Women Workers in Industry," "1930–Southern Summer School" Folder, Box 111, ALES Records.

76. Louise Leonard, "Director's Report," 1930, 3.

77. Ibid.

78. Leonard, "Director's Report 1930," 6; Dorothy Gardner is a pen name for Dorothy Worthington Butts, who wrote *Eastward of Eden,* which premiered on Broadway in 1947.

79. Louise Leonard, "School for Workers Who Have Moved from Mountain to Mill," *Mountain Life and Work,* Jan. 1931, "Southern Summer School, 1932" Folder, Box 111, ALES Records.

80. Ibid.

81. Hollace Ransdell, "Report of Dramatics Extension Program of the Southern Summer School for Women Workers in Industry: March 14–May 16, 1931," unpublished report, "Southern Summer School, 1931" Folder, Box 111, ALES Records.

82. Ibid., 3; Callie Crall, "Labor Dramatics in Louisville," unpublished article, "Southern Summer School, 1931" Folder, Box 111, ALES Records. My emphasis added.

83. Ransdell, "Report of Dramatics Extension Program," 4.

84. Ibid., 1.

85. Ibid., 2.

86. Ibid., 4.

87. Leonard, "Director's Report," 1931, 2.

88. Crall, "Labor Dramatics in Louisville."

89. Hollace Ransdell, *Job Huntin': A Tragi-comedy in One Act for Workers*, Southern Summer School for Women Workers in Industry, 1931.

90. Hollace Ransdell, *On the Picket: A One-Act Sketch*, Southern Summer School for Women Workers in Industry, 1931.

91. Ibid., 3–5.

92. Ibid., 3.

93. Ibid.

94. Ibid., 8.

95. Ibid., 9.

96. Ibid.

97. Ibid.

98. Ibid.

99. "Follow-Up Work," unpublished notes, M.P. "1930–Southern Summer School" Folder, Box 111, ALES Records.

100. Ibid.

101. Elsie Janison, "A School for Women Workers in Industry in the South," *School and Society*, 36, no. 928 (Oct. 8, 1932): 473–75.

102. Louise Leonard, Letter to Eleanor Coit, Aug. 3, 1932, Box 9, Folder 108, ALES Records.

103. Ibid., 1.

104. Ibid.

105. Leonard, "Director's Report, 1933," 1.

106. Gladys Tysinger, "Students," *News of the Southern Summer School for Women Workers in Industry* 4, no. 1 (Aug. 1933), 1, "Southern Summer School, 1933" Folder, Box 111, ALES Records.

107. Ibid.

108. Susie Grady, "Incidents in Routine," *News of the Southern Summer School for Women Workers in Industry* 4, no. 1 (Aug. 1933): 1–2, "Southern Summer School, 1933" Folder, Box 111, ALES Records.

109. Louise Leonard, Letter to Eleanor Coit, 2.

110. Emma Smith, "Schedule," *News of the Southern Summer School for Women Workers in Industry* 4, no. 1 (Aug. 1933): 2, "Southern Summer School, 1933" Folder, Box 111, ALES Records.

111. Mattie Thomas, "Dramatics," *News of the Southern Summer School for Women Workers in Industry* 4, no. 1 (Aug. 1933): 3, "Southern Summer School, 1933" Folder, Box 111, ALES Records.

112. Leonard, "Director's Report," 1933, 3.

113. Hollace Ransdell, *Bank Run: A Tragi-comic Sketch in One Act*, Southern Summer School for Women Workers in Industry, 1932.

114. Ibid., 1.

115. Ibid.

116. Ibid., 1–4.

117. Ibid., 4.

118. Ibid., 4–5.

119. Ibid., 5.

120. Hollace Ransdell, *World Economic Nonsense: A One-Act Skit,* Southern Summer School for Women Workers in Industry, 1933.

121. Ibid., 7.

122. Ibid.

123. Hollace Ransdell, *Mother Jones' Tin Pan Army: A Comic Sketch in One Act,* Southern Summer School for Women Workers in Industry, 1933.

124. Ibid., 3.

125. Ibid.

126. Ibid., 4.

127. Ibid.

128. Leonard, "Director's Report," 1933, 3.

129. Eleanor Coit, Letter to Floyd Joyce, March 8, 1933, Folder 108, Box 9, ALES Records; Eleanor Coit, Letter to Elizabeth Nord, March 31, 1933, Folder 108, Box 9, ALES Records.

130. Foner, *Women and the American Labor Movement,* 297.

131. Ruth Parsons, Letter to Eleanor Coit, March 8, 1933, Folder 108, Box 9, ALES Records.

132. Hollace Ransdell, Letter to Eleanor Coit, April 25, 1933, Folder 108, Box 9, ALES Records.

133. Ibid., 2.

134. Hollace Ransdell, Letter to Eleanor Coit, April 13, 1933, Folder 108, Box 9, ALES Records; Hollace Ransdell, Letter to Eleanor Coit, April 19, 1933, Folder 108, Box 9, ALES Records.

135. Leonard, "Director's Report," 1934, 1.

136. Ibid.

137. Leonard, "Director's Report," 1934, 1; "Central Committee Meeting Minutes," 1934, 1.

138. "Central Committee Meeting Minutes," 1934, 1.

139. Ibid.

140. "The Southern Summer School and the Affiliated Schools," unpublished notes, "Southern Summer School, 1934" Folder, Box 111, ALES Records.

141. Ibid. 2.

142. "Koch," *Fortnightly,* March 1, 1934, 1.

143. Leonard, "Director's Report," 1935, 1.

144. "Dramatics," *Mountain Top News,* 1, no. 4 (July 21, 1935): 5.

145. *Labor Drama: An Affiliated Schools for Workers Scrapbook (1936),* Box 38, Folder 2, ALES Records.

146. Ibid.

147. For contextualization, Frank Capra's screwball romantic comedy about a cheeky heiress, *It Happened One Night*, swept the Academy Awards in 1935.

148. Hollace Ransdell, "Dramatics Report," unpublished report, 1935, 10, "Southern Summer School, 1936" Folder, Box 111, ALES Records.

149. Ibid.

150. Ibid., 1.

151. Alice Hanson Cook, *Lifetime of Labor: The Autobiography of Alice H. Cook* (New York: Feminist Press at CUNY, 2000), 85–86; "Personals," *Springboard*, 1, no. 1 (Feb. 1938): 6.

152. Robert H. Zieger, *The CIO: 1935–1955* (Chapel Hill: University of North Carolina Press, 1995), 1–2.

153. Ibid., 87.

154. Later the publication was renamed *AFL-CIO News* once the organizations merged in 1955.

155. Titles included "Tomorrow's Factories Are Here Today with Automation—So Are New Problems for Labor," "Lack of Equality Hurts Canal Zone," and "Factory Din Splitting More Workers' Ears."

156. John Cort, "Labor's Glass House," *Commonweal*, April 4, 1958, 14–15.

157. Camp, Interview.

158. Hollace Ransdell, "Amateur Dramatics in the Labor Movement," *Labor Drama: An Affiliated Schools for Workers Scrapbook (1936)*, ALES Records.

159. Thomas Postlewait, "The Hieroglyphic Stage: American Theatre and Society, Post–Civil War to 1945," in *The Cambridge History of American Theatre*, ed. Don B. Wilmeth and Christopher Bigsby (Cambridge: Cambridge University Press, 1999), 188.

160. Hollace Ransdell, "The Soap Box Theatre," *The Crisis*, April 1935, 125.

Chapter 5

Epigraph: Zilphia Horton, "Drama Workshop Report," 1939, Box 58, Folder 3. HREC Records.

1. "About Us," Highlander Research and Education Center, http://highlandercenter.org/about-us/, last accessed Aug. 17, 2018.

2. "Timeline," Highlander Research and Education Center, http://highlandercenter.org/media/timeline/, last accessed Aug. 17, 2018.

3. William J. Moore, "The Determinants and Effects of Right-to-Work Laws: A Review of the Recent Literature," *Journal of Labor Research* 19, no. 3 (1998): 445–69; David T. Ellwood and Glenn Fine, "The Impact of Right-to-Work Laws on Union Organizing," *Journal of Political Economy* 95, no. 2 (1987): 250–73.

4. Myles Horton, "Southern Mountain School," Letter, 1932, in *The Long Haul: An Autobiography*, ed. Judith Kohl and Herbert R. Kohl (New York: Teachers College Press, 1998), 62.

5. Aimee Horton, "The Highlander Folk School: A History of the Development of its Major Programs Related to Social Movements in the South, 1932–1961," Ph.D. dissertation, University of Chicago, 1971, 23.

6. Myles Horton, "Southern Mountain School," Letter, 1932, in *The Long Haul*, 62.

7. Myles Horton, "A Community," in *The Long Haul*, 81.

8. Ibid.; Aimee Horton, "The Highlander Folk School," 52.

9. Aimee Horton, "The Highlander Folk School," 55.

10. Ibid., 347.

11. Ibid.

12. "Student Application for Admission to Highlander Folk School," 1934, Folder 11, Box 61, Highlander Research and Education Center Records, 1917–2005, Wisconsin Historical Society, University of Wisconsin–Madison (hereafter cited as HREC Records).

13. See Aimee Horton, "The Highlander Folk School"; Wendall A. Parris, "Highlander Folk School," *Negro History Bulletin* 21, no. 8 (May 1, 1958): 170; Frank Adams, "Highlander Folk School: Getting Information, Going Back and Teaching It," *Harvard Educational Review* 42, no. 4 (Dec. 1, 1972): 497–520; C. Alvin Hughes, "A New Agenda for the South: The Role and Influence of the Highlander Folk School, 1953–1961," *Phylon* 46, no. 3 (1985): 242–50, doi:10.2307/274832; Vicki K. Carter, "The Singing Heart of Highlander Folk School," *New Horizons in Adult Education and Human Resource Development* 8, no. 2 (1994): 4–24; and Stephen A. Schneider, *You Can't Padlock an Idea: Rhetorical Education at the Highlander Folk School, 1932–1961* (Columbia: University of South Carolina Press, 2014).

14. See Edna Nahshon, *Yiddish Proletarian Theatre: The Art and Politics of the Artef, 1925–1940* (Santa Barbara: Greenwood Press, 1998); Dorothy Chansky, *Composing Ourselves: The Little Theatre Movement and the American Audience* ([Carbondale: Southern Illinois University Press, 2005); Constance D'Arcy Mackay's *The Little Theatre in the United States* (New York: H. Holt and Company, 1917).

15. Jonnye West is also listed as "Elsie" in other writings about Highlander in 1932. Frank T. Adams, *James A. Dombrowski: An American Heretic, 1897–1983* (Knoxville: University of Tennessee Press, 1992), 70.

16. Anne Petty, "Dramatic Activities and Workers' Education at Highlander Folk School, 1932–1942," Ph.D. dissertation, Bowling Green State University, 1979.

17. Petty, "Dramatic Activities and Workers' Education"; Myles Horton, "Educational Theory: Mutual Education," 9, Folder 38, Box 2, Series 1, Myles Horton Papers, HREC Records.

18. Fount F. Crabtree, "The Wilder Coal Strike of 1932–33," master's thesis, George Peabody College for Teachers, 1937; Angela Smith, "Myles Horton, Highlander Folk School, and the Wilder Coal Strike of 1932," master's thesis, Middle Tennessee State University, 2003.

19. The title of the labor folk song "The Ballad of Barney Graham" refers to this union boss.

20. Aimee Horton, "The Highlander Folk School," 59.

21. John M. Glen, *Highlander: No Ordinary School 1932–1962* (Lexington: University Press of Kentucky, 1988).

22. Oral History Interview with Don West, Jan. 22, 1975, Interview E-0016. Southern Oral History Program Collection (#4007), Southern Historical Collection, Wilson Library, University of North Carolina at Chapel Hill.

23. *The Highlander Fling*, Dec. 1933, 1.

24. "Highlander Folk School Summer School Report and Summary of other Reports of Other Educational Activities, September 1933-4," Series VI, Box 2, Folder 7, HREC Records.

25. See W. Calvin Dickinson and Patrick D. Reagan, "Business, Labor, and the Blue Eagle: The Harriman Hosiery Mills Strike, 1933–1934," *Tennessee Historical Quarterly* 55 (1996): 240–55; James A. Hodges, *New Deal Labor Policy and the Southern Cotton Textile Industry, 1933–1941* (Knoxville: University of Tennessee Press, 1986).

26. "Highlander Folk School Summer School Report and Summary of other Reports of Other Educational Activities, September 1933-4," Series VI, Box 2, Folder 7, HREC Records.

27. "Highlander Folk School Summer School Report and Summary of other Reports of Other Educational Activities, September 1933-4"; "Play to be Given," *Fighting Eaglet* 2 (June 1934): 2, Folder 11, Box 61, HREC Records.

28. "Play to be Given," *Fighting Eaglet* 2 (June 1934): 2, Folder 11, Box 61, HREC Records; "Concerning Workers' Education," Folder 11, Box 61, HREC Records. The plays were titled either "Charity" or "Restless Feet" according to notes by Myles Horton, but no documentation exists confirming these titles. "Analytical Record of Student Activities," handwritten notes, Folder 11, Box 61, HREC Records.

29. See Chapter 3 and Richard J. Altenbaugh, *Education for Struggle: The American Labor Colleges of the 1920s and 1930s* (Philadelphia: Temple University Press, 1990).

30. Aimee Horton, "The Highlander Folk School," 57.

31. Petty, "Dramatic Activities and Workers' Education," 82.

32. "Labor Chautauqua: Plays, Mass Recitations, Songs by and for Workers," n.d., Brookwood Labor College Players, Folder 1, Box 58, HREC Records.

33. Ibid.

34. Elizabeth Hawes, "Mopping It Up," Folder 4, Box 57, HREC Records. There are two unpublished versions in the file. I reference the version with handwritten notes.

35. Ibid., 1.

36. Ibid., 6.

37. Ibid.

38. Zilphia Horton's work in folk music and music-based arts activism is well

documented and has been examined in great detail. See Carter, "The Singing Heart"; Alicia Ruth Massie-Legg, "Zilphia Horton, a Voice for Change," Ph.D. dissertation, University of Kentucky, 2014; Julia Schmidt-Pirro and Karen M. McCurdy, "Employing Music in the Cause of Social Justice: Ruth Crawford Seeger and Zilphia Horton," *Voices* 31, nos. 1–2 (2005): 32; and the numerous historical studies of Highlander Folk School.

39. Carter, "The Singing Heart," 5.

40. Massie-Legg, "Zilphia Horton," 63.

41. "One Slain in Flareup at Hosiery Mill Strike," *Chicago Daily Tribune*, Feb. 4, 1935, 12.

42. Glen, *Highlander,* 38.

43. Ibid.; Aimee Horton, "The Highlander Folk School," 123.

44. Aimee Horton, "The Highlander Folk School."

45. Letter to Coy, April 17, 1935, Folder 1, Box 58, HREC Records; Hazel Cunard, *We Ain't a-Goin' Back* (Barnesville, Ohio: Socialist Party of Ohio, 1934).

46. Letter to Coy.

47. "Report on Summer Activities," Folder 11, Box 61, HREC Records.

48. Zilphia Horton, Letter to Myles Horton, Nov. 1934, Box 1, Folder 2, Myles Horton Papers, HREC Records.

49. Editorial, *New Theatre* 1, no. 8 (Sept. 1934): 4; Douglas McDermott, "New Theatre School 1932–1942," *Speech Teacher* 14, no. 4 (Nov. 1965): 278–85.

50. McDermott, "New Theatre School 1932–1942," 283.

51. Ibid.

52. Ibid., 280.

53. Ibid., 283.

54. Lee Baxandall, "Brecht in America, 1935," *TDR* 12, no. 1 (1967): 69–87, doi:10.2307/1125294.

55. Colette A. Hyman, *Staging Strikes: Workers' Theatre and the American Labor Movement* (Philadelphia: Temple University Press, 1997).

56. Ibid. Fannia M. Cohn, "Social Drama: A Technique for Workers' Education," *Workers' Education Quarterly*, 1934, Folder 6, Box 7, Cohn Papers, Kheel Center for Labor-Management Documentation and Archives at M. P. Catherwood Library, Cornell University; Fannia M. Cohn, "The Workers' University of the International Ladies' Garment Workers' Union," *Life and Labor* (March 1920): 73–77.

57. Petty, "Dramatic Activities and Workers' Education," 100.

58. Massie-Legg, "Zilphia Horton," 65.

59. "Mock Anti-Labor Convention," *Our Verdict*, Feb. 5, 1936, Folder 11, Box 61, HREC Records.

60. "What's Taught—A Class Review," *Lookout*, June 7, 1936, 4, Folder 11, Box 61, HREC Records.

61. The Highlander Folk School," pamphlet, 1936, Folder 11, Box 61, HREC Records.

62. Erik S. Gellman and Jarod Roll, *The Gospel of the Working Class: Labor's Southern Prophets in New Deal America* (Champaign: University of Illinois Press, 2011); Donald H. Grubs, *Cry from the Cotton: The Southern Tenant Farmers' Union and the New Deal* (Little Rock: University of Arkansas Press, 1971); Jerold S. Auerbach, "Southern Tenant Farmers: Socialist Critics of the New Deal," *Labor History* 7, no. 1 (Jan. 1, 1966): 3–18, doi:10.1080/00236566608583975.

63. "Highlander Activities—1936," unpublished notes, 1936, Folder 11, Box 61, HREC Records.

64. Ibid.

65. "Songs," unpublished notes, Folder 11, Box 61, HREC Records.

66. "The Men Behind the Man Behind the Guns," unpublished script, Folder 2, Box 58, HREC Records.

67. "1st Worker (man)," untitled and unpublished skit, Folder 2, Box 58, HREC Records.

68. *Gumbo,* Highlander Folk School, n.d., Folder 1, Box 57, HREC Records.

69. Ibid., 4.

70. Ibid.

71. Ibid., 9.

72. Ibid.

73. Ibid.

74. Paul Green, *In Abraham's Bosom* (London: Allen & Unwin, 1929).

75. Lee Hays, Letter to Zilphia Horton, Folder 2, Box 58, HREC Records.

76. Ibid.

77. Ibid.

78. Aimee Horton, "The Highlander Folk School," 130.

79. Ibid.

80. "Highlander Folk School Review," Series 2, Folder 1, Box 2, Folder 1. HREC, 4.

81. Ibid.; Petty, "Dramatic Activities and Workers' Education," 106.

82. "Highlander Folk School Review," Series 2, Folder 1, Box 2, Folder 1. HREC, 4. Leo Huberman, *The Labor Spy Racket* (New York: Modern Age Books, 1937).

83. Ibid.

84. Ibid., 17–18.

85. Ruby Norris, *Labor Spy,* 7–8, Highlander Folk School, Folder 3, Box 57; Huberman, *The Labor Spy Racket.*

86. See Robert P. Weiss, "Private Detective Agencies and Labour Discipline in the United States, 1855–1946," *Historical Journal* 29, no. 1 (1986): 87–107.

87. Norris, *Labor Spy,* 4.

88. Ibid., 7.

89. Ibid., 10–11.

90. Ibid., 11.

91. Jean Carter, *Annotated List of Labor Plays* (New York: Affiliated Schools for Workers, 1938).

92. Arthur Vandenberg, qtd. in Milton Plesur, "The Republican Congressional Comeback of 1938," *Review of Politics* 24, no. 4 (1962): 525–62.

93. Alan Brinkley, *The End of Reform: New Deal Liberalism in Recession and War* (New York: Knopf Doubleday, 2011).

94. *Five Plays About Labor: Highlander Folk School* (Monteagle, TN: Highlander Folk School. Aug. 1939). Box 2, Eveline M. Burns Collection, Kheel Center for Labor-Management Documentation and Archives, M. P. Catherwood Library, Cornell University.

95. Ibid., 42–47.

96. Zilphia Horton, "Drama Workshop Report," 1939, 8, File 3, Box 58, HREC Records.

97. Petty, "Dramatic Activities and Workers' Education," 116–17.

98. *Five Plays About Labor,* 2; Aimee Horton, "The Highlander Folk School," 150–55.

99. Zilphia Horton, "Drama Workshop Report," 1939, 8.

100. Ibid.

101. Ibid., 2.

102. "News of the Screen," *New York Times,* June 2, 1938, 18.

103. "The Screen Calendar," *New York Times,* Oct. 9, 1938, 4; "Program for Today at the World's Fair," *New York Times,* July 5, 1940, 11.

104. John McDougal Burns, "Highlander School Uses Drama with Students to Spread Communism Doctrine in Tennessee," *Nashville Tennessean,* Oct. 19, 1939. "Highlander Folk School," Federal Bureau of Investigation, File 61-7511.

105. "Highlander Folk School," Federal Bureau of Investigation, File 61-7511.

106. She accidentally ingested carbon tetrachloride, typewriter cleaning fluid. See Massie-Legg, "Zilphia Horton," 79–80; Glen, *Highlander,* 138.

Chapter 6

Epigraphs: Lee Hays, "Dramatics at Commonwealth Must Serve Needs and Aspirations of Labor Audience," *Commonwealth College Fortnightly,* Jan. 15, 1938, 2. Fred Halford, Memorandum, Oct. 22, 1940, "Special Agent in Charge (Arkansas) to Special Agent in Charge (New York), Re: New Theatre League (formerly Commonwealth College); Mena, Arkansas; INTERNAL SECURITY," Bureau File 61-6156-13. Federal Bureau of Investigation.

1. Ruskin College, named after John Ruskin, was a British workers' college formed in 1899 in Oxford. It became a model for workers' education. See Valerie Quinney, "Workers' Education: A Confrontation at Ruskin College," *Journal of Education* (1983): 52–78.

2. See William Cobb's discussion for additional detail about the school's founding (36–45) and his discussion of life as a Commoner (111–26). William Cobb, *Radical Education in the Rural South: Commonwealth College, 1922–1940* (Detroit: Wayne State University Press, 2000).

3. Ibid., 111.

4. Ibid., 113; See additional discussion about Commonwealth's daily goings-on in Charlotte and Raymond Koch, *Educational Commune: The Story of Commonwealth College* (New York: Schocken Books, 1972).

5. Fulks, qtd. in Cobb, *Radical Education*, 115.

6. "On Being a Commonwealth Teacher," *Commonwealth College Fortnightly*, Nov. 15, 1933, 2.

7. See Foster Rhea Dulles and Melvyn Dubofsky, *Labor in America: A History* (Chicago: Harlan Davidson, 1993), 315–17; Mel van Elteren, *Labor and the American Left: An Analytical History* (Jefferson, NC: McFarland, 2011), 80–82.

8. By 1937, Communist Party members held leadership positions in roughly 40 percent of CIO-affiliated unions. Philip Dray, *There Is Power in a Union* (New York: Anchor, 2010), 444–45; Dulles and Dubofsky, *Labor in America*, 315; van Elteren, *Labor and the American Left*, 78–80.

9. Cobb, *Radical Education*, 173.

10. "Bearing False Witness from the Pulpit," *Commonwealth College Fortnightly*, Dec. 1, 1936, 2–3; "The One Man Circus," *Commonwealth College Fortnightly*, Jan. 1, 1937, 1, 4; "Preaches Violent Sermons," *Commonwealth College Fortnightly*, Jan. 15, 1937, 2.

11. "The One Man Circus," 1; "Preaches," 2.

12. "The One Man Circus," 4.

13. Luther D. Summers, "Communism and Commonwealth College Unmasked," pamphlet, Box 4, Clay Fulks Collection, Commonwealth College Collections. My emphasis added.

14. Ibid., 11.

15. A substantial portion of the testimony's transcript appears in in Cobb, 149–53.

16. The school had previously been targeted by Representative Gooch via a failed sedition bill in 1935. "Preaches," 2.

17. Cobb, *Radical Education*, 167; Koch and Koch, *Educational Commune*, 187–95.

18. Cobb, *Radical Education*, 172; Koch and Koch, *Educational Commune*, 196–200.

19. "Williams Active in State for Past Seven Years," *Commonwealth College Fortnightly*, Aug. 15, 1937, 4.

20. "Announce Reorganization: Claude Williams Elected Director," *Commonwealth College Fortnightly*, Aug. 15, 1937, 1.

21. Koch and Koch, *Educational Commune*, 197.

22. "Society News," *Commonwealth College Fortnightly*, Jan. 15, 1926, 2; "Student-Workers Give Japanese Play," *Commonwealth College Fortnightly*, March 16, 1926, 1; "School Stages Russian Play in Final Dramatics Program," *Commonwealth College Fortnightly*, May 1, 1926, 2.

23. "Irish Play Features Monthly Theatrical," *Commonwealth College Fortnightly*, Dec. 15, 1927, 1.

24. Ibid.

25. "Party Ends Happy Thanksgiving Day," *Commonwealth College Fortnightly,* Dec. 15, 1927, 1, 4; "Students Sing and Satirize," *Commonwealth College Fortnightly,* Jan. 1, 1927, 11; "Seminar Opened by Greek Drama Talk," *Commonwealth College Fortnightly,* Feb. 1, 1929, 1.

26. "Zeuch Protest Sets Commons A-Twitter," *Commonwealth College Fortnightly,* Feb. 15, 1929, 1.

27. "Program for 1929–30 at Commonwealth," *Commonwealth College Fortnightly,* April 1, 1929, 1; "Courses for New Quarter," *Commonwealth College Fortnightly,* Dec. 1, 1929, 3.

28. "For Services Rendered," *Commonwealth College Fortnightly,* March 1, 1929, 1.

29. "Commonwealth College: Suggested Three-Year Course of Study," *Commonwealth College Fortnightly,* Dec. 1, 1931, 2–3.

30. Ibid.

31. Cobb, *Radical Education,* 135.

32. "Three New Courses Offered for Spring," *Commonwealth College Fortnightly,* April 1, 1933, 1, 4.

33. "Commonwealth College Summer Session," *Commonwealth College Fortnightly,* May 15, 1934, 3–4.

34. "Quarter to Begin Monday, October 1," *Commonwealth College Fortnightly,* Sept. 1, 1934, 1.

35. "'Lock-Step' Opponent Views Commonwealth," *Commonwealth College Fortnightly,* Feb. 15, 1927, 1–2.

36. "Helen Marcel Bellman" *Commonwealth College Fortnightly,* Aug. 15, 1927, 2.

37. "Three New Courses Offered for Spring," *Commonwealth College Fortnightly.* April 1, 1933, 1, 4.

38. "Catalog Supplement, 1933–34," *Commonwealth College Fortnightly,* July 15, 1933, 2–7.

39. Sis Cunningham was one of the few Arkansan students. She later became a famous folk singer in her own right. "Neighbors View Efforts of Amateur Dramatics," *Commonwealth College Fortnightly,* Feb. 1, 1932, 1, 4; "Drama of Jobless Is Presented at College," *Commonwealth College Fortnightly,* June 1, 1932, 1–2; "Commoner's Comment," *Commonwealth College Fortnightly,* Aug. 15, 1932, 3.

40. "Ben Low to Direct Dramatics," *Commonwealth College Fortnightly,* Jan. 1, 1935, 2.

41. "Myra Page Comes to Commonwealth," *Commonwealth College Fortnightly,* Sept. 15, 1935, 1, 4.

42. Peter Frye, "Commonwealth Courses: Labor Drama," *Commonwealth College Fortnightly,* Oct. 15, 1935, 2, 4.

43. Ibid.

44. Ibid.

45. Brooks Atkinson, "Waiting for Lefty," *New York Times,* Feb. 11, 1935.

46. As an example of Fulks's commitment to drama, in 1930, he asked for and received a seven-month leave to manage a little theatre in Tulsa, OK. Clay Fulks, "Labor Dramatics at Commonwealth," *Commonwealth College Fortnightly*, Oct. 15, 1935, 4; "Fulks Hits Broadway," *Commonwealth College Fortnightly*, March 15, 1930, 2.

47. Fulks, "Labor Dramatics at Commonwealth," 4.

48. Ibid.

49. Ibid.

50. Ibid.

51. In an interview in 2012, his wife, English actress Thelma Ruby, asserted that Frye had never mentioned any theatre in Arkansas and that I likely had my Peter Fryes confused. However, Frye makes brief mention of his time at Commonwealth in his autobiography. Peter Frye and Thelma Ruby, *Double or Nothing* (London: Janus Publishing, 1997), 74–75.

52. "Drama Group Performs," *Commonwealth College Fortnightly*, Dec. 1, 1935, 4.

53. Alexander later founded the Bay Area Actors' Laboratory, which, like its more famous sibling, the Hollywood-based Actors' Lab, came under fire during the McCarthy era for teaching communist philosophies. "Communist Infiltration of the Motion Picture Industry, 1948, 1951–52," Hearing, House Un-American Activities Committee, Los Angeles, Federal Bureau of Investigation, Bureau File 100-325-22; "Students to Improvise Campus Entertainments," *Commonwealth College Fortnightly*, July 15, 1936, 3.

54. Hays, qtd. in Doris Willens, *Lonesome Traveler: The Life of Lee Hays* (Lincoln: University of Nebraska Press–Bison Books, 1993), 14.

55. Ibid.

56. Jim Capaldi, "Wasn't That a Time: A Conversation with Lee Hays," *Sing Out! The Folk Song Magazine*, 28, no. 5 (Oct. 1979), 2–5; Hays, qtd. in Willens, *Lonesome Traveler*, 20.

57. Willens, *Lonesome Traveler*, 60.

58. Capaldi, "Wasn't That a Time," 3.

59. Jean Carter, *Annotated List of Labor Plays* (New York: Affiliated Schools for Workers, 1938), 3.

60. "Arkansan Will Lead Labor Drama," *Commonwealth College Fortnightly*, Sept. 1, 1937, 2.

61. Lee Hays, "Workers' Dramatics," *Commonwealth College Fortnightly*, Sept. 1, 1937, 2.

62. Ibid.

63. Ibid.

64. Hays, qtd. in Robert Cochran, "'All the Songs in the World': The Story of Emma Dusenbury," *Arkansas Historical Quarterly* 44 (Spring 1985): 3–15, doi :10.2307/40027722.

65. "Dramatics Teacher Asks for Copies of Play Scripts," *Commonwealth College Fortnightly*, Oct. 15, 1937, 2.

66. "Plays Contributed in Response to Appeal," *Commonwealth College Fortnightly*, Jan. 1, 1938, 3.

67. "Director and Industrial Manager Visiting East," *Commonwealth College Fortnightly*, Nov. 1, 1937, 4.

68. "Dramatics Class Offers Skit by Florence Lasser," *Commonwealth College Fortnightly*, Nov. 15, 1937, 2.

69. Lee Hays, "Ninety-Seven Cents: A play written by students of Commonwealth College and presented by them December 4, at their college," *Commonwealth College Fortnightly*, 15 Dec. 15, 1937, 2–4.

70. Ibid.

71. Ibid.

72. See *Pins and Needles, In Union There Is Strength, Singing Jailbirds*, and *Waiting for Lefty*.

73. "Ninety-Seven," 3.

74. Ibid.

75. Ibid., 2.

76. Ibid., 4.

77. "Dramatics Class," 4.

78. "Two Classes Added as New Term Opens," *Commonwealth College Fortnightly*, Jan. 15, 1938, 1, 4.

79. "Dramatics Class," 2.

80. Ibid.

81. Ibid.

82. Ibid. My emphasis added.

83. Ibid.

84. Ibid.

85. Ibid., 2–3. "From 97¢ to Hushpuppy: Report of the Dramatics Director to the Second Annual Meeting of the Commonwealth College Association," Feb. 26, 1939, St. John Collection, Commonwealth College Collections.

86. Ibid., 2.

87. Ibid., 2.

88. Ibid., 1. Emphasis his.

89. Ibid., 2.

90. Ibid., 1.

91. Ibid., 2.

92. Lee Hays, "Toby," *Commoner*, Nov. 1938, 4.

93. Ibid., 4; Hays, "From 97¢ to Hushpuppy," 2.

94. Hays, "From 97¢ to Hushpuppy," 2.

95. Ibid., 5.

96. Ibid., 3.

97. Ibid.

98. Ibid.

99. Ibid., 4.

100. "Quarter to Begin Monday, October 1," *Commonwealth College Fortnightly*, Sept. 1, 1934, 1; "Around the Campus," *Commoner*, May 1938, 2.

101. "Backgrounds of Newcomers Include Varied Interests," *Commoner*, May 1938, 1.

102. "Marionettes for Unions," unpublished pamphlet, Commonwealth College, n.d., St. John Collection, Commonwealth College Collections.

103. "Dramatic Program to Include Puppet Work," *Commoner*, May 1938, 1.

104. Ibid.

105. Koch and Koch, *Educational Commune*, 198.

106. "Association Elects New Officers," *Commoner*, Sept.–Oct. 1939, 1.

107. Halford, Memorandum, Oct. 22, 1940, 2.

108. Lee Hays, "It Wasn't Easy," *People's Songs Bulletin*, Feb.–March 1948, 11–5.

109. Lee Hays, "Space Cantata," unpublished playtext, Box 5; "Corey," unpublished playtext, Box 5, Lee Hays Collection. Ralph Rinzler Folklife Archives and Collections, Center for Folklife and Cultural Heritage, Smithsonian Institution, Washington, DC.

Conclusion

1. "Minutes from Workers' Drama Conference," n.d., Box 10, Folder 19 (Theatre Institute), Brookwood Labor College Collection. Archives for Urban and Labor Affairs at Walter Reuther Library, Wayne State University.

2. See Manon van de Water's articles, "Constructed Narratives: Situating Theatre for Young Audiences in the United States," *Youth Theatre Journal* 14, no. 1 (2000): 101–13, and "Constance D'Arcy Mackay: A Historiographical Perspective," *Youth Theatre Journal* 9, no. 1 (1995): 79–91; Roger Bedard and John Tolch, *Spotlight on the Child* (New York: Greenwood Press, 1989); and Roger Bedard, "The Cultural Construction of Theatre for Children and Young Audiences: A Captive Eddy of Recursive Harmonies," *Youth Theatre Journal* 23, no. 1 (2009): 22–29, https://doi.org/10.1080/08929090902851551, for examples of essays that look critically at the historiographical conservatism present in studies of theatre for youth.

BIBLIOGRAPHY

Archival Collections

American Labor Education Service Records, 1927–1962. Kheel Center for Labor-Management Documentation and Archives at M. P. Catherwood Library, Cornell University (cited as ALES Records).

Archives held at the Highlander Research and Educational Center, New Market, TN (cited as HREC Archive).

Brookwood Labor College Collection. Archives for Urban and Labor Affairs at Walter Reuther Library. Wayne State University (cited as Brookwood Collection).

Claude Williams Papers. Archives for Urban and Labor Affairs, Walter Reuther Library, Wayne State University, Detroit, MI.

Commonwealth College Collections, University of Arkansas (cited as Commonwealth Collection).

Cornelia Barker Papers. Manuscript Archives and Rare Book Library, Robert W. Woodruff Library, Emory University.

Eleanor Gwinnell Coit Papers, 1913–1974. Five College Archives & Manuscript Collections. Smith College, Northampton, MA.

Ernest E. Schwarztrauber Papers, 1894–1953. Wisconsin Historical Society, University of Wisconsin–Madison (cited as Schwarztrauber Papers).

Eveline Burns Collection. Kheel Center for Labor-Management Documentation and Archives at M. P. Catherwood Library, Cornell University.

Highlander Collection. Tennessee State Library and Archives.

Highlander Research and Education Center Records, 1917–2005. Wisconsin Historical Society, University of Wisconsin–Madison (cited as HREC Records).

Lee Hays Collection. Ralph Rinzler Folklife Archives and Collections Center for Folklife and Cultural Heritage, Smithsonian Institution. Washington, DC (cited as Lee Hays Collection).

Papers of the MacKaye Family, 1751–1990. Rauner Special Collections Library, Dartmouth College (cited as MacKaye Family Papers).

Portland Civic Theatre Records, Oregon Historical Society.

Portland Labor Temple Records, Oregon Historical Society.

Southern Historical Collection and the North Carolina Collections. Wilson Library, University of North Carolina at Chapel Hill.

Selected Works

Adams, Frank T. "Highlander Folk School: Getting Information, Going Back and Teaching It." *Harvard Educational Review* 42, no. 4 (Dec. 1, 1972): 497–520.

———. *James A. Dombrowski: An American Heretic, 1897–1983*. Knoxville: University of Tennessee Press, 1992.

Ahrens, Gale, ed. *Lucy Parsons: Freedom, Equality & Solidarity: Writings and Speeches, 1878–1937*. Chicago: Charles H. Kerr, 2004.

Altenbaugh, Richard J. "'The Children of a Militant Labor Progressivism': Brookwood Labor College and the American Labor College Movement of the 1920s and 1930s." *History of Education Society* 23, no. 4 (1983): 395–411, http://www.jstor.org/stable/368076.

———. *Education for Struggle: The American Labor Colleges of the 1920s and 1930s*. Philadelphia: Temple University Press, 1990.

———. "Proletarian Drama: An Educational Tool of the American Labor College Movement." *Theatre Journal* 34, no. 2 (1982): 197–210, http://www.jstor.org/stable/3207450.

Altenbaugh, Richard, and Rolland G. Paulston. "Work People's College: A Finnish Folk High School in the American Labor College Movement." *Paedagogica Historica, International Journal of the History of Education* 18 (1978): 238–56, http://dx.doi.org/10.1080/0030923780180201.

"American Fund for Public Service Records, 1922–1941." New York Public Library. http://archives.nypl.org/mss/74.

Ashbaugh, Carolyn. *Lucy Parsons: An American Revolutionary*. Chicago: Haymarket Books, 2013.

Auerbach, Jerold S. "Southern Tenant Farmers: Socialist Critics of the New Deal." *Labor History* 7, no. 1 (Jan. 1, 1966): 3–18, https://doi.org/10.1080/00236566608583975.

Baker, Jean H. *Sisters: The Lives of America's Suffragists*. New York: Hill and Wang, 2006.

Balser, Diane. *Sisterhood and Solidarity: Feminism and Labor in Modern Times*. Boston: South End Press, 1987.

Barrow, Clyde W. "Counter-Movement within the Labor Movement: Workers' Education and the American Federation of Labor, 1900–1937." *Social Science Journal* 27, no. 4 (Jan. 1, 1990): 395–417, https://doi.org/10.1016/0362-3319(90)90015-C.

———. "Playing Workers: Proletarian Drama in the Curriculum of American Labor Colleges, 1921–1937." *Journal of Arts Management and Law* 20, no. 4 (1991): 5–29, https://doi.org/10.1080/07335113.1991.9942865.

———. "Playing Workers: Proletarian Drama in the Curriculum of American Labor Colleges, 1921–37." In *Paying the Piper: Causes and Consequences of Art Patronage*, edited by Judith H. Balfe, 94–118. Urbana: University of Illinois Press, 1993.

Baxandall, Lee. "Brecht in America, 1935." *TDR (1967–1968)* 12, no. 1 (1967): 69–87, https://doi:10.2307/1125294.

Bedard, Roger L. "The Cultural Construction of Theatre for Children and Young Audiences: A Captive Eddy of Recursive Harmonies." *Youth Theatre Journal* 23, no. 1 (2009): 22–29, https://doi.org/10.1080/0892 9090902851551.

Bedard, Roger L., and C. John Tolch. *Spotlight on the Child: Studies in the History of American Children's Theatre.* New York: Greenwood Press, 1989.

Bittner, Egon. "Radicalism and the Organization of Radical Movements." *American Sociological Review* 28, no. 6 (1963): 928–40, http://www.jstor.org.ezproxy1.lib. asu.edu/stable/2090312.

Black, Cheryl. *The Women of Provincetown, 1915–1922.* Tuscaloosa: University of Alabama Press, 2002.

Blair, Karen J. "Pageantry for Women's Rights: The Career of Hazel MacKaye, 1913–1923." *Theatre Survey* 31 (1990): 23–46, http://dx.doi.org/10.1017/S004 055740000096X.

Bloom, Jonathan D. "Brookwood Labor College: The Final Years, 1933–1937." *Labor's Heritage* 2, no. 2 (1990): 24–43.

Boisvert, Raymond D. *John Dewey: Rethinking Our Time.* New York: SUNY Press, 1998.

Boris, Eileen, and Annelise Orleck. "Feminism and the Labor Movement: A Century of Collaboration and Conflict." *New Labor Forum* 20 (2011): 33–41.

Brinkley, Alan. *The End of Reform: New Deal Liberalism in Recession and War.* New York: Knopf Doubleday, 2011.

Brody, David. *In Labor's Cause: Main Themes on the History of the American Worker.* New York: Oxford University Press, 1993.

———. *Labor Embattled: History, Power, Rights.* Urbana: University of Illinois Press, 2005.

———. "The Old Labor History and the New: In Search of an American Working Class." *Labor History* 20. no. 1 (1979): 111–26, https://doi.org/10.1080 /00236567908584522.

———. "Radical Labor History and Rank-and-File Militancy." *Labor History* 16, no. 1 (1975): 117–26, https://doi.org/10.1080/00236567508584325.

Brovkin, Vladimir N. *Russia After Lenin: Politics, Culture and Society, 1921–1929.* East Sussex: Psychology Press, 1998.

Calhoun, Arthur. "The Place of Dramatics in the Promotion and Maintenance of Workers' Education." *The Promotion and Maintenance of Workers' Education: Third Annual Conference of Teachers in Workers' Education at Brookwood, February 19–22, 1926.* Local No. 189 of American Federation of Teachers. N.d.

———. "The Social Significance of Labor Dramatics." *Workers' Education* (May 1926): 18–20.

Camp, Miriam Bonner. Interview with Mary Frederickson. #4007 (1976).

Southern Oral History Program Collection, Southern Historical Collection, Wilson Library, University of North Carolina at Chapel Hill.

Canning, Charlotte. *The Most American Thing in America: Circuit Chautauqua as Performance.* Iowa City: University of Iowa Press, 2005.

Capaldi, Jim. "Wasn't That a Time: A Conversation with Lee Hays." *Sing Out! The Folk Song Magazine* 28, no. 5 (Oct. 1979): 2–5.

Carter (Ogden), Jean, and Jesse Ogden. *Everyman's Drama: A Study of the Noncommercial Theatre in the United States.* New York: American Association for Adult Education, 1938.

———. *The Play Book: An Elementary Book on Stage Technique with Nine Plays of Various Types and Some Suggestions for Creative Use of Plays and Playing.* San Diego: Harcourt, Brace and Company, 1937.

Carter, Vicki K. "The Singing Heart of Highlander Folk School." *New Horizons in Adult Education and Human Resource Development* 8, no. 2 (1994): 4–24, https://doi.org/10.1002/nha3.10061.

Chambers, Jonathan. Review of *Staging Strikes: Workers' Theatre and the American Labor Movement* by Collette Hyman. *Theatre History Studies* 19 (1999): 200–202.

Chansky, Dorothy. *Composing Ourselves: The Little Theatre Movement and the American Audience.* Carbondale: Southern Illinois University Press, 2005.

Chappell, Drew. "Constructions of Revolt of the Beavers and Notions of the Child Audience: Controversy in the Federal Theatre Project." *Youth Theatre Journal* 21, no. 1 (2007): 41–53, https://doi.org/10.1080/08929092.2007.10012595.

"Chronology of IWW History." Industrial Workers of the World, http://www.iww.org/en/history/chronology. Accessed Aug. 15, 2018.

Cobb, William H. *Radical Education in the Rural South: Commonwealth College, 1922–1940.* Detroit: Wayne State University Press, 2000.

Cochran, Robert. "'All the Songs in the World': The Story of Emma Dusenbury." *Arkansas Historical Quarterly* 44 (Spring 1985): 3–15, https://doi.org/10.2307/40027722.

Cocks, Catherine, Peter Holloran, and Alan Lessof. *Historical Dictionary of the Progressive Era.* Lanham, MD: Scarecrow Press, 2009.

Cohn, Fannia M. "Social Drama: A Technique for Workers' Education." *Workers' Education Quarterly,* 1934 Cohn Papers, Folder 6, Box 7, Kheel Center for Labor-Management Documentation and Archives at M. P. Catherwood Library, Cornell University.

———. "The Workers' University of the International Ladies' Garment Workers' Union." *Life and Labor* (March 1920): 73–77.

"Communist Infiltration of the Motion Picture Industry, 1948, 1951–52." Hearing. House Un-American Activities Committee. Los Angeles. Federal Bureau of Investigation. Bureau File 100-325-22.

Cook, Alice Hanson. *Lifetime of Labor: The Autobiography of Alice H. Cook.* New York: Feminist Press at CUNY, 2000.

Cort, John. "Labor's Glass House." *Commonweal* (Apr. 4, 1958), 14–15.

Crabtree, Fount F. "The Wilder Coal Strike of 1932–33." Master's thesis, George Peabody College for Teachers, 1937.

Crain, Marion. "Feminizing Unions: Challenging the Gendered Structure of Wage Labor." *Michigan Law Review* 89, no. 5 (1991): 1155–1221, https://doi.org /10.2307/1289551.

Cunard, Hazel. *We Ain't a-Goin' Back.* Barnesville, Ohio: Socialist Party of Ohio, 1934.

Dail, Chrystyna. *Stage for Action: U.S. Social Activist Theatre in the 1940s.* Carbondale: Southern Illinois University Press, 2016.

Dawley, Alan. *Struggles for Justice: Social Responsibility and the Liberal State.* Cambridge: Harvard University Press, 1991.

De Man, Henry. "Labor's Challenge to Education." *New Republic* (March 2, 1921), 16–18.

Denning, Michael. *The Cultural Front: The Laboring of American Culture in the Twentieth Century.* New York: Verso, 1998.

Dewey, John. *Art as Experience.* New York: Minton, Balch and Company, 1934.

———. *Democracy and Education: An Introduction to the Philosophy of Education.* New York: Macmillan, 1922.

———. *Education and Experience.* New York: Macmillan, 1938.

———. *Individualism, Old and New.* New York: Minton, Balch and Company, 1930.

———. *Liberalism and Social Action.* New York: Putnam, 1963.

———. *The Public and Its Problems.* Athens, Ohio: Swallow Press, 1954.

Dickinson, Calvin, and Patrick D. Reagan, "Business, Labor, and the Blue Eagle: The Harriman Hosiery Mills Strike, 1933–1934." *Tennessee Historical Quarterly* 55 (1996): 240–55.

"Dramatics." *Mountain Top News* 1, no. 4 (July 21, 1935).

Dray, Philip. *There Is Power in a Union.* New York: Anchor, 2010.

Dubofsky, Melvyn. *The State and Labor in Modern America.* Chapel Hill: University of North Carolina Press, 1994.

Dubofsky, Melvyn, and Joseph Anthony McCartin. *We Shall Be All: A History of the Industrial Workers of the World.* Urbana: University of Illinois Press, 2000.

Duffy, Susan. *American Labor on Stage: Dramatic Interpretations of the Steel and Textile Industries in the 1930s.* Westport, CT: Greenwood Press, 1996.

Dulles, Foster Rhea, and Melvyn Dubofsky. *Labor in America: A History.* Chicago: Harlan Davidson, 1993.

Dunsany, Lord. *Five Plays.* Holicong, PA: Wildside Press, 2002.

Dwyer, Richard. "Workers' Education, Labor Education, Labor Studies: An Historical Delineation." *Review of Educational Research* 47, no. 1 (1977): 179–207, http:// www.jstor.org/stable/1169973.

Egbert, Donald Drew. *Social Radicalism and the Arts, Western Europe: A Cultural History from the French Revolution to 1968.* New York: Knopf, 1970.

Ellwood, David T., and Glenn Fine. "The Impact of Right-to-Work Laws on Union Organizing." *Journal of Political Economy* 95, no. 2 (1987): 250–73.

Elteren, Mel van. *Labor and the American Left: An Analytical History*. Jefferson, NC: McFarland, 2011.

Evans, Alice. "Waiting for Lefty." *New Theatre*, April 1935.

Fearnow, Mark. *The American Stage and the Great Depression: A Cultural History of the Grotesque*. Cambridge: Cambridge University Press, 1997.

Finan, Christopher. *From the Palmer Raids to the Patriot Act: A History of the Fight for Free Speech in America*. Boston: Beacon Press, 2007.

Five Plays About Labor: Highlander Folk School. Monteagle, TN: Highlander Folk School, Aug. 1939. Box 2. Eveline M. Burns Collection. Kheel Center for Labor-Management Documentation and Archives, M. P. Catherwood Library, Cornell University.

Flanagan, Hallie. *Arena*. New York: Duell, Sloan, and Pearce, 1940.

———. *Shifting Scenes of the Modern European Theatre*. New York: B. Blom, 1972.

Flanagan, Hallie, Margaret Ellen Clifford, and Whittaker Chambers. *Can You Hear Their Voices? A Play of Our Time*. Experimental Theatre of Vassar College, 1931.

Flood, Gerhard Rangvald. "History and Educational Program of the Portland Labor College." Master's thesis, Oregon State University, 1940.

Folino White, Anne. *Plowed Under: Food Policy Protests and Performance in New Deal America*. Bloomington: Indiana University Press, 2015.

Foner, Philip Sheldon. *Women and the American Labor Movement: From the First Trade Unions to the Present*. New York: Free Press, 1982.

Frederickson, Mary. "Recognizing Regional Differences: The Southern Summer School for Women Workers." In *Sisterhood and Solidarity: Workers' Education for Women, 1914–1984*, edited by Joyce L. Kornbluh and Mary Frederickson, 147–82. Philadelphia: Temple University Press, 1984.

Friedman, Bonchi. *Miners*. In *Staged Action: Six Plays from the American Workers' Theatre*, edited by Lee Papa, 159–84. Ithaca: ILR Press, 2009.

Frye, Peter. "Commonwealth Courses: Labor Drama." *Commonwealth College Fortnightly*, Oct. 15, 1935, 2, 4.

Frye, Peter, and Thelma Ruby. *Double or Nothing*. London: Janus, 1997.

Fuoss, Kirk. *Striking Performances: Performing Strikes*. Jackson: University Press of Mississippi, 1997.

Gall, Gregor. *Sex Worker Unionization: Global Developments, Challenges and Possibilities*. London: Palgrave Macmillan UK, 2016.

Gellman, Erik S., and Jarod Roll. *The Gospel of the Working Class: Labor's Southern Prophets in New Deal America*. Urbana: University of Illinois Press, 2011.

Gilmore, Glenda Elizabeth. *Defying Dixie: The Radical Roots of Civil Rights, 1919–1950*. New York: W. W. Norton, 2008.

Glaspell, Susan Keating. *The People*. In *The People and Close the Book: Two One-act Plays*. New York: Frank Shay, 1918.

Glassberg, David. *American Historical Pageantry: The Uses of Tradition in the Early Twentieth Century*. Chapel Hill: University of North Carolina Press, 1990.

Glen, John M. *Highlander: No Ordinary School, 1932–1962*. Lexington: University Press of Kentucky, 1988.

Goldman, Harry, and Mel Gordon. "Workers' Theatre in America: A Survey 1913–1978." *Journal of American Culture* 1, no. 1 (1978): 169–81, https://doi.org/10.1111/j.1542-734X.1978.0101_169.

Green, Paul. *In Abraham's Bosom*. London: Allen & Unwin, 1929.

Grubbs, Donald H. *Cry from the Cotton: The Southern Tenant Farmers' Union and the New Deal*. Chapel Hill: University of North Carolina Press, 1971.

Gutman, Herbert G. *Power and Culture: Essays on the American Working Class*. New York: New Press, 1992.

———. "Work, Culture, and Society in Industrializing America, 1815–1919." *American Historical Review* 78, no. 3 (1973): 531–88, https://doi.org/10.2307/1847655.

Haberland, Michelle. *Striking Beauties: Women Apparel Workers in the U.S. South, 1930–2000*. Athens: University of Georgia Press, 2015.

Halford, Fred. Memorandum, Special Agent in Charge (Arkansas) to Special Agent in Charge (New York). Oct. 22, 1940. "Re: New Theatre League (formerly Commonwealth College); Mena, Arkansas; INTERNAL SECURITY." Bureau File 61615613. Federal Bureau of Investigation.

Harding, Warren Gamaliel. *Rededicating America: Life and Recent Speeches of Warren G. Harding*. Indianapolis: Bobbs-Merrill Company, 1920.

Hays, Lee. "Commonwealth College Labor Songs: A Collection of Old and New Songs for the Use of Labor Unions." Mena, AR: Commonwealth College, 1938.

———. "It Wasn't Easy." *People's Songs Bulletin*, Feb.–March 1948, 11–15.

———. "*One Bread, One Body; An Original Labor Play in 3 Scenes*. Mena, AR: Commonwealth College, 1938.

Heller, Rita. "Blue Collars and Bluestockings: The Bryn Mawr Summer School for Women Workers, 1921–1938." In *Sisterhood and Solidarity: Workers' Education for Women*, edited by Joyce Kornbluh and Mary Frederickson, 107–46.

Hewett, Rebecca Coleman. "Progressive Compromises: Performing Gender, Race, and Class in Historical Pageants of 1913." PhD diss., University of Texas at Austin, 2010, http://hdl.handle.net/2152/ETD-UT-2010-05-967.

———. "'Sing Me a Song with Social Significance': Cultural Labor as Public Performance in *Pins and Needles*." Master's thesis, University of Texas at Austin, 2004.

"Highlander Folk School." Federal Bureau of Investigation, File 61-7511.

Hodges, James A. *New Deal Labor Policy and the Southern Cotton Textile Industry, 1933–1941*. Knoxville: University of Tennessee Press, 1986.

Hogan, J. Michael. *Rhetoric and Reform in the Progressive Era*. East Lansing: Michigan State University Press, 2003.

Hollis, Karyn. *Liberating Voices: Writing at the Bryn Mawr Summer School for Women Workers*. Carbondale: Southern Illinois University Press, 2004.

Horton, Aimee Isgrig. *The Highlander Folk School: A History of Its Major Programs, 1932–1961*. New York: Carlson, 1989.

———. "The Highlander Folk School: A History of the Development of its Major Programs Related to Social Movements in the South, 1932–1961." PhD diss., University of Chicago, 1971.

Horton, Myles, Judith Kohl, and Herbert R. Kohl. *The Long Haul: An Autobiography*. New York: Teachers College Press, 1998.

Howlett, Charles F. "Brookwood Labor College and the Struggle for Peace and Justice in America." *Encyclopedia of Peace Education*. Lewiston, ME: Edwin Mellen, 1993.

Huberman, Leo. *The Labor Spy Racket*. New York: Modern Age Books, 1937.

Hughes, Alvin. "A New Agenda for the South: The Role and Influence of the Highlander Folk School, 1953–1961." *Phylon* 46, no. 3 (1985): 242–50, doi:10.2307/274832.

Hyman, Colette A. *Staging Strikes: Workers' Theatre and the American Labor Movement*. Philadelphia: Temple University Press, 1997.

———. "Women, Workers, and Community: Working-Class Visions and Workers' Theatre in the 1930s." *Canadian Review of American Studies* 23, no. 1 (1992): 15–38, http://dx.doi.org/10.3138/CRAS-023-01-02.

———. "Workers on Stage: An Annotated Bibliography of Labor Plays of the 1930s." *Performing Arts Resources* 12 (1987): 171–95.

Jenison, Elsie. "A School for Women Workers in Industry in the South." *School and Society* 36, no. 928 (Oct. 8, 1932).

Johnston, Robert D. *The Radical Middle Class: Populist Democracy and the Question of Capitalism in Progressive Era Portland, Oregon*. Princeton: Princeton University Press, 2003.

Kessler-Harris, Alice. *In Pursuit of Equity: Women, Men, and the Quest for Economic Citizenship in Twentieth-Century America*. New York: Oxford University Press USA, 2001.

———. *Out to Work: A History of Wage-earning Women in the United States*. New York: Oxford University Press, 2003.

———. *A Woman's Wage: Historical Meanings and Social Consequences*. Lexington: University Press of Kentucky, 1990.

———. *Women Have Always Worked: A Historical Overview*. Old Westbury, NY: Feminist Press; New York: McGraw-Hill, 1981.

Kingsbury, Susan M. "Original Plan for a Summer School for Women Workers in Industry, Bryn Mawr, Pennsylvania." *Women Workers at the Bryn Mawr Summer School*, 265–70. New York City: Affiliated Summer Schools for Women Workers in Industry and American Association for Adult Education, 1929.

Kline, Herbert. "Writing for Workers Theatre." *New Theatre* (Dec. 1934): 22–25.

Kloppenberg, James T. *Uncertain Victory: Social Democracy and Progressivism in European and American Thought, 1870–1920.* New York: Oxford University Press, 1986.

Koch, Charlotte, and Raymond Koch. *Educational Commune: The Story of Commonwealth College.* New York: Schocken Books, 1972.

Koch, Friedrich. *Carolina Folk-plays.* New York: Henry Holt, 1922.

Kornbluh, Joyce L., and Mary Frederickson. *Sisterhood and Solidarity: Workers' Education for Women, 1914–1984.* Philadelphia: Temple University Press, 1984.

Kronish, Amy, and Costel Safirman. *Israeli Film: A Reference Guide.* Santa Barbara: Praeger, 2003.

Labor Drama: An Affiliated Schools for Workers Scrapbook. 1936. ALES Records.

Labor's Reward. In *Treasures III Social Issues in American Film, 1900–1934.* Chatsworth, CA: National Film Preservation Foundation; distributed by Image Entertainment, 2007. Film.

Lembcke, Jerry. "Labor and Education: Portland Labor College, 1921–1929." *Oregon Historical Quarterly* 85, no. 2 (1984): 117–34.

Leonard, Louise. "School for Workers Who Have Moved from Mountain to Mill." *Mountain Life and Work.* Jan. 1931, Box 111, "Southern Summer School, 1932" Folder, ALES Records.

———. "The South Begins Workers' Education." *American Federationist*, Nov. 1928. Box 111, "Southern Summer School 1928" Folder, ALES Records.

———. "Workers' Education in the South." *Vassar Quarterly* (1935): 2–6. Mary Cornelia Barker papers, Manuscript Archives and Rare Book Library, Robert W. Woodruff Library, Emory University, Atlanta, GA.

Leonard, Thomas C. *Illiberal Reformers: Race, Eugenics, and American Economics in the Progressive Era.* Princeton: Princeton University Press, 2016.

Leuchtenburg, William E. "Progressivism and Imperialism: The Progressive Movement and American Foreign Policy, 1898–1916." *Mississippi Valley Historical Review* 39, no. 3 (1952): 483–504, doi:10.2307/1895006.

———. *The White House Looks South: Franklin D. Roosevelt, Harry S. Truman, Lyndon B. Johnson.* Baton Rouge: LSU Press, 2005.

Levine, Ira. *Left-Wing Dramatic Theory in the American Theatre.* Ann Arbor: UMI Research Press, 1985.

Levine, Lawrence W. *Highbrow/Lowbrow: The Emergence of Cultural Hierarchy in America.* Cambridge: Harvard University Press, 1988.

Lorwin, Lewis Levitzki, and Jean Atherton Flexner. *The American Federation of Labor: History, Policies, and Prospects.* Washington, DC: Brookings Institution, 1933. 225–28.

Luff, Jennifer. *Commonsense Anticommunism: Labor and Civil Liberties Between the World Wars.* Chapel Hill: University of North Carolina Press, 2012.

Mackay, Constance D'Arcy. *The Little Theatre in the United States.* New York: H. Holt, 1917.

"MacKaye, Hazel." *American Women: The Official Who's Who Among the Women of the Nation, 1935–36*, edited by Durward Howes, 96. Los Angeles: Richard Blank, 1935.

MacKaye, Hazel. *The Enchanted Urn: A Fantasy in Pantomime*. New York: Woman's Press, 1924.

——. *Good Will, the Magician: A Peace Pageant for Children*. New York: National Child Welfare Association, 1924.

——. "Plays for Workers." *Workers' Education*, May 1926, 11–17.

——. *The Quest of Youth; A Pageant for Schools*. Vol. 33. Washington, DC: Bureau of Education, 1924.

MacKaye, Percy. *Caliban by the Yellow Sands: Shakespeare Tercentenary Masque*. Garden City, NY: Doubleday, 1916.

——. *Epoch: The Life of Steele MacKaye, Genius of the Theatre, in Relation to His Times and Contemporaries*. New York: Scholarly Press, 1968.

"Marxist Internet Archive." www.marxists.org/archive/index.htm. Accessed Aug. 17, 2018.

Massie-Legg, Alicia Ruth. "Zilphia Horton, a Voice for Change." PhD diss., University of Kentucky, 2014.

Mathews, Jane DeHart. *The Federal Theatre, 1935–1939: Plays, Relief, and Politics*. Princeton: Princeton University Press, 1967.

May, Martha. "Bread Before Roses: American Workingmen, Labor Unions, and the Family Wage." In *Families in the U.S.: Kinship and Domestic Politics*, edited by Karen V. Hansen and Anita Ilta Garey, 143–56. Philadelphia: Temple University Press, 1998.

McConachie, Bruce. Review of *Canadian Workers Theatre, 1929–1940*, by Toby Gordon Ryan; *Theatres of the Left, 1880–1935: Workers' Theatre Movements in Britain and America*, by Raphael Samuel, Ewan MacColl, and Stuart Cosgrove; *Left-Wing Dramatic Theory in American Theatre*, by Ira A. Levine. *Theatre Journal* 38, no. 4 (1986): 502–4. JSTOR, https://doi.org/10.2307/3208306.

McCormick, La Rue, and Malca Chall. *Activists in the Radical Movement, 1930–1960: The International Labor Defense, the Communist Party*. Oakland: University of California Press, 1980.

McDermott, Douglas. "New Theatre School 1932–1942." *Speech Teacher* 14, no. 4 (1965): 278–85, https://doi.org/10.1080/03634526509377465.

"Miss Hazel MacKaye, A Pageant Director." [Obituary.] *New York Times*. Aug. 12, 1944.

Montgomery, David. *Beyond Equality: Labor and the Radical Republicans, 1862–1872*. Urbana: University of Illinois Press, 1967.

——. *The Fall of the House of Labor: The Workplace, the State, and American Labor Activism, 1865–1925*. Cambridge: Cambridge University Press, 1989.

——. "Labor and the Republic in Industrial America: 1860–1920." *Le Mouvement Social* (1980): 201–15.

———. *Workers' Control in America: Studies in the History of Work, Technology, and Labor Struggles.* Cambridge: Cambridge University Press, 1979.

Moore, William J. "The Determinants and Effects of Right-to-Work Laws: A Review of the Recent Literature." *Journal of Labor Research* 19, no. 3 (1998): 445–69.

Murphy, Brenda. *The Provincetown Players and the Culture of Modernity.* Cambridge: Cambridge University Press, 2005.

Murphy, Paul L., Kermit Hall, and David Klaassen. *The Passaic Textile Strike of 1926.* Belmont, CA: Wadsworth, 1974.

Muste, A. J. "Ritual in Mass Education or Dramatizing the Labor Movement." American Federation of Teachers. Local 189. *Mass Education for Workers: Second Annual Conference of Teachers in Workers' Education at Brookwood,* February 20–22, 1925. Katonah, NY: American Federation of Teachers, 1925.

———. "Workers' Education in the United States." *Religious Education* 24, no. 8 (1929): 738–45, https://doi.org/10.1080/0034408290240808.

Nahshon, Edna. *Yiddish Proletarian Theatre: The Art and Politics of the Artef, 1925–1940.* Santa Barbara: Greenwood Press, 1998.

Neufeld, Maurice F., Daniel J. Leab, and Dorothy Swanson. *American Working Class History: A Representative Bibliography.* New York: Bowker, 1983.

"New Theatre League Schools." *New Theatre* (April 1935): 22.

Norris, Norman Dale. *The Promise and Failure of Progressive Education.* New York: R&L Education, 2004.

Norton, Helen G. "Brookwood in Its First Decade." *Labor Age* (May 1931): 18–19.

———. "Drama at Brookwood." *Labor Age* (May 1926): 16–19.

———. *A Survey of Brookwood Students, 1921–1931.* Katonah, NY: Brookwood Labor College.

Odets, Clifford. *Waiting for Lefty.* In *Waiting for Lefty and Till the Day I Die; Two Plays.* New York: Random House, 1935.

Pageant of Athena. Boston: Merrymount Press, 1915.

Palmer, Gladys. *The Industrial Experience of Women Workers at the Summer Schools, 1928–1930.* No. 89. Washington, DC: Women's Bureau, United States Department of Labor, 1930.

Papa, Lee, ed. *Staged Action: Six Plays from the American Workers' Theatre.* Ithaca: ILR Press, 2009.

———. "'We Gotta Make up Our Minds': *Waiting for Lefty,* Workers' Theatre Performance and Audience Identification." *Text and Performance Quarterly* 19, no. 1 (1999): 57–73.

Parris, Wendall A. "Highlander Folk School." *Negro History Bulletin* (May 1, 1958): 170.

Pels, Dick. "The Dark Side of Socialism Hendrik de Man and the Fascist Temptation." *History of the Human Sciences* 6, no. 2 (1993): 75–95.

"Personals." *Springboard* 1, no. 1 (Feb. 1938): 6.

Peters, Paul, and George Sklar. *Stevedore.* London: Jonathan Cape, 1934.

Petty, Anne W. "Dramatic Activities and Workers' Education at Highlander Folk School, 1932–1942." PhD diss., Bowling Green State University, 1979.

Pinski, David. *A Dollar: A Comedy in One Act.* New York: Samuel French, 1920.

The Playground. Executive Committee of the Playground Association of America, 1922.

Plesur, Milton. "The Republican Congressional Comeback of 1938." *Review of Politics* 24, no. 4 (1962): 525–62.

Postlewait, Thomas. "The Hieroglyphic Stage: American Theatre and Society, Post-Civil War to 1945." In *The Cambridge History of American Theatre*, vol. 2, 1999, 107–95.

Preece, Harold. "The South Stirs." *The Crisis* 48 (Oct. 1941): 318.

Quinney, Valerie. "Workers' Education: A Confrontation at Ruskin College." *American Journal of Education* (1983): 52–78.

Ransdell, Hollace. "Amateur Dramatics in the Labor Movement." *Labor Drama: An Affiliated Schools for Workers Scrapbook*. 1936. ALES Records.

——. *Bank Run: A Tragi-comic Sketch in One Act.* Southern Summer School for Women Workers in Industry, 1932.

——. "Greasing the Rails for Passaic Strikers." *Labor Defender* (Jan. 1927): 5, 15.

——. "Guilty! of What?" *Labor Defender* (May 1927): 69–70.

——. "Jack Rubenstein and 'Whitey' Adamchesky." *Labor Defender* (June 1927): 85, 95.

——. *Job Huntin': A Tragi-comedy in One Act for Workers.* Southern Summer School for Women Workers in Industry, 1931.

——. *Mother Jones' Tin Pan Army: A Comic Sketch in One Act.* Southern Summer School for Women Workers in Industry, 1933.

——. "Negro Miners Plead for Union Sympathy." *Labor's News: The News Magazine of the Labor Movement*. Vol. 15. New York: Federated Press, 1928.

——. *Oh Mr. Yaller Dog Take Him Away: A One-Act Sketch Taken from Life in a Mill Village.* Southern Summer School for Women Workers in Industry, 1929.

——. *On the Picket Line: A One-Act Sketch.* Southern Summer School for Women Workers in Industry, 1931.

——. *Prisoners of the Passaic Strike.* Joint Committee for Passaic Defense (American Civil Liberties Union and the International Labor Defense), 1926.

——. "The Soap Box Theatre." *The Crisis* (April 1935): 122–24.

——. "The State versus Thomas Regan, Textile Worker." *Labor Defender* (April 1927): 54.

——. *Work and Wealth: A Modern Morality Play.* Southern Summer School for Women Workers in Industry, 1929.

——. *World Economic Nonsense: A One-Act Skit.* Southern Summer School for Women Workers in Industry, 1933.

Robinson, James W. "The Expulsion of Brookwood Labor College from the Workers' Education Bureau." *Labour History* 15 (1968): 64–69.

Rome, Harold. *Pins and Needles.* New York: Florence Music, 1937.

Salstrom, Paul. *Appalachia's Path to Dependency: Rethinking a Region's Economic History, 1730–1940.* Lexington: University Press of Kentucky, 2015.

Sandler, Mark. "Workers Must Read: The Commonwealth College Library, 1925–1940." *Journal of Library History* 20, no. 1 (1985): 46–69.

Schachat, Lillian. "Brookwood Presents *The Weavers.*" *Brookwood Review* (Jan. 1925): 3.

Schmidt-Pirro, Julia, and Karen M. McCurdy. "Employing Music in the Cause of Social Justice: Ruth Crawford Seeger and Zilphia Horton." *Voices* 31, nos. 1–2 (2005): 32.

Schneider, Stephen A. *You Can't Padlock an Idea: Rhetorical Education at the Highlander Folk School, 1932–1961.* Columbia: University of South Carolina Press, 2014.

Schwartz, Michael. *Class Divisions on the Broadway Stage: The Staging and Taming of the I.W.W.* New York: Palgrave Macmillan, 2014.

Schwarztrauber, Ernest. "Education of Dramatic Work in Labor Colleges." *Workers' Education Yearbook* (1924): 141–42.

Scott, Ann Firor. "After Suffrage: Southern Women in the Twenties." In *The Myth of Southern History: Historical Consciousness in Twentieth-century Southern Literature,* 81–100. Nashville: Vanderbilt University Press, 1970.

Seidman, Joel I. "The Yellow Dog Contract." *Quarterly Journal of Economics* 46, no. 2 (1932): 348–61, http://dx.doi.org/10.2307/1884803.

Semuels, Alana. "The Racist History of Portland, the Whitest City in America." *Atlantic* (July 22, 2016).

Sicherman, Barbara, and Carol Hurd Green. *Notable American Women: The Modern Period.* Cambridge: Harvard University Press, 1980.

Smith, Angela. "Myles Horton, Highlander Folk School, and the Wilder Coal Strike of 1932." Master's thesis, Middle Tennessee State University, 2003.

Smith, Hilda Worthington. *Women Workers at the Bryn Mawr Summer School.* New York City: Affiliated Summer Schools for Women Workers in Industry and American Association for Adult Education, 1929.

"Southern School for Women Workers Closing Third Session." *Women's Wear Daily* (Aug. 22, 1929). Box 111. "Southern Summer School 1929" Folder. ALES Records.

"Southern Summer School for Women Workers in Industry." Pamphlet. N.d. Baltimore: Southern Summer School for Women Workers in Industry. Cornelia Barker Papers, Manuscript Archives and Rare Book Library, Robert W. Woodruff Library, Emory University. Atlanta, GA.

"Staff Gossip." *News of Southern Summer School for Women Workers in Industry* 1, no. 1 (Feb. 1930): 3.

Sternhill, Zeev. *Neither Right nor Left: Fascist Ideology in France.* Princeton: Princeton University Press, 1995.

Stokes, Elizabeth Dilling. *The Red Network: A "Who's Who" and Handbook of Radicalism for Patriots.* New York: Arno Press, 1936.

Taylor, Philip M. *Munitions of the Mind: A History of Propaganda.* 3rd ed. Manchester: Manchester University Press, 2003.

Thomas, M. Carey. "Address by M. Carey Thomas." *Women Workers at the Bryn Mawr Summer School.* New York City: Affiliated Summer Schools for Women Workers in Industry and American Association for Adult Education, 1929, 255–64.

Tippett, Thomas. *Mill Shadows: A Drama of Social Forces in Four Acts.* Katonah, NY: Brookwood Labor College, 1932.

———. "What Price Coal." Unpublished playtext. 1926. Box 57, Folder 7, HREC Records.

———. *When Southern Labor Stirs.* London: Jonathan Cape, 1931.

Toller, Ernst. *Man and the Masses [Masse Mensch].* Translated by Louis Untermeyer. Garden City, NY: Doubleday, Page & Co., 1924.

Triece, Mary E. *Protest and Popular Culture: Women in the U.S. Labor Movement, 1894–1917.* Boulder: Westview Press, 2001.

Tyack, David. "Ways of Seeing: An Essay on the History of Compulsory Schooling." *Harvard Educational Review* 46, no. 3 (Sept. 1, 1976): 355–89, https://doi.org/10.17763/haer.46.3.v73405527200106v.

Tyler, Gus. *Look for the Union Label: A History of the International Ladies' Garment Workers' Union.* Armonk, NY: M. E. Sharpe, 1995.

van de Water, Manon. "Constance D'Arcy Mackay: A Historiographical Perspective." *Youth Theatre Journal* 9, no. 1 (1995): 79–91, https://doi.org/10.1080/08929092.1995.10012468.

———. "Constructed Narratives: Situating Theatre for Young Audiences in the United States." *Youth Theatre Journal* 14, no. 1 (2000): 101–13, https://doi.org/10.1080/08929092.2000.10012521.

Walker, Samuel. *In Defense of American Liberties: A History of the ACLU.* Carbondale: Southern Illinois University Press, 1999.

Ward, Winifred. *Creative Dramatics for the Upper Grades and Junior High School.* New York: D. Appleton and Company, 1929.

Weisbord, Albert. *Passaic: The Story of a Struggle Against Starvation Wages and for the Right to Organize.* Brooklyn, NY: AMS Press, 1976.

Weiss, Robert P. "Private Detective Agencies and Labour Discipline in the United States, 1855–1946." *Historical Journal* 29, no. 1 (1986): 87–107.

"Who's Who" in Pageantry. Boston: American Pageant Association, 1914.

Wiebe, Robert H. *The Search for Order, 1877–1920.* New York: Hill and Wang, 1967.

Willens, Doris. *Lonesome Traveler: The Life of Lee Hays.* Lincoln: University of Nebraska Press—Bison Books, 1993.

"Williams Active in State for Past Seven Years." *Commonwealth College Fortnightly,* Aug. 15 1937, 1, 4.

Wolf, Friedrich. *Floridsdorf.* Verlag Genossenschaft Ausländ. Arbeiter in der UdSSR, 1935.

The Women of Summer. Directed by Suzanne Bauman and Rita Heller. National Endowment for the Humanities. Filmmakers Library, 1986. Film.

Woodworth, Christine, Elizabeth A. Osborne. *Working in the Wings: New Perspectives on Theatre History and Labor.* Carbondale: Southern Illinois University Press, 2015.

Zieger, Robert H. *The CIO: 1935–1955.* Chapel Hill: University of North Carolina Press, 1995.

INDEX

STUDIES IN
THEATRE HISTORY AND CULTURE